Teaching Hemingway and War

# TEACHING HEMINGWAY

Mark P. Ott, Editor
Susan F. Beegel, Founding Editor

Teaching Hemingway's *The Sun Also Rises*
EDITED BY PETER L. HAYS

Teaching Hemingway's *A Farewell to Arms*
EDITED BY LISA TYLER

Teaching Hemingway and Modernism
EDITED BY JOSEPH FRUSCIONE

Teaching Hemingway and War
EDITED BY ALEX VERNON

# Teaching Hemingway and War

Edited by Alex Vernon

The Kent State University Press    Kent, Ohio

Copyright © 2016 by The Kent State University Press, Kent, Ohio 44242
All rights reserved
Library of Congress Catalog Card Number 2015009652
ISBN 978-1-60635-257-1
Manufactured in the United States of America

"Hemingway, PTSD, and Clinical Depression" by Peter L. Hays was originally published in his book *Fifty Years of Hemingway Criticism* (Scarecrow Press, 2014) and appears courtesy of Scarecrow Press.

*Library of Congress Cataloging-in-Publication Data*
Teaching Hemingway and war / edited by Alex Vernon.
   pages cm. — (Teaching Hemingway)
   Includes bibliographical references and index.
   ISBN 978-1-60635-257-1 (pbk. : alk. paper) ∞
   1. Hemingway, Ernest, 1899–1961—Study and teaching. 2. War in literature. 3. War and literature. I. Vernon, Alex, 1967– editor.
   PS3515.E37Z89175 2015
   813'.52—dc23
                                2015009652

Well the reason you are so sore you missed the war is because the war is the best subject of all. It groups the maximum of material and speeds up the action and brings out all sorts of stuff that normally you have to wait a lifetime to get.
—Ernest Hemingway, letter to F. Scott Fitzgerald, 25 December 1925

The title of this book is *A Farewell to Arms* and except for three years there has been war of some kind almost ever since it has been written. Some people used to say, why is the man so preoccupied and obsessed with war, and now, since 1933 perhaps it is clear why a writer should be interested in the constant, bullying, murderous, slovenly crime of war. . . . I believe that all the people who stand to profit by a war and who help to provoke it should be shot on the first day it starts by accredited representatives of the loyal citizens who will fight it. . . . If, at the end of the day, there was any evidence that I had in any way provoked the new war or had not performed my delegated duties correctly, I would be willing, if not pleased, to be shot by the same firing squad and be buried wither with or without cellophane or be left naked on a hill.
—Ernest Hemingway, "The Author's 1948 Introduction to A Farewell to Arms"

# Contents

Foreword
    MARK P. OTT      ix
Introduction
    ALEX VERNON      1

## Part 1: The Great War

The Violence of Story: Teaching *In Our Time* and Narrative Rhetoric
    ALEXANDER HOLLENBERG      15

"Our Fathers Lied": The Great War and Paternal Betrayal in Hemingway's *In Our Time*
    LISA TYLER      30

Connective Gestures: Mulk Raj Anand, Ernest Hemingway, and the Transnational Worlds of World War I
    RUTH A. H. LAHTI      41

Character Construction and Agency: Teaching Hemingway's "A Way You'll Never Be"
    PETER MESSENT      60

## Part 2: The Spanish Civil War

Seeing Through Fracture: *In Our Time, For Whom the Bell Tolls*, and Picasso's *Guernica*
    THOMAS STRYCHACZ      77

Hemingway and the Spanish Civil War: The Writer's Maturing View
    MILTON A. COHEN      92

"What you were fighting for": Robert Jordan On Trial in the Classroom
    STEVEN A. NARDI      107

Teaching *The Spanish Earth* in a War Film Seminar
    ALEX VERNON      122

## Part 3: Trauma Tales

Hemingway, PTSD, and Clinical Depression
    PETER L. HAYS      133

"Shot . . . crippled and gotten away": Animals and War Trauma in Hemingway
    RYAN HEDIGER      143

The Poetics of Hemingway's *Death in the Afternoon:* Restaging the Experience of Total War
    CHRISTOPHER BARKER      157

"In Another Country" and *Across the River and into the Trees* as Trauma Literature
    SARAH WOOD ANDERSON      172

## Part 4: Ernest Hemingway Seminar

Introduction
    ALEX VERNON      189

Perceptions of Pain in *The Sun Also Rises*
    JOSEPHINE REECE      195

A Farewell to the Armed Hospital: Military-Medical Discourse in Frederic Henry's Italy
    ZACK HAUSLE      209

Pilar's Turn Inward: Storytelling in Hemingway's *For Whom the Bell Tolls*
    ANNA BROADWELL-GULDE      224

Appendixes      238
Works Cited      247
Selected Bibliography      255
Contributors      259
Index      262

# Foreword

Mark P. Ott

How should the work of Ernest Hemingway be taught in the twenty-first century? Although the "culture wars" of the 1980s and 1990s have faded, Hemingway's place in the curriculum continues to inspire discussion among writers and scholars about the lasting value of his work. To readers of this volume, his life and writing remain vital, meaningful, and still culturally resonant for today's students.

Books in the Teaching Hemingway Series build on the excellent work of founding series editor Susan F. Beegel, who guided into publication the first two volumes of this series, *Teaching Hemingway's* A Farewell to Arms, edited by Lisa Tyler (2008), and *Teaching Hemingway's* The Sun Also Rises, edited by Peter L. Hays (2008). To promote their usefulness to instructors and professors—from high schools, community colleges, and universities—the newest volumes in this series are organized thematically, rather than around a single text. This shift attempts to open up Hemingway's work to more interdisciplinary strategies of instruction through divergent theories, fresh juxtapositions, and ethical inquiries, and to the employment of emergent technology to explore media beyond the text.

*Teaching Hemingway and War,* edited by Alex Vernon, speaks to issues of intense interest to students and scholars today: war, trauma, loss. The expertise and insight Vernon displayed in his groundbreaking work *Hemingway's Second War: Bearing Witness to the Spanish Civil War* (2011) is evident throughout this volume. These far-ranging essays explore Hemingway's biography, his wartime wounding, the Great War, the Spanish Civil War, his short fiction, his novels, and his one film. This volume demonstrates that in today's classrooms and lectures halls Hemingway's work is being taught in more thoughtful and innovative ways than ever before. Indeed, the essays showcase the creativity, wisdom, and insight of authors from varied backgrounds united in their passion for sharing Hemingway's work with a new generation of students.

# Introduction

Alex Vernon

In "Soldier's Home," a story from Hemingway's first major book of fiction, *In Our Time,* Harold Krebs returns home from the Great War, having "been at Belleau Wood, Soissons, the Champagne, St. Mihiel and in the Argonne" (*CSS* 111)—in other words, having fought in every major battle the Marines faced. In those actions, over a period of five and a half months, the Fourth Marine Brigade, attached to the Second Division of the American Expeditionary Force and generally maintaining a full strength of 8,469, took combat casualties of 2,232 dead and 9,056 wounded (McClellan 10, 65).[1] Apparently escaping physical injury himself, Krebs witnessed a sheer devastation of bodies.

Back home, interpersonal communication fails him. He sits on the front porch of his childhood home, not quite back inside, not quite back out in the world, turning to a first-generation history of the war and finally learning about his own experiences. The story itself turns here, in this paragraph falling at its midpoint: "He looked forward with a good feeling to reading all the really good histories when they would come out with good detail maps" (*CSS* 113). For the first time Krebs looks *forward,* pleasantly anticipating a morsel of his future, the word *good* repeated a fourth time two sentences later.

Immediately after this paragraph we go inside, into Krebs's bedroom with his mother, where the story's dialogue begins. The prior narrative consisted of reflections and general descriptions of Krebs's days and evenings. But when "he sat there on that porch reading a book on the war," the narrative literally falls into time and place (*CSS* 113), landing into *story,* understood as a sequence of embodied actions and events. Hemingway synchronizes the story's grounding with the beginning of Krebs's personal story's grounding, a process whose necessity Krebs *feels*, as underscored by his preoccupation with the need for better maps. His desire for more complete historical narratives likewise expresses his desire for a more coherent personal narrative. The movement into history becomes the movement into the future as Krebs stumbles toward a more-or-less integrated self that can get on with it. He goes inside, confronts his family, and then—assuming we can accept the promise of the final paragraph's conditional posture ("He would go to Kansas City. . . . He would go over to the schoolyard" [*CSS* 116])—renters the world.

In a sense, cultural historians of twentieth-century warfare have been following Krebs's lead. If there is a subfield of literary theory devoted to understanding war, we can safely say it began with studies of the Great War, through works such as Paul Fussell's *The Great War and Modern Memory* (1975), Eric J. Leed's *No Man's Land: Combat and Identity in World War I* (1979), and Sandra M. Gilbert and Susan Gubar's "Soldier's Heart: Literary Men, Literary Women, and the Great War" (1983), followed in the 1990s by Samuel Hynes's *A War Imagined: The First World War and English Culture* (1990), Geoff Dyer's *The Missing of the Somme* (1994), Jay Winter's *Sites of Memory, Sites of Mourning: The Great War in European Cultural History* (1996), and Joanna Bourke's *Dismembering the Male: Men's Bodies, Britain, and the Great War* (1996). World War I continues to serve as a cornerstone to which literary and cultural studies return, as seen in Vincent Sherry's *The Great War and the Language of Modernism* (2004), Santanu Das's *Touch and Intimacy in First World War Literature* (2005), Steven Trout's *On the Battlefield of Memory: The First World War and American Remembrance, 1919–1941* (2010), and Beth Linker's *War's Waste: Rehabilitation in World War I America* (2011), four books appearing before the centennial. War trauma studies likewise really begin with the Great War.

In 2013, I had occasion to ruminate on a potential upper-level undergraduate course called Topics in Literary Theory: War Studies. One of my solutions involved class readings and work on World War I, followed by individual student projects examining texts from later wars in a particular contextual or through a specific theoretical trajectory—by linking, for example, war disability studies on narratives of the 1920s to a text from the 1970s. I also considered including a selection of Hemingway's work alongside these scholarly studies. Conveniently enough for students of Ernest Hemingway and war, his initiation into twentieth-century war was the century's own initiation. I can easily imagine a student, for example, bringing together Gilbert and Gubar's "Soldier's Heart" essay and Hemingway's "Soldier's Home" story with Tim O'Brien's Vietnam

War story "The Things They Carried" (which also ends conditionally) and its companion story, "Love."

Hemingway went to the Great War, as many soldiers do, straight out of childhood: "I was very ignorant at nineteen and had read little," he relates in the introduction to the anthology *Men at War*, published during the Second World War. "I would have given anything for a book like this which showed what all the other men that we are a part of had gone through and how it had been with them" (*MAW* xiv). Hemingway was at the time engaging in his layman's counterintelligence-gathering services for the United States out of Cuba, eventually turning his fishing boat *Pilar* into a clandestine patrol boat. He had already witnessed, and to various degrees participated in, the First World War, the Greco-Turkish War, the Spanish Civil War, and the Second Sino-Japanese War, and would in due course accompany the Allied invasion and liberation of Europe as a war correspondent.

Veterans of the Spanish Civil War were the first to enter Paris, with armored cars bearing the names of battles of the precursor war against European fascism, battles Hemingway had written about: Guadalajara, Madrid, Teruel, Ebro. He must have found this fact sweetly if bitterly apt. The first page of his introduction to *Men at War* attributes the cause of the World War II to the failure of the Allied powers in Spain, to "the Democracies' betrayal of the only countries that fought or were ready to fight to prevent it" (*MAW* xi). Within a year, Philippe Lelerc, the French general responsible for sending the company into Paris, was on his way to Indochina, with propaganda posters heralding, "Yesterday Strasbourg, Tomorrow Saigon, Join in!" Had Hemingway maintained his faculties and not taken his own life in 1961, one wonders how he might have responded to the United States' role in the war in Vietnam. His compatriots from Spain certainly heeded that call: Robert Capa died there in 1954, Martha Gellhorn covered the war in 1966, and Joris Ivens might very well have invited him, in 1967, to work on *The 17th Parallel*—the Vietnamese war's equivalent to *The Spanish Earth*—as, thirty years earlier, Ivens had invited him to journey to China to produce *The 400 Million*.

We should all be extremely grateful that Hemingway declined the 1938 China trip in order to write *For Whom the Bell Tolls*. This novel came to my mind on a visit to a Vietnamese museum lionizing the militia and villagers who created and inhabited the Vinh Moc wartime tunnel complex. Above a celebratory mural, in English, was inscribed the famous phrase from *Hamlet*, "to be or not to be." This reference to the suicide soliloquy (as I had been accustomed to understanding it)—the same moment in the play which gave Hemingway the novel's working title of "The Undiscovered Country"—puzzled me until I ran across Samuel Johnson's annotations to the soliloquy . It isn't necessarily that Hamlet contemplates suicide, but, argues Johnson, that he knows that any action he takes against the king his uncle may well result in his death:

> Hamlet, knowing himself injured in the most enormous and atrocious degree, and seeing no means of redress, but such as must expose him to the extremity of hazard, meditates on his situation in this manner: *Before I can form any rational scheme of action under this pressure of distress,* it is necessary to decide, whether, *after our present state, we are* to be or not to be. That is the question, which, as it shall be answered, will determine, *whether 'tis nobler,* and more suitable to the dignity of reason, *to suffer the outrages of fortune* patiently, or to take arms against them, *though perhaps* with the loss of life. (emphasis in original)²

For Jordan, the issue transcends the bridge mission at hand: is it nobler to risk death for the Spain of the Spanish Republic or to deny conscience's call? Extratextually, the 1940 novel can be read less as a historical gesture than as a contemporaneous call for resolve by all those opposed to fascism, not just Spain's defeated antifascists.

As my digressions and speculations indicate, readers of this volume do not need cursory information on Hemingway's war experiences. We continue to enjoy new war-focused biographies, chiefly of Hemingway in the First World War—most recently Steven Florczyk's *Hemingway, the Red Cross, and the Great War* (2013). We even have a book-length study of Hemingway's weeks in China, Peter Moreira's *Hemingway on the China Front: His WWII Spy Mission with Martha Gellhorn* (2007). We should hope, someday, for a solid literary biography of Hemingway's Second World War involvement and writings, and for a study of his evolving relationship with war based strictly on his complete published letters. Students who need semester-friendly introductions have several solid print resources: Michael Reynolds's "Ernest Hemingway 1899–1961: A Brief Biography," in Linda Wagner-Martin's *Historical Guide to Ernest Hemingway* (2000); Seán Hemingway's introduction to *Hemingway on War* (2003); and the chapters on World War I, the Spanish Civil War, and World War II in *Ernest Hemingway in Context*, by Debra Moddelmog and Suzanne del Gizzo (2013).

Some of Hemingway's short pieces can also help introduce students to Hemingway and war, perhaps connecting them more immediately and urgently than through fiction's filter: his raw, pained preface to Luis Quintanilla's *All the Brave,* written in Spain during the death throes of the Spanish Republic that he supported so energetically, and his powerful article, "A Veteran Visits the Old Front," in which Hemingway, who had just turned twenty-three, sounds like a much older man. In *Men at War*, he writes that "no mechanized vehicle is any better than the heart of the man who handles the controls. So learn about the human heart and the human mind in war from this book. There is much about them in here" (*MAW* xx). It is essential that students do not allow a lack of war or military experience to impede their critical imaginative interactions. What is literature for if not the sympathetic consideration of the unfamiliar?

Hemingway's own career authorizes all of us in this venture, as he did not participate in most of the military actions he writes about. Writing of *The Red Badge of Courage*, whose author was born after the American Civil War, Hemingway judges that "that . . . boy's dream of war . . . was to be truer to how war is than any war the boy who wrote it would ever live to see" (*MAW* xvii), and he includes Stephen Crane's novel in its entirety in *Men at War*. For all its preparatory research, Crane's Civil War novel remarkably avoids the trap that, according to Geoffrey Dyer, catches most historical Great War novels of being "more precisely written about" than the survivors' own memoirs and quasi-autobiographical fictions: "they almost inevitably bear the imprint of the material from which they are derived, can never conceal the research on which they depend. . . . they feel like secondary texts" (78–79). Crane refuses insistence on historical detail (he never bothers saying anything more precise than "rifle," for example), giving the narrative a necessary looseness, yet also, because of his critical distance from the events, manages to structure and control it such that Hemingway praises it for being "as much of one piece as a great poem is" (*MAW* xvii). Hemingway learned from Crane to trust his imagination in locating his war stories outside his personal history, while bringing to bear what Crane couldn't teach: a disciplined attitude toward drawing on his own experiences. Hemingway wrote what he knew but also what he did not know, and from that skillful concocting comes the magic. Hemingway's great accomplishment in novels like *A Farewell to Arms* and *For Whom the Bell Tolls* is exactly this stirring together of experience and invention. As he writes, "Learning to suspend your imagination and live completely in the very second of the present minute with no before and no after is the greatest gift a soldier can acquire. It, naturally, is the opposite of all those gifts a writer should have. That is what makes good writing by good soldiers such a rare thing and why it is so prized when we have it" (*MAW* xxvii). Hemingway was never a soldier, though he spent enough time in combat zones to render this assessment an indirect, not-so-subtle, and deserved self-appreciation.

I was a soldier once, seeing combat in the brief Persian Gulf War of 1990–91 (the first U.S.-Iraq war), which was my path to Hemingway. In the late 1990s, before the recent wars in Iraq and Afghanistan, I needed a dissertation topic. I realized that the Vietnam-era generation of veterans-turned-professors faced retirement, and at the time these were the scholars mostly carrying the torch of war literature. So I pursued a professional opportunity. If one commits to studying American war literature, well, one must work to some extent on Hemingway. What started as career strategy has become a joy.

The cliché that good texts always surprise you with new discoveries and questions I have found exceedingly the case with Hemingway's oeuvre. Having written about and for years discussed with students the strange infusion of the martial with the maternal in *A Farewell to Arms*, having read the novel an untold number of times, how could I have missed until the most recent iteration of the Hemingway seminar this pregnant passage from the wounded soldier and expectant father?—"Valentini had done a fine job. I had done half the retreat on foot and swum part of the Tagliamento with his knee. It was his knee all right. The other knee was mine. Doctors did things to you and then it was not your body any more. The head was mine, and the inside of the belly. *It was very hungry in there. I could feel it turn over on itself*" (*FTA* 231; emphasis added). That particular class saw my first close reading of the novel's pre-op enema passage, which strangely mixes spirituality, whoredom, mendacity, physical penetration, and Catherine's scene-controlling submission. The conservation, seemingly inspired by her physical evacuation of Frederic, ends with the self-evacuation of her own ego: "There isn't any me any more" (*FTA* 106). This same class also produced my first close reading of Robert Jordan's fantasizing of taking Maria to a Madrid coiffeur in *For Whom the Bell Tolls* (345–46), which paves the way, just a few pages later, for her recounting to him her head-shearing by rapacious Falangists, an event he imagines resubjecting her to by having her tell the tale to entertain a crowd of pipe-smoking, presumably male, university students. The two tonsorial scenes we read somewhat in light of *The Garden of Eden*, a veteran's tale rarely characterized as such.

Whatever resistance to Hemingway students might bring to my classes falls away quickly. I may be a victim of my own naïvely wishful thinking, but I find that embracing an engaged classroom attitude, proceeding *as if*, is more energizing and constructive than any alternative. The texts are so rich that the first discussion day shakes up dismissive ideas about his machismo, his autobiographical fiction, his love of war, his simple style. As an exercise in close attention, I have students date by year and season the opening chapters of *A Farewell to Arms* in preparation for the first class. This exercise, together with a thirty-second lecture about Hemingway's weeks with the Red Cross in Italy versus Frederic Henry's years in the Italian Army (Steven Florczyk claims that the area in which Hemingway's unit operated was so quiet that it "is unlikely that Hemingway would have been called upon to sit behind the steering wheel of an ambulance other than to pose for a photograph" [59]), begins to divorce writer from protagonist and introduces students to a different way to think about the writer's style. Henry doesn't know why he signed up; he treats Catherine rather callously; he doesn't know why he didn't visit the Abruzzi on leave as he had planned; and we don't learn his full name in English until relatively late, after his wounding—and after the class's first day's reading. All of these easily identifiable signals help rouse the students' curiosity. By the time we have reached Henry's declaration of his farewell to arms, the students are ready to consider the moment's ambiguity. Is this really a heroic commitment to pacifism, a specific rejection of the politics and strategy of the Great War, or merely a portrayal of a tired, confused soul's understandable retreat into life's simple pleasures of food, drink, and love? What on earth do we make of the shooting of the sergeant? Does this novel really express an uncomplicated relationship to war for its writer?

Upper-level literature students do not need as much guidance, as they are already primed to practice a hermeneutics of suspicion. When I begin courses for these students with *In Our Time* or *The Garden of Eden*, the genre experimentation of the former and the gender experimentation of the latter instantly engage them.

If this introduction appears to privilege the major novels (excepting "Soldier's Home"), the essays that follow range widely among Hemingway's stories, novels, nonfiction, and his one film.

Part 1 treats some Hemingway works of the Great War. Whatever particular interests drew you to this volume, I encourage you to read Alex Hollenberg's essay on *In Our Time* as an excellent discussion of the art and ethics of reading, of the violence inherent in interpretation, that you might even assign to your students. It also provides a deft jolt to those of us, like me, habituated to unifying the stories for our students through Nick Adams's consciousness. When Hollenberg argues that Nick's repeated application of the word *tragic* to the future fishing of the swamp in "Big Two-Hearted River" indicates how he is already turning his own experiences into a text, I then wonder about the word's pointing to tragedy as the genre that exposes and enacts the hero's own flaws and culpabilities. Accordingly, in the story's swamp-as-war-memory metaphor, Nick defers thinking about not only what happened to him in war but also his actions, his behavior, and his responsibility, whatever they might be.

Lisa Tyler asks students to read the stories of *In Our Time* through the cultural context of the war's generational betrayal, a betrayal that extended to a resentment of the home front generally. Her contextual evidence is chiefly from British literature, and though one might be quick to differentiate European disillusionment from America's brief and victorious experience of the war, it would take little classroom time to establish a similar sensibility among some U.S. veterans by introducing a choice poem or two from Cummings (e.g., "next to of course god america i," "my sweet old etcetera," or "I sing of Olaf glad and big") or even from Hemingway (e.g., "Killed Piave—July 8—1918," "[All armies are the same . . . ]," "Shock Troops," "To Good Guys Dead"). The misogynist ditty "The Lady Poet with Foot Notes" footnotes the line "One lady poet's husband was killed in the war" with the vituperation, "It sold her stuff" (*CP* 77). Depending on the aims of the course being taught, one could easily take the idea of generational and home-front betrayal beyond that particular war. One could also challenge the idea of widespread veteran disillusion and aimlessness, as Trout so effectively does in *On the Battlefield of Memory* (2).

Ruth Lahti's "Connective Gestures" offers two approaches to us and our students: a close reading of physical action and a transnational juxtaposition of texts. Pairing *A Farewell to Arms* with Mulk Raj Anand's Great War novel, *Across the Black Waters*, "illuminates," as she puts it, "the presence of 'nation' as a shaping force in both Hemingway's and Anand's texts, thereby encouraging students to think critically about how national power entangles itself in representations of war" (41). Anand's novel is also of interest because Anand missed the First World War and instead bases the novel's descriptions of that war on his months of International Brigade service in Spain. Peter Messent has found that a structuralist method can equip students to analyze a narrative. His examination of Nick Adams's character in "A Way You'll Never Be" through a consideration of Schlomith Rimmon-Kenan's *Narrative Fiction: Contemporary Poetics* models for students the authority and indeed responsibility of all readers to adapt and refine, rather than straightforwardly apply, whatever critical apparatus we employ.

Thomas Strychacz conveys us from the Great War to the Spanish Civil War—from Part 1 to Part 2—by way of Picasso's monumental *Guernica*. If compositionally the painting echoes the first-impression mishmash of *In Our Time*, it also brings students to a conversation about vision and power in *For*

*Whom the Bell Tolls*. I reluctantly added this novel to my Hemingway seminar syllabus a decade ago, daunted by my own ignorance at that time about the Spanish Civil War. I could have used Milton Cohen's essay, "Hemingway and the Spanish Civil War: The Writer's Maturing View," as a primer on the war and an introduction to Hemingway's writing about it. Teachers in the same boat will find Cohen's essay useful in choosing the best point of entry for teaching that war in Hemingway.

The next essay in Part 2 focuses on Robert Jordan. Inspired by James Gee's *What Video Games Have to Teach Us about Learning and Literacy*, Steven Nardi turns teaching the novel into a low-stakes interactive game by having the class put Jordan on trial for needlessly endangering the lives of others to become "an enemy not only of the Spanish people but of the international community." In addition to the terms of the Non-Intervention Pact and the slightly later 18 U.S. Code § 959 of 1948 (Enlistment in Foreign Service), we might provocatively frame a discussion in the spirit of George Monbiot's contention that George Orwell's service in Spain could have resulted in life in prison under the United Kingdom's Terrorism Act of 2006, "for fighting abroad with a 'political, ideological, religious, or racial motive'" (Monbiot). Part 2 concludes with my contribution on teaching the Hemingway and Ivens' film *The Spanish Earth* in a war film seminar. This essay situates the film in the overall course design and offers my own critical reflections, for which the class meeting served as springboard and which pull together several of the course's strands of discussion.

In a sense, Part 3 takes us back to where studies of war in Hemingway began, with the wound and trauma postulations of Edmund Wilson and Philip Young. In Moddelmog and del Gizzo's recent book, *Ernest Hemingway in Context*, Peter Hays contributes a biographical piece, "Ailments, Accidents, and Suicide"; his essay in the present collection extends this discussion by ruminating on the overlapping postwar afflictions of post-traumatic stress disorder (PTSD), traumatic brain injury (TBI), and the kind of wounding psychiatrist Jonathan Shay has termed *moral injury*. The title of Ryan Hediger's essay, "Shot . . . Crippled and Gotten Away: Animals and War Trauma in Hemingway," immediately brings to mind images from Hemingway's "A Natural History of the Dead." Hediger mentions this story and several others while focusing his attention on the rarely taught "Get a Seeing-Eyed Dog," as well as on *For Whom the Bell Tolls*. Hediger concludes by turning student attention to "Barking at Death," James Plath's essay on Hemingway's 1933 safari. Following Plath, Hediger quotes the experimental nonfiction *Green Hills of Africa* and posits that hunting animals in Africa helped Hemingway put his wounding and mortality into a healthy perspective. Christopher Barker writes of a different salubrious 1930s animal encounter, and its companion experimental nonfiction accounting, in Hemingway's bullfighting book. "The Poetics of Ernest Hemingway's *Death in the Afternoon*: Restaging the Experience of Total War" also shares Ruth Lahti's transnational approach by placing Hemingway's works in juxtaposition to Ernst Jünger's *Storm of Steel*. Earlier, I recommended all users of this book to visit its first essay; I likewise recommend visiting Sarah Anderson's "'In Another Country' and *Across the River and into the Trees* as Trauma Literature." Anderson's cogent work gives us a solid case for incorporating the neglected novel into our teaching, especially in war or trauma literature courses. She also reminds us that war literature expresses the human condition, not just the veteran condition.

The three best final essays from that senior seminar class appear in Part 4 of this volume, both as evidence of what our students are capable of and as smart, provocative, well-written contributions to Hemingway studies in their own right. Josephine Reece's disquisition on war and bullfighting in *The Sun Also Rises* warrants a reckoning-with by anyone working on the subject. Zack Hausle, a philosophy major, employs Michel Foucault's idea of *biopower* "as a useful lens of analysis for understanding *A Farewell to Arms*" (209). Finally, Anna Broadwell-Gulde investigates the representation and valuation of Pilar's oral storytelling in *For Whom the Bell* Tolls, a novel dominated by Robert Jordan's unspoken storytelling.

Toward its end, the introduction to *Men at War* comments on its own rhetoric of wartime editorializing:

> If matters of this sort intrude themselves into an introduction to a book of narratives of men at war, it must be remembered that we are at war and an impersonal, detached, and purely objective introduction could only be a literary curiosity. This introduction is written by a man, who, having three sons to whom he is responsible in some ways for having brought them into this unspeakably balled-up world, does not feel in any way detached or impersonal about the entire present mess we live in. Therefore, be pleased to regard this introduction as absolutely personal rather than impersonal writing. (*MAW* xxvi–xxvii)

Hemingway's essay states baldly how it does what we want our students' essays to do: Be significant. Matter. Like Hemingway's anthology, *Teaching Hemingway and War* appears in a time of war for the United States, if at the close rather than the opening. The ongoing civil war in Syria has drawn frequent comparison to the Spanish Civil War on the blogosphere. Fully one-third of the essays in the 2013 *War in Ernest Hemingway's* For Whom the Bell Tolls offer comparative perspectives on contemporary wars. Several contributors to this volume remind us that we might see veterans in our classrooms, and that, these days, teaching war literature possesses a clear if unfortunate poignancy that is both pedagogically useful and ethically important. It matters.

It matters whether or not one's nation or people—or any other nation or people—is at war. It matters because the world is still all balled up, and we citizens of it are responsible to one another. It matters because war literature isn't just about war; it's about people. Fascination with Hemingway's biography, with his wartime wounding and consequent travels to wars in his person and in his writing, evidence as much.

## Notes

1. The calculations of casualties are taken from the "Fourth Brigade casualties" chart in chapter 18 of McClellan, while those of brigade strength are drawn from chapter 1.

2. Long determined to edit Shakespeare's plays, Johnson finally published his edited and annotated edition in eight volumes in 1765. This annotation of Hamlet's soliloquy comes from *Hamlet* III.i, in vol. 1 of William Shakespeare, *The Plays of William Shakespeare,* ed. Samuel Johnson, 8 vols. (London: J. and R. Tonson, et al., 1765).

# Part One

# The Great War

# The Violence of Story

Teaching *In Our Time* and Narrative Rhetoric

Alexander Hollenberg

There are certain privileges in life, not the least of these is the ability to teach literature to a roomful of students who, had they been living a century ago, probably would have been conscripted into what was then the world's bloodiest and most gruesome of wars. And even if they hadn't, they would have known someone who had—someone who experienced atrocity, who was stuck in the mud of the trenches, who charged machine guns, who came home shell-shocked, or who didn't come home at all. For most students, however, such images and words are not revelatory. They crop up in the weeks approaching Veterans Day and Remembrance Day, inundating us with a cultural narrative that is always tragic, at times heroic, and irreversibly slipping away—perhaps a little too quickly and a little too comfortably.

How do we come to understand World War I in the classroom? How do we interpret the myriad experiences of war without reducing their integrity as experiences, without resorting to the platitudes that somehow make war even more distant and wholly *other* to ourselves? I'm not sure it's at all possible to really *know* war unless you've been in it or are close to someone who has. Certainly, I've been fortunate enough to find safe harbor in the literary life, but I know several students who either plan to enlist in the military or already have. If we can't fully know war in the classroom, then, together, we can at least begin to understand the ways narrative reconstructs its experiences and subsequently solicits our responses.

Such are the issues with which I wrestle when I prepare to teach Ernest Hemingway's *In Our Time*. To teach it is to engage in an implicit act of remembrance, a reimagination of the many types of lives marked by war. I have taught this short-story cycle at most undergraduate levels: in American surveys, modernist courses, and advanced research seminars. And no matter what their stage of study, students are generally struck by the text's formal properties. Indeed, *In Our Time*'s multiplicity of narratives—stories and interchapters—forces us to face head-on our assumptions of and expectations for narrative coherency. The text's internal disjunction offers an especially productive opportunity to illustrate to students the ways in which an understanding of narrative technique is central to the text's rhetorical effects. If I'm teaching freshmen or sophomores, I might initially ask them to describe the experience of reading such a form. If I'm teaching more advanced students, I will ask them whether they think Hemingway's form makes an argument. In both cases, students (like many critics before them) will typically hone in on the issue of unity (for critiques of the book's unity, see Barloon's "Very Short Stories" and Trout's "Antithetical Icons?"). Most argue that the stories' very separation from one another is what begs connection—it is our responsibility, they imply, to show how the text thematically coheres. The point here is not to mire the students in a debate about the role of literary interpretation (not yet, anyway); rather, through this introductory questioning, it's possible to suggest to students that such narrative patterning bears a specific relationship to the short-story cycle's content. In other words, as students contemplate the structural complexities of *In Our Time*, they become enmeshed in the very difficulties, and perhaps impossibilities, of making clear sense of a world ensnared by the experience of war. From this perspective, the text becomes a world oftentimes absent of cause and effect, conventional narrative logic, and reason. And this absence begets an irrational world in which the inhumanity of war becomes, absurdly, "a most pleasant business" (*CSS* 64).

In a work that juxtaposes the dehumanizing violence of war with so many other forms of violence—the ritualized violence of bullfights, the state-sanctioned violence of executions, the self-inflicted violence of a father who cuts his own throat, the emotional violence that veterans enact upon themselves and others—I want my students to consider how language might also be violent and how Hemingway's narrative might be suspicious of its own rhetorical power.

I begin to flesh out these ideas by introducing Hemingway's theory of the iceberg, a concept of which many students will already have a cursory awareness: "If a writer of prose knows enough about what he is writing about he may omit things that he knows and the reader, if the writer is writing truly enough, will have a feeling of those things as strongly as though the writer had stated them. The dignity of movement of an ice-berg is due to only one-eighth of it being above water" (*DIA* 192). What's so provocative about this aesthetic theory, with respect to a discussion on the relationship between narrative rhetoric and war, is its implicit meditation on interpretive responsibility. To ask students simply what Hemingway means by this statement misses out on an important pedagogical opportunity. We can easily call attention to the surface meaning of this theory of omission, a minimalist metaphor arguing that removing language can actually strengthen the work. But if students have already begun to read *In Our Time,* they will likely intuit in this statement more than a mere imperative for how to write well and truly. And especially keen members of the class, without much prodding from me, will observe that it's somewhat odd for an author (someone who makes his living from words) to suggest the possibility of narrative *without* much language.

Two points are essential to communicate to students at this early stage. First, such a theory has everything to do with Hemingway's modernist context. He wrote *In Our Time* in the shadow of World War I. And as in every other war, leaders have had to use language to persuade others of the necessity of that war. If I have time, I quote to the class Frederic Henry's self-conscious meditation from *A Farewell to Arms,* in which he expresses his embarrassment at "the words sacred, glorious, and sacrifice and the expression in vain" (*FTA* 184). Like Frederic, Hemingway's iceberg theory implies a particular reluctance toward language: words can be disingenuous, and narrative has as much potential to lie as it does to communicate the truth of experience. The second (and related) essential point is that such an aesthetic solicits a mode of active reading. Insofar as Hemingway's iceberg is a response to that sort of bombastic language that not only conceals truth but has no respect for it in the first place, the omissions and overwhelming reticence of *In Our Time* solicit readers to make inferences, to read into and reconstruct the text's meaning for themselves. But before I send students off believing that they can make Hemingway's text mean whatever they want it to mean (that old gem), I complicate my point. We can never *know* exactly what's omitted—what a character like Nick Adams or Harold Krebs refuses to say or even think. That knowledge is only ever an imperfect reconstruction, a *feeling* of those things, never the things themselves. The iceberg is thus as much an entreaty for responsible reading as it is a strategy for writing. We slowly become aware of the immediate need to interpret and the way the text simultaneously limits that act.

Students intuitively recognize narrative's power, even if they cannot perfectly articulate it. They know how it can be used to label, to categorize, to mark, as well as to insult, to degrade, and to hurt. As an act of interpretation, narrative imposes, or at least attempts to impose, a particular set of values upon the world. Does a soldier who "run[s] the searchlight up and down . . . two or three times" to silence screaming refugees (*CSS* 11) bear any resemblance to the reader who searches for enlightenment and enlightened readings? I think so, uncomfortable as the thought is. When we teach students to interpret, we teach them to be creative, but implicit in such an act is the imposition of oneself upon the otherness of the text. In interpretation—in the reading of narrative—there is thus risk: the risk of overextending the self, of overwhelming the other and turning it into a mere instrument of our own rhetorical purposes. To begin to think of the parallels between violence *in* stories and the violence *to* stories is no easy task, but it is an essential exercise, especially for those students who are trying to deepen their understandings of how texts operate through the interpretive demands they make upon their readers.

This certainly takes time, and when I teach *In Our Time,* I typically spend about six hours of lecture and moderated discussion gradually building students' awareness of the text through three key frames: contextual, structural, and stylistic. Within each of these smaller modules, I attempt to show students not only how Hemingway's text describes a world consumed by war and its effects but also the ways its discourse responds to and challenges that world.

### Context in Letters and Language

My contextual argument focuses specifically on the language of soldiers. I show students real examples of soldiers' letters home during World War I. Fortunately, these are readily available all over the internet, and a quick search will produce some fascinating results. Because I teach in Canada, I'm partial to the Canadian Letters and Images Project, which has assembled an impressive collection of letters, diary entries, and poems from more than 280 World War I soldiers. What's especially encouraging is the number of new blogs and websites arising not from institutional sources but from the descendants of soldiers who have reconstructed detailed personal histories of their ancestors. Through many of these sources, I'm able to find both transcribed and scanned copies of original letters, the latter being especially important because they make censorship immediately palpable for students. Just seeing these soldiers' letters, and the extremely low-tech forms of censorship enforced upon language, obliges students to encounter the very limits of narrative expression during the war. I show them, for example, a "letter" written on 8 June 1917, by Robert Quick, a ship's cook serving on the USS *Pueblo,* which is not much of a letter at all. Rather, it is a form full of ready-made statements that instructs soldiers to "place a cross opposite expressions you wish to use." The options are not especially expansive. Quick was fortunate enough to mark "I am well," "Glad to know you are well," "Love," and, perhaps most telling, "I regret that owing to the censorship regulations, I am unable to give any further news or information." I then show students another letter, from 29 June 1915, this one actually written out in long form by Douglas Maclean, a member of the New Zealand Expeditionary Force in Gallipoli. As with any literary text, we read this slowly and closely, and it manifests as a compelling testimony to the exigency of narrative expression during wartime as well as to the frustrating silences imposed on such expression: "Dear Father, I suppose there is not much that I can write that will pass the censor's hands but I have been lucky enough to acquire a piece of paper and envelope and might as well use them." And Maclean was right—about a quarter of the second page of his letter is crudely scribbled out by a black pencil.

Together, we observe the many forms of censorship that soldiers endured and the historical conditions that prevented these young men from being able to tell their stories adequately to their loved ones. Following this activity, we discuss how much of *In Our Time* exposes the very inadequacy of language itself to describe experience. Frequently, when characters try to speak, we realize the difficulty they have in conveying their emotions or explaining the traumas they have faced. I suggest, moreover, that this reticence is not a trait exclusive to the male veterans that populate Hemingway's text—Nick Adams, Krebs, the kitchen corporal, and the others. Just as often it is refugee mothers, or the American girl from "Cat in the Rain," or Krebs's sister Helen, whose stories remain poignantly *un*told but nonetheless scratch at the text's traumatic surface, and, in their numerous iterations, refuse to go gently. Because such silences manifest as a limit to the knowability of experience, imposing a unifying source for the trauma becomes an ethically risky interpretive venture. The task is not simply to figure out what's *not* said—as if there's some code to break, or key to unlock these texts—but rather to understand *how* these narrative silences work to place us in a parallel state of confusion, anxiety, or even desperation.

An effective way to shift the conversation from the historical reality of censorship to the ways that narrative's limitations are constituted through the text is to spend some time analyzing chapter 2. Because the passage is so brief, this exercise offers students a great opportunity to practice and experiment with their close reading skills. I also hand out, as a companion piece, Hemingway's 1922 *Toronto Star* dispatch, "A Silent, Ghastly Procession," upon which he based his vignette. As a relatively straightforward entry point, I ask students to note the differences in the way the two texts narrate the same event. Such an exercise is particularly useful for encouraging more cautious students to participate as we linger on the concrete particulars of language without immediately launching into the more abstract philosophical arguments that can, understandably, be intimidating. One of the key ideas I suggest is that Hemingway's literary writing does not simply mimic reportage. Though his style focuses on the reduction of language, we quickly observe that Hemingway's modernism is something quite different from journalistic standards of the time. Whatever he might have learned from the style sheet of the *Kansas City Star*, he also learned what not to do. In that respect, students will identify a major difference in how the two texts are introduced. Whereas the *Toronto Star* dispatch familiarizes the reader with moderately lengthy sentences that answer the *who*, *what*, *when*, *where*, and *why* of the story, chapter 2 of *In Our Time* employs tight declarative sentences that bear more relation to imagism than journalism. Indeed, students also note that the dispatch is much more emotive and sentimental. By using and repeating adjectival and adverbial supplements ("staggering," "silent," "blindly"), Hemingway pushes into the territory of the melodramatic, while many note a certain condescension in the description of "brilliant, peasant costumes" (*BL* 51). I neither confirm nor deny this interpretation, but I do build upon it by asking the class to consider the major perspectival difference between the two texts. The dispatch is by no means disinterested, but it does employ an outsider's perspective of the refugees; we read from above and look below. Although we are told the procession is "never-ending," we are also told where it will end—"There is only Macedonia and Western Thrace to receive the fruit of the Turk's return to Europe" (*BL* 52)—and so that initial qualifier appears overwrought and potentially disingenuous.

My purpose here is not to criticize Hemingway's early journalism but to show how the mitigation of this external focalization in *In Our Time* changes the narrative's function. Thus, I compare with the class the endings of the two pieces, asking them how their narrative techniques diverge. In the *Star*, Hemingway writes: "Nearly half a million refugees are in Macedonia now. How they are to be fed nobody knows, but in the next month all the Christian world will hear the cry: 'Come over into Macedonia and help us!'" (*BL* 52). But chapter 2 of *In Our Time* concludes as follows: "Women and kids were in the carts crouched with mattresses, mirrors, sewing machines, bundles. There was a woman having a kid with a young girl holding a blanket over her and crying. Scared sick looking at it. It rained all through the evacuation" (*CSS* 71).

The interchapter builds up to a powerful image of agony and fear without ever blatantly editorializing on that fact. Moreover, we are offered neither distance from the event nor the comfort of full knowledge that such focalizing distance can sometimes include. We cannot see exactly who is "scared sick." The omission of the grammatical subject makes the scene partly unknowable to readers, while at the same time it solicits our participation in the tragedy through the inferential activity that such omission requires. The simplification of the grammar in this sentence produces a recalcitrance that causes the reader to hesitate over a straightforward reading that would identify the girl as the one who is scared sick and not, for example, an anonymous narrator-observer.

In its reworking of old material, this fictional narrative implicitly underscores the rhetorical violences we can perform when we make stable narratives out of the most senseless, incoherent, and dehumanizing of situations. Hemingway's style here solicits from the reader a hermeneutics of indeterminacy, where access to the other is simultaneously offered and withheld. We cannot fully witness or extricate ourselves from the terrible scene. Like the soldiers' censored letters, which blatantly dramatize the limitations of language imposed within a wartime context, the narrative technique brings us uncomfortably close to such terrible moments but also suppresses knowledge and interpretive mastery over the experience.

Structural Parataxis

As students begin to understand the ways *In Our Time* responds to its wartime context, they seem to find Hemingway's choice of genre even more provocative. After several hours' worth of lecturing and close reading, I find it useful to revisit students' initial misgivings over the short-story cycle's disjunction. To prepare for this module, I ask students to submit a short reading response to Peter Donahue's "The Genre Which Is Not One: Hemingway's *In Our Time*, Difference, and the Short Story Cycle," an essay that argues for the "un-fixed nature" of Hemingway's chosen genre (161). Through this assignment, students begin to recognize that genre is more than a vessel for ideas; it shapes narrative logic. In advanced seminars, I also assign Stephen Clifford's "Hemingway's Fragmentary Novel: Readers Writing the Hero in *In Our Time*," as it provides both some compelling revisions of the 'Hemingway hero' and a prolonged meditation on how the text's pluralism interacts with the values readers bring to the process of interpretation. I begin our conversation by asking a simple question. Is there a central character in this text? The obvious answer is Nick

Adams, but I push students to consider that (a) Nick Adams is not present in many of the narratives, (b) in several cases where we might assume that a protagonist is Nick, that assumption is never fully substantiated by the text, and (c) that since the larger storyworld of *In Our Time* encompasses a multiplicity of voices, focusing primarily upon Nick's experiences risks imposing textual unity at the cost of fully attending to the experiences of those others. It is here that students begin to recognize that the ways in which we approach a text as readers, and the interpretive work we do upon it (not only to find meaning but to make meaning), have particular consequences.

If first-time readers are ready to make the cycle's disparate narratives connect to each other through certain thematic links, my line of questioning asks them to consider not only what meanings are missed in that search for unity but, more importantly, how that search may violate the text. I imagine that when instructors ask their students if the narratives of *In Our Time* have anything in common, the most frequent answer they will receive is "violence." This is a great answer, but perhaps not for the reason students will expect: Hemingway's omissions, both within and between stories, are tantalizing, begging to be filled in, and yet that process of *filling in* necessitates interpretive force. It means turning the unknowable into the knowable, compelling a recalcitrant text to connect with itself. Hemingway's genre brings the potential power of interpretation to the fore and thus more fully implicates us within the consuming violences of "Our Time."

Having tested the waters of some complex ethical negotiations and abstract thinking regarding the responsibilities of interpretation, students need to be brought back to solid critical ground. I therefore suggest to them that the genre is a version of parataxis writ large, a *structural parataxis*. If parataxis is a technique that emphasizes the separateness of each individual sentence and limits causation—where that which comes before is not actively constructed as having a causal relationship to that which comes after—*structural parataxis* implies that there is no clear causative line between the cycle's narratives, that characters do not simply recur, and that the interchapters do not specifically illuminate what comes between them. Indeed, when we look closely at *In Our Time*, its structure reiterates the very transience of coherence. Students may notice, for example, the prevalence of mothers and babies in the cycle's earlier sections. But to impose a straightforward connection between the mother of "Indian Camp," who undergoes a caesarean performed with a "jack-knife" and "nine-foot, tapered gut leaders" (*CSS* 69), and the refugee woman of chapter 2, the reader must willfully forget the very fact of their difference—the historical and geographical differences between Adrianople and Michigan, the Karagatch road and Ojibway woodlands. Such diversity of historical experience is accentuated by the cycle's parataxis, and together these elements implicitly resist our gestures of symbolic assimilation or, rather, assimilation-by-symbol.

To emphasize the potential integrity of each narrative is to ask students to contemplate how we use others (texts, characters, people) as instruments for our own rhetorical purposes. From this perspective, the interchapters are not merely positive transitional moments—connectives that inform our reading through a process of *mapping on similarities*—but spaces of friction, where interpretation is halted in the moment, where we are made hyperaware of the differences between figures we would assume to be compatible, and where our own critical attempts to explicate the text force us to perform the very difficulty of understanding difference. Faced with a cycle whose structure is especially representative of a plurality of experiences, whose narration even of "war" is fragmented into different wars, times, regions, and voices, students grapple with the fact that a single narrative arc cannot (and, perhaps, should not) contain such plurality. To better consolidate this structural argument, I quote to them from William James's *A Pluralistic Universe*:

> Pragmatically interpreted, pluralism or the doctrine that it is many means only that the sundry parts of reality *may be externally related*. . . . Things are "with" one another in many ways, but nothing includes everything, or dominates over everything. The word "and" trails along after every sentence. Something always escapes. "Ever not quite" has to be said of the best attempts made anywhere in the universe at attaining all-inclusiveness . . . However much may be collected, however much may report itself as present at any effective centre of consciousness or action, something else is self-governed and absent and unreduced to unity. (321–22; emphasis in original)

Such pragmatism may come as a shock to some, but for others James's idea of the "and," with its explicit critique of conceptual perfection, bears a productive relationship with Hemingway's generic choice. To conceive of *In Our Time*'s separate interchapters as a series of "ands" that constitute its structural parataxis is to recognize the particularity of each narrative experience and resist the conflation of those particular experiences into universalizing and generalizing interpretations. And yet the interchapters, as James would intuit, are "with" the other narratives in many ways. They are both conjunctive and disjunctive, connecting themselves to other narratives and insisting on the limits of that connection.

This foray into Jamesian pluralism helps students articulate the ways in which the cycle's structural representation of war complicates our desire to understand war. Such attention to the nontotalizing rhetorical effects of the text's structure stimulates many students to think about the potential violences of an interpretation that would conflate certain characters' narration of war into *the* experience of war: Nick's "separate peace" on the Italian front (*CSS* 105), they note, is *not* the same as Harold Krebs's involvement at Belleau Wood, Soissons, the Champagne, St. Mihiel, and the Argonne. Students begin to recognize the value-laden assumptions implicit in their initial desire to unify the text, and instead see the war—like the text—as a multitude of oftentimes unshareable experiences.

### Of Style and Soldiers

As we move forward, I begin to pay more prolonged attention to particular narratives, and as edifying as it might be to give every story and interchapter its due, time's winged chariot doesn't stop even for English professors. Still, this is why teaching *In Our Time* can be so rewarding—its narrative variety all but ensures that the text you teach one semester won't be the same text you teach the next. If, up to this point, I have tried to render the cycle in fairly broad strokes, in this module I focus on the ways certain stories interact with the text's structural arguments. I also remind my students of what it means to think of narrative as a form of rhetoric, a concept that, in most of my courses, I tend to reiterate until it sticks. I use James Phelan's definition from *Experiencing Fiction*, which stresses that narrative is the action of "somebody telling somebody else on some occasion and for some purpose(s) that something happened" (3). Because this definition is straightforward, students can easily digest it, but it is also valuable because it highlights that narrative is an interactive communicative experience between tellers, listeners, context, event, and function. Such interactivity is key because it reminds students that their interpretations must account for narrative discourse. That is, attending to the nuances of *how* a text is constructed helps us sort out the judgments and values expressed through that particular telling.

In "Soldier's Home," for example, we examine how Hemingway handles focalization to represent Krebs's sense of loss. Krebs's story is one of a traumatized interior. Home late from the war, having missed out on the pageantry that greeted other soldiers returning to the United States, he withholds himself from others, hardly speaking because he senses no one will listen to him unless he exaggerates his experience: for Krebs, talking about the war means lying about it. Still, more provocative is this story's implication that even efforts to speak "truly" about war will emerge as lies. Krebs craves a return to a smooth life, a life without complication: "All of the times that had been able to make him feel cool and clear inside himself when he thought of them; the times so long back when he had done the one thing, the only thing for a man to do, easily and naturally, when he might have done something else, now lost their cool, valuable quality, and then were lost themselves" (*CSS* 111). Students will readily pick up that this passage is focalized through Krebs's consciousness, and when I ask about the consequences of such focalization, they are prepared to answer because of earlier work we've done on context and structure. The passage is, in a sense, unreadable: we cannot perfectly know the "something" that Krebs has lost. And the word *thing*, students point out, is especially ironic. Despite Krebs's gesture to a concrete and observable reality—a "thing" he can hold onto—that reality is lost, not only to him, but to the reader as well.

I push this conversation a bit further, so as not to rest merely on the idea of ambiguity. What Krebs wants, I point out, is a certain simplicity of life where he can look at the "patterns" of girls' clothing and get a girl without having "to work to get her" (*CSS* 112). But Hemingway's style communicates a larger structural irony. Hemingway represents Krebs's consciousness through a cadenced, rhythmically predictable, and paratactic style. In one paragraph, the anaphora "He did not want" is repeated five times (112–13), producing an aural and tonal simplicity and an accretion of negatives that signify a person who can no longer expend the constructive effort of imagining other people (girls) as real. Krebs's vision of the ideal simple life may be at odds with the simplicity of the text. Where we actively attend to the protagonist and at least *try* to intuit dimensionality, Krebs cannot do the same thing for the girls he putatively desires. This type of stylistic argument is beneficial for students because it amplifies the deleterious effects of Krebs's wartime experience. As he is unable to interpret the reality of others beyond their surfaces, he is essentially *other* to the close reader. In turn, this may help to account for certain sympathetic readings of Krebs's mother. If Hemingway's style conditions us to recognize the limitations of Krebs's mode of reading others, then that style may also solicit skepticism toward the silences that Krebs's focalization imposes on his mother. As conversation continues, students find themselves able to make larger contextual connections as well. They note, for example, that Krebs's postwar trauma is exacerbated by the text's "loss" of words themselves, insofar as it limits the reader's ability to reconstruct the depths of his experience.

"Soldier's Home" is also a valuable story to teach because of its proximity to the interchapter preceding it. If Krebs alludes to the obscure "something else" of his wartime experience (*CSS* 111), I ask my students whether they think the interchapter helps to explain what that omission may be. In other words, does the interchapter elucidate the story and give us a sense of what soldiers such as Krebs had to endure? Is it a saying of the unsaid? Written from the perspective of a soldier under bombardment at Fossalta, it is certainly visceral. But I like talking about this narrative with my students because it also contemplates the ethical limits of storytelling. The protagonist prays to Jesus as he is shelled, promising that if he survives, he will tell the world about Him. But after the onslaught, the soldier visits a prostitute and the narrative ends with one of *In Our Time*'s most provocative sentences: "*And he never told anybody*" (*CSS* 109; italics in original). I explain to my class that this story operates as a mode of imagistic witnessing, a concise and penetrating depiction of trench warfare. And yet I also point out that this final line imbues the text with a certain paradoxical quality only possible in fiction: this soldier refuses to tell the personal story that we have just, somehow, been told. Here, my students encounter the ethics of narrative silence, which implicitly asks how a character's choice *not* to tell a story interacts with (and sometimes works at cross-purposes to) the reader's need to understand. Robyn Warhol's work on the "antinarratable," or tellings that are proscribed by social convention (224), may provide extra fodder for class discussion. And Adam Zachary Newton's argument, that to attend to the hermeneutic ethics of a text is to learn "the paradoxical lesson that 'getting' someone else's story is also a way of losing the person as 'real'" (19), may further inspire students to think about the consequences implicit in the twin acts of telling and listening.

Once I've put these complex issues out into the ether, I go back the text. When I ask students to comment upon the way chapter 7 handles perspective, the closest of readers will notice the shift from third-person singular—"He lay very flat and sweated and prayed oh jesus christ get me out of here"—to first-person plural—"We went to work on the trench and in the morning the sun came up and the day was hot and muggy and cheerful and quiet" (*CSS* 109). Subtle as it is, the switch from "he" to "we" marks the narrator not as *heterodiegetic* (a noncharacter narrator) but *homodiegetic* (a character narrator). What the "we" implies is actually quite dramatic. Whereas readers will expect certain types of narrators to be able to access the consciousness of a protagonist, a narrator who is part of that character's world (in this case, a fellow soldier) would not have such interior access. In other words, Hemingway's small narrative dramatizes the communication of this desperate soldier's consciousness as a product of another soldier's imagination. When I ask my students, Why do we tell stories?—an unfairly loaded question—they generally assume that the reason is to gain an understanding and sense of the narrator's world—to *know* the other. And yet, chapter 7's narrative paradox shows us that the process of understanding and knowing someone inevitably involves imaginative leaps, a reading into and reconstruction of otherness that is not necessarily sanctioned by the person whose experience it is.

In this way, my lectures proceed through an exciting discussion of the intersection of narrative ethics and war. Is it possible to narrate such trauma without reducing it? How does one describe an experience for which words were never enough? There are a host of pedagogical pathways that an instructor may take at this point. I sometimes linger over "A Very Short Story," to show how Hemingway mobilizes romantic tropes in order to undercut them; in its depiction of Luz, a nurse who falls out of love with a young soldier after the Armistice, the story demonstrates the banal pain that comes from holding on too tightly to heroic narratives after the war. I also like to return to "On the Quai at Smyrna," both to remind students that the cycle reaches far beyond World War I and to show that Hemingway's handling of the second person perspective—"*You* remember the harbor" (*CSS* 64; emphasis added)—emphasizes the scene as a singular experience even as it simultaneously suggests the possibility of sharing that experience with an interlocutor. "Quai" beckons us to move in and out of soldiers' experiences, enacting moments of commensurability and incommensurability, understanding and disgust, implicitly asking us how judgment is constituted in the midst of empathy.

After exposing themselves to the many hostilities of *In Our Time*, several of my students tell me that they find some sanctuary in "Big Two-Hearted River." Much like Nick Adams himself, they are comforted by this storyworld, which juxtaposes so sharply against the rest of the cycle. Hemingway's famous declaration, in *A Moveable Feast*, that "the story was about coming back from the war but there was no mention of the war in it" can help to consolidate this point (75). But how safe a narrative space is it? I point out that the larger cycle, in a sense, conditions our responses to this final story: we are prepared by the rest of the text to intuit war's violent reach almost everywhere, not only in "the burned-over country" that Nick leaves behind (*CSS* 163), but also in the "satisfactory hiss" of a mosquito conflagrated by Nick's match (169); the grasshopper, hooked so precisely by Nick, spitting up "tobacco juice" (175); and the trout offal "tossed . . . ashore for the minks to find" (180). Even the story itself is fractured by chapter 15, the story of the hanging of Sam Cardinella, who loses control of his sphincter muscle just after a priest tells him, "Be a man, my son" (171). Here, violence manifests as a mode of narrative interruption and threatens to become a perpetual fact of modern experience.

The clearest sign that this narrative operates as something more than a safe space, however, is the swamp, where "the fishing would be tragic" (*CSS* 180). When I ask my students why Nick refuses to fish the swamp, I ask them to focus on diction. Why does Hemingway repeat the word *tragic* in two consecutive sentences? I want them to think about the connotations of such a literary word amidst the Michigan backcountry. *Tragic* defamiliarizes because it shows Nick to be an *interpreter* of his world. He begins to read his setting metaphorically—as a literary text rather than the literal world. If, for Hemingway, "learning to suspend your imagination and live completely in the very second of the present minute . . . is the greatest gift a soldier can acquire" (*MAW* xxvii), then Nick's language here is an attempt to identify a new, "writerly" version of himself away from the war. Despite the swamp's threatening presence, the literary diction signals a shift away from the intense focus on the material world (eating, fishing, sleeping), and suddenly toward a world of imaginative possibility. The swamp is described as a space "smooth and deep" that "it would not be possible to walk through," and where there is only a "half light" (*CSS* 180). This lack of clarity—of enlightenment—signals the swamp as unknowable, as a form of otherness. It represents a potential threat to the sense of cohesion and strength that Nick has found alone within the forest. If he is beginning to find a stable sense of self, the swamp is a reminder that such self-contained stability is only temporary. He must at some point allow others and otherness to become a part of his experience again. Thus, by conceiving the swamp *as* text, Nick begins to recognize the necessity of engaging with unknowability, of reading and interpreting others, even if such engagement bears tragic risks. In turn, this line of thinking can prompt students to nuance their own ideas about the text. Instead of only asking how the text critiques violence, they begin to observe how *In Our Time* reimagines responsibility to and for the other. It is a responsibility that involves a recognition of both our desire to connect and the inevitable limitations of that connection, of our proximity and our dislocation from the text's violently plural space.

These strategies for teaching *In Our Time* are by no means exhaustive, but I've found that they encourage students to think deeply and critically about the ways narrative responds to its context and the ways such responses are constituted through the interpretive work we perform upon texts. Moreover, to teach this short-story cycle is to teach not only how a range of actors came to experience modern warfare but to show students that the violence of war also occasioned new modes of storytelling that cast doubt on the capacity of narrative to function as an instrument of knowledge. This early Hemingway work demonstrates a radical suspicion of its own raw materials—of language itself—and how we marshal those materials for particular rhetorical purposes. If the undergraduate classroom offers a safe creative space where we, along with our students, can tease out the implications of our close encounters with textual otherness, *In Our Time* reminds us that such encounters are never fully estranged from the world beyond the text, and that to interpret is to also participate in the violence of story.

# "Our Fathers Lied"

## The Great War and Paternal Betrayal in Hemingway's *In Our Time*

Lisa Tyler

> If any question why we died,
> Tell them, because our fathers lied.
> —Rudyard Kipling, "Epitaphs"

In his short story collection *In Our Time,* Ernest Hemingway crafts a work in which, like others involved in World War I, he ultimately holds his own father, and fathers in general, responsible for the carnage and suffering he witnessed. "For as the early glamour of battle dissipated and late Victorian fantasies of heroism gave way to modernist visions of unreality, it became clear that this war to end all wars necessitated a sacrifice of the sons to the exigencies of the fathers" (Gilbert 280). In teaching *In Our Time,* an instructor would need first to establish that such a literary tradition of writing about paternal betrayal exists, and then to ask students to examine the evidence supporting the contention that *In Our Time* belongs within that tradition.

### Paternal Betrayal in the Great War

In *A War Imagined: The First World War and English Culture,* an eminently useful work for preparing lecture notes on the theme of paternal betrayal in World War I, Samuel Hynes identifies what he calls "the theme of the Old Men—the conviction that the war had empowered the elderly to send the young to their deaths" (246). Hynes traces this theme through a range of British cultural artifacts, from magazine and newspaper articles to a painting, *He Gained a Fortune but He Gave a Son,* by the futurist artist C. R. W. Nevinson.

In *Sexchanges,* the second volume of *No Man's Land: The Place of the Woman Writer in the Twentieth Century,* Sandra Gilbert and Susan Gubar document the ways in which the anger of World War I soldiers at their fathers broadens in many literary works of the period to become a fury at those on the home front in general, transforming into a hatred specifically of the women who did not have to serve and who seemed to benefit from the relative freedom they experienced during the Great War. But Hemingway mentions women in only a couple of stories in *In Our Time,* focusing instead almost exclusively on fathers. It is important to point out to students that, as Hynes notes, the term *Old Men* indicates gender—"there were no Old Women, because women were not perceived as having power"—and also implies a certain class: "Wartime and post-war explosions of wrath against the Old Men were not directed at Old Farmers, or Old Postmen, after all: the term meant those men beyond service age who had the power to send young men to their deaths" (248).

Anger over the fathers' perceived betrayal is the theme of some of the finest literature of the Great War. Wilfred Owen's poem "The Parable of the Old Man and the Young" (readily available online) retells the biblical story of "Abram" and Isaac. Preparing to sacrifice his son at God's request, Abram "builded parapets and trenches there, / And stretched forth the knife to slay his son" but is interrupted by an angel, who assures him it is not necessary to kill Isaac and indicates that he should kill "the Ram of Pride" instead: "But the old man would not so, but slew his son, / And half the seed of Europe, one by one" (42). Owen died just before the war's end.

Although Owen's poem is deservedly the best-known work in this vein, it is not the only one. Rudyard Kipling, who lost his eighteen-year-old son John (Hitchens 43–44), wrote the couplet that forms the epigraph of this essay; it, too, is readily available online. Siegfried Sassoon spent part of the war hospitalized for shell shock and wrote several poems on similar themes; they, too, can easily be accessed online for students to review independently or for the instructor to present during class. The soldier in Sassoon's "Remorse," for example, has experienced horrors he cannot discuss: "'there's things in war one dare not tell / Poor father sitting safely at home, who reads / Of dying heroes and their deathless deeds'" (*Counter-Attack* 57). His poem "Survivors" describes the home front's condescending assurance regarding the returning soldiers—"No doubt they'll soon get well"—and ends with a dark image of angry sons: "Men who went out to battle, grim and glad; / Children, with eyes that hate you, broken and mad" (*Counter-Attack* 55).

Instructors wishing to teach a survey of war literature could easily locate other works on the same theme. In her disturbing 1922 short story "The Fly," Katherine Mansfield, whose younger brother Leslie died in the service (Tomalin

139), depicts a father, known only as "the boss," who has lost a son in the war. A Mr. Woodifield, who has also lost a son, tells him that in visiting his own son's grave, he and his family had discovered the grave of the boss's son nearby. After his departure, the boss thinks for a moment of his son before becoming distracted by a fly in his inkpot. He first saves the fly but then torments it, dropping ink on it until it dies: "He's a plucky little devil, thought the boss, and he felt a real admiration for the fly's courage. That was the way to tackle things; that was the right spirit. Never say die; it was only a question of . . ." (Mansfield 601). As Gilbert and Gubar observe, "Mansfield's message is clear: as flies to wanton fathers are 'the boys' to 'the bosses' who have sacrificed their sons in war and do not even know how to mourn them properly"( 281).

Similarly, Edith Wharton, made a Chevalier of the Legion of Honor in recognition of her volunteer service to war refugees, depicts an American father, John Campton, learning to appreciate his son George's sacrifice in her short novel *A Son at the Front*. John's ex-wife challenges him, saying "What do you suppose those young men out there think of their fathers, safe at home, who are too high-minded and conscientious to protect them?" (184).

### Fathers in Hemingway's *In Our Time*

Hemingway seems to share this terrible fury over a perceived paternal betrayal. I am not the first to note its presence in *In Our Time*. Robert Gajdusek pronounces the collection "a carefully integrated study of patriarchal failure" (172), and Bickford Sylvester argues that an important theme running throughout the work is the "child who grows to young adulthood disappointed by every expected source of leadership and support in the older generation" (77).

An instructor could begin the discussion of *In Our Time* by asking students first to identify the literal and metaphorical fathers in the collection and then to talk about how they are depicted. *In Our Time* begins with patriarchal figures (first an officer and then a doctor) literally tearing children away from their hysterical mothers (in "On the Quai at Smyrna" and "Indian Camp") and ends with a king (surely a classic patriarchal figure) in an absurdist rose garden straight out of Lewis Carroll, saying in all innocence, "Of course the great thing in this sort of an affair is not to be shot oneself!" (*CSS* 181). Sylvester aptly pronounces the Greek king "the crowning father figure in Hemingway's collection" (78). If there is nevertheless a faint whiff of nostalgia about this collection, it's interesting to note that in this final story, the king is in a garden, one to which Nick Adams can no more return than could the first Adam.

Hemingway's disdain for the king's self-interested attitude is most clearly evident in a statement the writer makes in his September 1935 *Esquire* article, "Notes on the Next War: A Serious Topical Letter": "No one man nor group of men incapable of fighting or exempt from fighting should in any way be given the power, no matter how gradually it is given them, to put this country or any country into war" (*BL* 178). He demonstrates the strength of this feeling by repeating the sentiment two months later in "The Malady of Power: A Second Serious Letter": "Now is the time to make it impossible for any one man, or any hundred men, or any thousand men, to put us in a war in ten days—in a war they will not have to fight" (*BL* 198).

In "Soldier's Home," the nearest thing to a confrontation between a soldier and his father occurs only obliquely. Astute students will quickly notice that Krebs's father is the only family member who does not appear directly in the story, yet it's his father who prompts Krebs's mother to confront him about what he will do with his life. And it's clear that while his mother is concerned about Krebs's morality ("I know the temptations you must have been exposed to"), his pragmatic father is concerned about more material matters: "He thinks you have lost your ambition, that you haven't got a definite aim in life" (*CSS* 115). Critics tend to be very hard on Krebs's mother, who is admittedly cloying in her sentimentality, but they fail to mention that she largely acts as a mouthpiece for her husband. Hemingway is kinder, specifically pointing out that she "did not say this in a mean way" and "seemed worried" (115). And although Krebs says he doesn't love her, he concedes that this is in part because he doesn't love anybody. He resists her invocation of God, the ultimate patriarch, by insisting, "I'm not in His Kingdom," but he does seem to have some genuine feelings for her. Krebs "had felt sorry for her" and ultimately consoles himself by deciding he will "get a job and she would feel all right about it" (116). His father is the stricter parent, the one who "can't read his *Star* if it's been mussed" (114), and Krebs, convinced that his father would never have allowed him to take out the car without persuasion, twice insists to his apparently kinder and gentler mother, "I'll bet you made him" (114). Finally, it is his father, not his mother, whom Krebs ultimately rejects completely: "He would not go down to his father's office. He would miss that one" (116).

A similar rejection of paternal advice occurs in chapter 13 of *In Our Time*, when the narrator tries to persuade Luis to stop dancing and drinking, since he will have to fight a bull that night. Luis resists, saying, "Oh leave me alone. You're not my father" (*CSS* 149). Curiously, in a later edition, "father" is changed to "mother"—an emendation that instructors may wish to bring to students' attention. We might interpret the narrator's behavior as loving concern if it were not for the coda, in which we learn from the narrator's conversation with Maera that if Luis does not kill his bulls, Maera and the narrator will end up having to fight them. What seems like fatherly concern is unmasked to reveal protective self-interest. Similarly, in "The Battler," two older men—first the brakeman and then Ad Francis—seem friendly initially only to surprise the naïve Nick when they later turn on him. Both of them call him "kid" before they abruptly resort to violence.

The racetrack story "My Old Man" might initially seem a more positive portrayal of a loving father-son relationship, but even here the father sacrifices his son's needs to his own principles. As Michael Reynolds observes, "It is his first story in which the father fails the son" (*Paris Years* 58–59). It was certainly not the last. At the hanging depicted in chapter 15 of *In Our Time*, Sam Cardinella is so frightened he cannot walk and loses control of his bowels. One of the two priests who is present says, "Be a man, my son," advice that is undercut by the final sentence of the vignette: "The priest skipped back onto the scaffolding just before the drop fell" (*IOT* 143). The "son" is enjoined to be a man, but the "father" seems all too preoccupied with his own personal safety.

### "The Doctor and the Doctor's Wife" as Prelude to War

Every literal and metaphorical father in the collection eventually reveals himself to be at best coldly self-interested and at worst ruthlessly violent toward mothers and sons. Perhaps the key story for this interpretation of *In Our Time* is "The Doctor and the Doctor's Wife," which, according to David Seed, "reveals the differences between his parents in a way which paves the way for his adult engagement with life" (22)—a particularly troubling observation when we consider that the doctor is completely unable to express his emotions and instead turns to playing with guns, "indulging in a fantasy of violence" (Davis 148). Critics are often hard on the doctor's wife, but for Davis, the doctor surely presents the more dangerous model to follow: "as she counsels peace and mildness, the doctor prepares his weapon" (149). Oddly, however, some critics seem to feel the doctor is not violent enough. Michael Reynolds, for example, complains that "Doctor Adams failed the test, his capacity for violence too diluted by civilizing forces" (*Paris Years* 187). Should the doctor have shot his wife for the sin of disagreeing with him? Should a wife who doubts her husband's interpretation of events be punished? Would a murderous Doctor Adams have passed the supposed "test"?

In contrast to his wife, the doctor denies losing his temper and thus demonstrates his own fundamental emotional dishonesty: "She may not be able to face the truth, or may not know it, but he knows the truth and does not speak it" (Arnold 147). As Thomas Strychacz tellingly observes:

> The standoff in the garden between the doctor and Dick Boulton . . . does not merely happen to resemble the standoff between the Austro-Hungarian Empire and the Allies but may actually help explain it. The story describes a complex dynamic of humiliation and aggression emerging out of a history of territories annexed and dispossessed. . . . The doctor can either 'fight like a man' or be shamed; his response to shame is to pick up the shotgun. These early stories are testimony to Hemingway's profound understanding of the workings of masculine psychology and to his caustic critique of the limitations it imposes. We should not miss the pertinence of his critique to the psychology of the men who led nations into the Great War. (71)

If Strychacz's response seems strained or extreme, it may be useful to review with students the research on shame conducted by Thomas J. Scheff and Suzanne M. Retzinger. In their book *Emotions and Violence: Shame and Rage in Destructive Conflicts,* they suggest that shame is a common result of alienation and impaired social bonds: "When important bonds are damaged, shame results; when shame is not acknowledged, the attack is warded off with anger" (97)—an anger that, coupled with unacknowledged shame, is more likely than unalloyed anger to lead to violence. Scheff and Retzinger make the same link Strychacz does: "The European nations in the period 1870–1945 bear a strong resemblance to the dysfunctional families so clearly described by theorists of family systems" (163). Scheff and Retzinger attribute Hitler's appeal to Germans' shame and resulting rage over the aftermath of World War I. Furthermore, "the unbearably high levels of individual and collective violence in our era may be a consequence of the increasing repression of shame and the associated denial of social bonds" (139).

In shame resulting from a humiliating dispute over contested territory, then, Dr. Adams picks up his shotgun—and Europe goes to war. As Larry E. Grimes writes of "The Doctor and the Doctor's Wife," "the presence of the shotgun is terrifying because it represents the only kind of power the doctor has left—the power to destroy. . . . All he has within and before him is death and annihilation" (154). Nick, in choosing to go with his father, chooses death, chooses war, chooses violence.

"A separate peace"

True, Nick later (in chapter 6 of *In Our Time*) renounces violence to declare, in his famous phrase, "You and me, we've made a separate peace" (*CSS* 105). But renouncing violence is only the first step in making peace (Ruddick 161). Even in this vignette, Hemingway recognizes that Nick's declaration is too facile; it's the only place in the interchapters where the word *peace* even appears (Hagemann 54), a point easily made by asking students to prepare for class by locating every instance of the word they can find (or by referring them to the *Concordance to Hemingway's* In Our Time compiled by Peter L. Hays). It's particularly interesting to ask students to compare Hemingway's vignette to the treatment given the same subject by Doris Lessing, born twenty years later, in a novel first published only after Hemingway's death:

> Having lived through a war when half the human race was engaged in murdering the other half, murdering more vilely, savagely, cruelly, than ever in human history, what does it mean to say: I don't believe that violence achieves anything?
>
> Every fibre of Martha's body, everything she thought, every movement she made, everything she was, was because she had been born at the end of one world war, and had spent all her adolescence in the atmosphere of preparations for another which had lasted five years and had inflicted such wounds on the human race that no one had any idea of what the results would be.
>
> Martha did not believe in violence.
>
> Martha was the essence of violence, she had been conceived, bred, fed, and reared on violence. (Lessing 195)

Surely part of the point Hemingway is making in *In Our Time* is that what is true of Lessing's Martha is also true of Nick: He had been conceived, bred, fed, and reared on violence.

"Now there is no peacetime"

The same point that Hemingway makes in *In Our Time* about the omnipresence of violence is also made by contemporary scholars in feminist peace studies. In "War Is Not Just an Event: Reflections on the Significance of Everyday Violence," Chris J. Cuomo argues that "war is a presence, a constant undertone, white noise in the background of social existence, moving sometimes closer to the foreground of collective consciousness in the form of direct combat yet remaining mostly as an unconsidered given" (42). If this idea of permanent war strikes students as anachronistic, too *politically correct* for someone like Hemingway, it's worthwhile to note something Hemingway himself wrote years later, about 16 October 1949, in a letter to John Hemingway, his eldest son, then a captain in the U.S. Army: "We never had a member of the family soldiering in peace time but I suppose now there is no peacetime" (*SL* 682).

Writing of chapter 6 of *In Our Time*, in which Nick declares his separate peace, Wendolyn E. Tetlow suggests that the imagery of the twisted iron bedstead hanging from the exploded house across the street from Nick dramatizes the way in which war invades the sanctity of the home—as students might realize if asked specifically what that image might mean in the context of *In Our Time*. In any case, as Tetlow points out, preceding stories have made clear that the home was invaded by "the quiet violence of his parents' marriage" long before the war: "Each interchapter reveals in detail one aspect of war that is also to appear in more subtle form in the supposedly tranquil life of a doctor's son in northern Michigan" (130, 132). It is not coincidental that Ernest once referred to the state of his parents' marriage as "an armed neutrality" (Baker, *Life Story* 10). The instructor might want to ask students what parallels they see between the war and violence in the interchapters and the private life in the short stories.

## Violence Begins at Home

Hemingway does not distinguish between private and public as Tetlow tries to; Hemingway sees violence as all-pervasive in modern culture and indistinguishable from what Tetlow rather coyly calls "the privacy of the bedroom" (33). It is in the sexual act that violence takes place in "Up in Michigan" (which Hemingway wanted to include in *In Our Time*); it is literally in the bedroom that Doctor Adams loads his gun in "The Doctor and the Doctor's Wife." And in "Fathers and Sons" the cycle continues. Nick's young son recalls the gifts his grandfather gave him: "an air rifle and an American flag" (*CSS* 376), emblems of violence and nationalism. Violence, Hemingway seems to be saying, begins at home.

Thomas J. Scheff, in *Bloody Revenge: Emotions, Nationalism, and War*, writes that "war is not just *out there*, separate from us; it is also *in here*, inside of us" (12; emphasis in original). As he elaborates, "when leaders of nations and their followers face large-scale, emotionally charged conflicts, they utilize the only dispute tactics they know—the ones they learned, beneath the level of awareness, in their families" (34). Even Tetlow concedes that "a strong suggestion of the connection between private frustration and brutality is obvious" (99). It is interesting to draw students' attention to Jessica Benjamin's speculation "that the insistence on maintaining the separation between public and private simply repeats the splitting of father and mother" (204).

To help students make for themselves that connection between the violence of war and the violence of Nick's family, the instructor might want to consider assigning a carefully selected passage or two from Virginia Woolf's *Three Guineas,* her 1938 discussion of how to prevent war. Woolf, a fellow modernist, contends "that the public and the private worlds are inseparably connected; that the tyrannies and servilities of the one are the tyrannies and servilities of the other" (142). Thus she writes of fathers, as well:

> It is a solemn sight always—a procession, like a caravanserai crossing a desert. Great-grandfathers, grandfathers, fathers, uncles—they all went that way ... The questions that we have to ask and to answer about that procession during this moment of transition are so important that they may well change the lives of all men and women forever. For we have to ask ourselves, here and now, do we wish to join that procession, or don't we? On what terms shall we join that procession? Above all, where is it leading us, the procession of educated men? (61–62)

Asking students how Hemingway might answer Woolf's question should help them recognize that Nick Adams fears joining the procession Woolf describes, becoming exactly like the father who sent him off to war.

### Patrophobia and Literary Allusion

*In Our Time* depicts Nick's *patrophobia,* his fear of becoming his father, a term I have adapted from Adrienne Rich's *matrophobia* ("the fear not of one's mother or of motherhood, but of becoming one's mother" [235]). Nick is clearly afraid of his own impending fatherhood in "Cross-Country Snow," but it is not the only story raising this theme. In "The Three-Day Blow," in a discussion with Nick, one of the books that Bill halfheartedly defends—"It ain't a bad book, Wemedge" (*CSS* 87)—is *The Ordeal of Richard Feverel,* an 1859 work by George Meredith that instructors might find useful to summarize for students. In Meredith's novel, a father, Sir Austin Feverel, has a "System" for raising his son Richard that ultimately destroys Richard's marriage, deranges and kills his wife, and breaks his will. "'First be virtuous,' he tells his son, 'and then serve your country with heart and soul'" (79). The instructions sound a little like those of Clarence Hemingway, and they would no doubt have sounded bitterly ironic immediately after the Great War.

One of the more sympathetic characters in Meredith's novel, a maternal servant who nursed Richard as an infant, "spoke to the effect that the wickedness of old people formed the excuse for the wildness of young ones" (244). It's clear that Richard's father, Sir Austin Feverel, is humorless (173) and almost diabolical in his efforts to control his son's life. Meredith comments blandly of Sir Austin that "his excessive love for [Richard] took a rigorous tone" (174) and later philosophizes:

> It is difficult for those who think very earnestly for their children to know when their children are thinking on their own account. The exercise of their volition we construe as revolt. Our love does not like to be invalidated and deposed from its command, and here I think yonder old thrush on the lawn, who has just kicked the last of her lank offspring out of the nest to go shift for itself, much the kindest of the two, though sentimental people do shrug their shoulders at these unsentimental acts of the creatures who never wander from nature. (257)

It might be helpful to explain to students that Hemingway describes Nick's father as both "sentimental" and "cruel" in "Fathers and Sons" (*CSS* 370), a story that takes its title from Ivan Turgenev's novel of deadly intergenerational conflict.

Perhaps most chilling of all to Hemingway, Sir Austin, shortly after Richard tries his hand at writing poetry, "told Lady Blandish that Richard had, at his behest, done what no poet had ever been known to be capable of doing: he had, with his own hands, and in cold blood, committed his virgin manuscript to the flames" (Meredith 87). No wonder Nick insists of this novel, "I couldn't get into it" (*CSS* 87).

During the same conversation with Bill in "The Three-Day Blow," Nick goes on to praise two other novels, one of which is Hugh Walpole's *Fortitude*, an Edwardian novel. The instructor might want to offer a brief summary of that novel and explain that its young male protagonist, who has been abused by his alcoholic, sadistic father, is haunted by the fear that he is doomed to repeat his father's errors: "Peter watched his father and his grandfather. Here were the three of them alone. What his grandfather was his father would one day be, what his father was, he ... yes, he must escape" (128; ellipses in original). Peter, who eventually becomes the author of three novels, is so tormented by his father during his childhood that "there were times when he thought of ending it all" (123). After Peter's mother dies, he holds his father responsible for her death (143). He associates what "the Parent" calls "Learning to Be a Man" with "torture" (70) and asks himself, "Were his father and grandfather mirrors of his own future years?" (115).

### Fathers, Sons, and the Truth about War

Lest students dismiss this theme of patrophobia as irrelevant to *In Our Time*, the instructor should note that the father-son relationship Walpole's novel depicts is clearly the salient point of this "fine" novel for Nick, who tells Bill, "That's a real book. That's where his old man is after him all the time" (*CSS* 87). Perhaps Nick feels the same. Like Peter, Nick does not want to become like his father, to repeat his father's mistakes. No wonder, in "Cross-Country Snow," Nick seems so uneasy about his impending fatherhood.

To bring that point home, the instructor might want to ask students to read as supplementary material the introduction Hemingway wrote for *Men at War: The Best War Stories of All Time*. In that introduction, which Ernest dedicated to his own three sons, John, Patrick, and Gregory Hemingway, he wrote:

> This introduction is written by a man, who, having three sons to whom he is responsible in some ways for having brought them into this unspeakably balled-up world, does not feel in any way detached or impersonal about the entire present mess we live in. . . .
>
> This book has been edited in order that those three boys, as they grow to the age where they can appreciate it and use it and will need it, can have the book that will contain truth about war as near as we can come by it, which was lacking to me when I needed it most. (*MAW* xxiii)

By writing about the war as truthfully and as honestly as he could, in *In Our Time* and in many of his other works, Hemingway seemed to want to stop the violence by breaking the cycle of father-son repetition—to prepare his sons better than his father had prepared him. He wanted to replace the legacy of violence with a legacy of truth.

# Connective Gestures

Mulk Raj Anand, Ernest Hemingway, and the Transnational Worlds of World War I

Ruth A. H. Lahti

A challenge for teachers of American war literature, one that has gained urgency in the post-9/11 twenty-first century, is that of resituating this traditionally nation-centered genre more fully within its global contexts. Too often, a focus on the American soldier's experience can occlude alternate literary perspectives and hide war's radically transnational ground: after all, wars represent a time and space in which the boundaries of a nation are most imperiled, yet most fiercely asserted. In spite of, and indeed because of, Hemingway's monumental status in and influence on American war fiction, his war writing serves as an ideal entry point to the project of "worlding" American war fiction. As my experience teaching both general education and upper-level literature courses at a large public American university has affirmed, students' familiarity with Hemingway—even if only a passing familiarity—serves as a springboard for identifying an American perspective on war and then jumping more comfortably into texts that present global views of U.S. wars.

To prompt thinking about how teachers and students can use Hemingway's work to imagine the transnational dimensions of war, I present here a comparative—or, as I would rather put it, connective—look at Hemingway's *A Farewell to Arms* (1929) and Mulk Raj Anand's *Across the Black Waters* (1939), with an eye toward demonstrating how this approach allows us to register the diversity of human experiences in World War I. This pairing illuminates the concept of "nation" as a shaping force in both Hemingway's and Anand's texts, thereby encouraging students to think critically about how national power entangles itself in representations of war. Just as Ernest Hemingway is a central figure in the development of American literature since the twentieth century, so Mulk Raj Anand is considered a founding father of modern Indian literature. The protagonists of their novels, Frederic Henry and Lal Singh, reflect significant viewpoints on and experiences of World War I respective to their national and social contexts. Yet these novels simultaneously convey how the lines of war bleed: War becomes not only a clashing point but a flashpoint of transnational connection, ranging from the unexpected joy of cultural sharing to the painful ethical crisis of apprehending and killing an other. Laying bare these complex vectors of affiliation within war through a connective approach enables students to begin to move beyond simplistic notions of "us" and "them"; this process also demythologizes war by emphasizing war as a fundamentally human event. Here, I present this Hemingway-Anand unit as I have prepared it for an introductory-level war literature course that I am currently developing, and at the end of the essay I list a selection of secondary texts that would be useful in adapting this model for an upper-level course.

## Brief Rationale

Before delving into the literature itself, I will briefly explain how this approach to teaching Hemingway relates to current aims in the study of war literature. To do so, I must first clarify what I mean by a transnational approach to Hemingway, since *transnational* is a term whose meaning remains diffuse despite the considerable critical cachet it has recently gained. Like methods used to explore the concept of gender, transnational approaches are centrally concerned with uncovering, and thereby denaturalizing, the ways that certain imaginary concepts align with forms of power to influence how people live—and specifically in the case of the transnational are concerned with the many ways that the imaginative power of "nation" joins the economic and geopolitical realities of nation-states to structure human interactions. Thinking beyond "nation" is central to transnational work, and much of this scholarship is therefore committed to tracing complex legacies of violence and inequality that intersect postcolonial, world, and empire studies.

Teaching (and even thinking) on this transnational, global scale can be daunting, calling for a narrower and more manageable focus on specific aspects of the two novels for classroom purposes. Zoning in on characters' bodily gestures is one way to investigate how the transnational plays out in these novels. Recent scholarship on both Hemingway and World War I suggests the benefits of paying attention to characters' bodies in literature. Works by Thomas Strychacz and Alex Vernon demonstrate how characters physically perform gender in Hemingway's works, while Santanu Das, in *Touch and Intimacy in First World War Literature,* movingly makes the case for reorienting our knowledge about the war through the concept of touch. I extend this important work through attention to the ways in which bodies at war in literature choreograph relationships specifically to national power, as characters enact what Kurt Vonnegut famously calls, in his subtitle to *Slaughterhouse-Five,* "a duty-dance with death." Though it pulls together complicated insights from areas such as postcolonial, feminist, and performance theory, the close reading of gesture translates easily into the classroom. Simply put, I ask students, "What are the characters actually *doing* in this scene, and what does this add to our knowledge about World War I?" This back-to-basics kind of thinking about literary characters has generally made a great deal of sense to my students, and it not only reminds them to think carefully about characters as representations but also highlights the critical, telling details of individuals at war that can fade into the background in war's grand narratives.

Finally, a point on the project of comparison. As my transnational approach may suggest, I find it important in the classroom to be aware of the words I use in bringing the texts together; in other words, while the term *comparative* (or *comparison*) is useful in many projects for identifying the similarities and differences of two texts, I try, in reading Anand and Hemingway's texts together, to resist both the tendency to flatten the connection into an equation of the experiences contained in each novel or the temptation to position the authors' perspectives as fully discrete. With the object of understanding World War I, these texts circle the same irretrievable past in ways that unevenly correspond to this central event, and while both authors circulated within modernist groups following the war, their individual relationships to World War I were filtered through and motivated by their respective national—specifically in Anand's case, proto-national—contexts. In seeking to grasp this difference and connection, I am influenced by historians of traumatic events such as Michael Rothberg and Marianne Hirsch (both of whom have focused on the Holocaust). Hirsch puts the task at hand in an inspirational way that merits inclusion at length:

> The challenge may be how to account for contiguous or intersecting histories without allowing them to occlude or erase each other, how to turn competitive or appropriative memory into more capacious transnational memory work.... Such a reparative approach to memory would be open to connective approaches and affiliations—thinking different historical experiences in relation to one another

to see what vantage points they might share or offer each other for confronting the past without allowing its tragic dimensions to overwhelm our imagination in the present and the future. (20, 24–25)

This approach to war literature avoids seeking truth or ultimate authenticity in either Hemingway's or Anand's novels on the war. Instead it invites us to think within the novels' shared register of World War I in a complex way that does not collapse into a melancholic lament for the painful past but encourages scholars and students to seek shared conditions of war that continue to have relevance today.

## Opening Methods

To lay the groundwork for our discussions and to provide students with the conceptual toolbox that they will need to interpret literary language, I begin each semester with self-reflexive writing prompts on the key concepts of the course and instruction on close-reading methods. In the first exercise, asking students to write about the course topics allows them to pause, reflect, and express what they already know about these topics, which generally empowers them—particularly those who aren't English majors—and helps them begin to make connections between literature, war, and their own knowledge and experiences. In addition, this activity provides me with a class pulse that helps me determine what I may need to spend more time covering. In my course on war literature, for example, I ask my students to write quietly for ten minutes or so in response to the following questions (which I collect at the end of class):

- How many ways can you define the word *war*? Brainstorm and list.
- What are some things that war literature can tell us that history cannot? Why read literature about war?

For our second meeting, I compile the responses from the students' writing and use their insights to open a classroom conversation about the event of war and literature. This activity prompts students to begin broadening their ideas of what *war* means, and it also helps them, at the beginning of the semester, to appreciate what is unique about literature as a source of information about the past. While the history of wars is a necessary context for understanding Hemingway's and Anand's novels, I find it important in my literature classroom to promote literary representation as its own entry point into the past, one that isn't ultimately grounded in the *telos* of historiography. Toward this end, I also spend time during the first week teaching students how to understand literary language, equipping them with the methods of close reading and having them work on the sentence level to identify such elements as figurative language, diction, literal content and structure, style, characterization, tone, and point of view. In my classes on war literature, texts that have worked well for these close-reading activities are Tim O'Brien's "How to Tell a True War Story" and William Faulkner's 1949 Nobel Prize Speech, with the latter being especially useful in its gestures toward global contexts.

Contexts

For readers not familiar with Mulk Raj Anand (1905–2004) or his novel *Across the Black Waters*, I'll briefly provide Anand's historical and social contexts, as well as pointing to the synergies between his Western Front novel and Hemingway's representations of the Italian front. Together with R. K. Narayan and Raja Rao, Anand is widely considered one of the founding fathers of modern Indian fiction written in English, or Indo-Anglian fiction. Anand, born in 1905 in Peshawar during the period of British rule in India, traveled to England in 1925, where he earned his doctorate in philosophy, took an active part in workers' rights movements and the Indian nationalist movement, and became a prominent member of writers' circles in London, including the Bloomsbury group. Though widely studied in postcolonial scholarship, Anand's impact on modernism and global politics is less known, as is his high public presence in England during the 1930s, through his job at the BBC with George Orwell. Anand is a pivotal figure in global modernisms for his role in introducing the world to the cruelty of the British colonial system in India, for his pioneering representation of the perspective of the outcast in Indian society (particularly in his acclaimed 1935 novel, *Untouchable*), and for his part in claiming the English language for India through his innovative blending of English and Indian idioms in his writing (Bluemel 68).

*Across the Black Waters* is the second novel in Anand's *Village Trilogy*, a series that follows the character Lal Singh, or Lalu, from his peasant upbringing in an Indian village, through the horrors of serving in World War I, to his later involvement in the Indian nationalist movement. In an interesting point of convergence, both Anand and Hemingway witnessed the Spanish Civil War, and it was during this period in Spain that Anand drafted *Across the Black Waters*. Like Hemingway, Anand was not a combatant in World War I. Instead, he based his descriptions of trench warfare on his own brief experience in the trenches in Spain before being removed to serve as a journalist (George 89). While *A Farewell to Arms* takes place between late summer 1915 and April 1918, *Across the Black Waters* depicts actions in France during the fall and winter of 1914 to 1915. Neither author was there at those times. This fact—that Hemingway and Anand both write about World War I from indirect experiences of the war—is an important one, and pointing it out can help redirect students' and scholars' expectations that war literature must be written by soldiers in order to have the ring of authenticity.

Anand's novel is regarded as the first of the few books written by an Indian author that represents the point of view of an Indian soldier in the Lahore Division of the British Indian Army regiment serving in France during World War I (George 89). *Across the Black Waters* opens with the Indian sepoys approaching Marseilles after their long journey from India to France on a British ship, a journey that Lalu is overjoyed to have survived in light of "his own and the family's prejudice that all who went beyond the mountains or across the black waters were destined for hell" (Anand 169). Lalu has dreamed of shaking off the dust of his small peasant village and seeing what he calls *Vilayat*, the lands of the white *Sahibs* whom he has known only peripherally as figures of colonial authority in India. Much of the early portion of the novel charts Lalu's fascination with "Franceville" and its superiority to his home village, from the sight of French women as the men parade down the street during their disembarkation, to his observations about farming practices in Europe, to the new sights of explosions and airplanes in the sky. Of these new experiences, Anand writes, "they had begun to believe that *Vilayat* was an unrelieved paradise and, encouraged by all the privileges of journey in ships and railways through foreign lands which they had never enjoyed before, heartened by the kindness of people everywhere, they had grown to the dignity of human beings and forgotten the way in which they had always been treated as so much cattle in India" (26–27). However, Lalu's view of France, the *Sahibs,* and the governments of Europe transforms as he encounters the realities of the war. Upon reaching the trenches and experiencing battle and the deaths of his comrades, Lalu's outlook turns bleak, and he thinks of the sepoys as "ghosts from another, warmer world, transplanted into this creeping wet, cold autumnal underworld of 'Franceville', they who had never suffered shell fire, who had no experience of high explosives, who had never seen steel birds fly in the air, who had never been taught anything but the bayonet charge which had been so useful for generations on the frontier" (129). The novel closes with Lalu being injured in an attack and captured by the Germans, and while we do not receive any additional information about his fate in *Across the Black Waters,* his presence in the final novel in the trilogy assures us of his survival.

The protagonists Frederic Henry and Lalu Singh immediately share an important feature: both are outsiders within the European theatres of World War I, though their lands of origin confer different statuses on each. Throughout *A Farewell to Arms*, characters consistently remark on Frederic's American nationality, an identity that affords him advantages in various situations, such as when he is injured on the battlefield and receives treatment through the preferential aid of a British officer (*FTA* 58–61). Lalu is likewise identified as an outsider to the war, though he shares his outsider status with the rest of the Lahore Division serving in France. Despite this outsider status, Frederic and Lalu also share another characteristic: both were educated in the language of their commanding officers. As an architecture student in Italy, Frederic has learned the Italian he needs to communicate with those around him, while Lalu has learned English from his education in British schools in India. In this way, both characters are also insiders to the war, and Frederic and Lalu serve as translators at several points in each novel.

Frederic's and Lalu's insider/outsider status reflects the complicated crossing histories pulled together by World War I. Lalu's status as a colonial subject of the British Empire in particular helps to recontextualize the imperial history also shaping Hemingway's novel. This usefully introduces the history of empires as a necessary context for understanding World War I, providing an opportunity to discuss how the war becomes a turning point for several empires, including the Ottoman Empire and the Austro-Hungarian Empire, as well as putting strain on the British Empire. More specifically, reading *Across the Black Waters* opens discussions about the damaging effects of the British imperial system in India and can prompt students to think about the continued effects and consequences of imperial (or neo-imperial) conquest today. In teaching this text, it is also necessary to discuss how the racial and class dynamics of the British Empire align with and ultimately strengthen the caste system in India. This history has real effects on the characters: Lalu explains, for example, that he had to join the army to avoid being imprisoned for his taboo relationship with his landlord's daughter. He also states, more generally, "For when [the Indian sepoys] first joined the army, these legionaries did so because, as the second, third, or fourth sons of a peasant family, overburdened with debt, they had to go on and earn a little ready cash to pay off the interest on the mortgage of the few acres of land, the only thing which stood between the family and its fate" (Anand 168). This rationale for joining the British Indian Army stands in contrast to Frederic's more mysterious motivations for joining the Italian army; from his ability to consistently draw sight drafts from his grandfather, we know that whatever his reasons are for joining up, Frederic isn't motivated by financial necessity. Overall, in the complex overlay between "empire" and "nation" constituting World War I, "nation" remains a powerful force for characters in these two novels, not in the least because the friction between nations serves as a catalyst for the war. Moreover, the concept of "nation" mediates the central characters' relationships to their countries of origin: for Frederic, the United States is part of a shadowy past which he moves beyond yet to which his identity remains tethered, while for Lalu, the idea of an Indian nation is always just beneath the surface of his meditations on the British Empire.

Finally, an important discussion to have with students before moving into the novels themselves concerns the representation of violence. Particularly because studying the gestures of war inevitably produces a close focus on graphic scenes of violence, I try to prepare students to grapple meaningfully with these scenes—to honor the discomfort they may feel with the graphic descriptions while at the same time asking themselves, What purpose does the representation serve? Talking to them at the beginning of the course about the issues surrounding violence in literature and letting them know that the authors may intend for them to feel "empathic unsettlement" (to use Dominick LaCapra's term from trauma theory) can help us as a class to understand the painful experiences involved in war while retaining an ethical distance from the violence portrayed. Of course, given the increasing numbers of veterans in our classrooms and the other forms of violence experienced by many students during their lives that may be called up by the literature, it's especially critical to have this conversation from the outset.

### Connective Gestures

Reading Hemingway and Anand together would work well within a war literature course or a global literature course, and could be combined with readings from other global fiction, short stories, and poetry dealing with war by authors such as W. E. B. DuBois, Pramoedya Ananta Toer, Kenzaburo Oe, Marianne Moore, Langston Hughes, Toni Morrison, Ha Jin, Susan O'Neill, Bao Ninh, Helen Benedict, and Yusef Komunyakaa. From a logistical standpoint, the activity of focusing on the novels' gestures would take place after the students have read the two novels, in the third week of a three-week unit on World War I, for example. I plan to assign each aspect of war listed below to groups of students, asking them to prepare brief ten-minute presentations during which they would: (1) present a selected quotation from each novel that in some way shows characters enacting their topic; (2) present an analysis of each quotation, using the close-reading strategies they have learned; and (3) develop a set of questions to ask the class about how the two quotations relate to one another. Such presentations have been successful in generating ideas in my previous courses, and I typically follow up, reinforce, and extend the ideas that the student groups present through my moderation of class discussion. While I require students to select their own passages for analysis, here I provide paired passages. These suggested pairings could also be adapted into a writing activity to be assigned ahead of time, in which students would individually complete the close readings of both quotations and then develop questions about the two passages' relation to one another. While in the scope of this essay I cannot cover the full range of topics that we would consider in the classroom, I can present here three dimensions of the war experience that I hope for students to better understand. In addition, I include possible questions to prompt discussion about the gestures made during the scene, as well as my brief thoughts about the gestures' significance. Other rich topics to examine through characters' gestures in both Anand and Hemingway include: mobility in war; class, caste, and hierarchy in war; religious ritual and war; and enacting grief and loss.

I. The Body in Battle

> With instantaneous resolution, the boy stooped low like a lion on the prowl and charged him with his bayonet, fixing him with such force that the butt of his rifle resounded back on his chest. The man gnashed his teeth and groaned as he fell. Lalu groped for his victim, to finish him, murmuring: *"Jahanam!* Hell. . . ." He had longed for a wristwatch. He undid the leather strap and, trembling, took the watch and let the hand drop, still warm, on the German's side. (Anand 148)

> I opened up my holster, took the pistol, aimed at the one who had talked the most, and fired. I missed and they both started to run. I shot three times and dropped one. The other went through the hedge and was out of sight. I fired at him through the hedge as he ran across the field. The pistol clicked empty and I put in another clip. I saw it was too far to shoot at the second sergeant. He was far across the field, running, his head held low. I commenced to reload the empty clip. (Hemingway, *FTA* 204)

Most traditionally, war literature focuses on scenes of battle, and these descriptions convey the body's extreme vulnerability and raise ethical questions surrounding methods of warfare. *Across the Black Waters* brings the body at war into full view through repeated descriptions of Lalu and his comrades in action against the Germans; in contrast, *A Farewell to Arms* largely turns away from battlefield description, presenting instead Frederic's limited viewpoint from the periphery of the battlefield upon his wounding and then, later, on the dangers of friendly fire and of one's own military police. Hemingway's choice not to describe directly the carnage of the battlefield itself comes into clearer view alongside Anand's text, and reading the two texts together allows us to appreciate Hemingway's departure from the traditional war story form while also, through Anand's vivid descriptions, keeping palpable for today's students the extreme bodily stakes of the World War I battlefield. Further, the texts together map out a much more variegated system of hierarchies and power differentials within spaces of battle than either would alone. Students will better perceive Frederic's relative mobility and agency within areas of war when they connect his experience to the scenes of Lalu's tightly regimented and controlled options for movement, which are limited not only by military command but also by racial politics; *Across the Black Waters* depicts the differences imposed between the Indian soldiers and their white counterparts, where the former are allowed only rifles and denied machine guns. Moreover, students will see that Lalu, as a rifleman in the trench, faces danger with much more regularity than does Frederic in the ambulance corps. Of course, these comparisons do not correspond evenly across the different terrains and armies, yet for students they bring up important questions about hierarchy and race in war. While both Hemingway and Anand describe the chaos and confusion of the battle experience, it becomes clear that the experience of Lalu and the other sepoys is marked by additional layers of confusion: the Indian troops have not been trained for battle in Europe; their imperial commanders do not relay basic information; and even when information is available, language barriers prevent them from fully grasping the situation. Overall, the sense of each man's bodily and spiritual isolation as he fights for his life crosses through the additional filters of Frederic's and Lalu's national and imperial affiliations.

These two passages mark the occasions where the protagonists kill someone in a space of war. The passage from *A Farewell to Arms* comes as Frederic and the other ambulance drivers are in retreat and two sergeants ignore Frederic's orders and take off on their own. The passage from *Across the Black Waters* follows the sepoys as they are ordered to attack the German line and, in an interesting parallel, continues with Lalu witnessing one of his Indian officers killing an Indian soldier who refuses to take part in the offensive. Both of these scenes startlingly emphasize how the conditions of war force the participant to act quickly and according to his training—Hemingway's detached, mechanical description of Frederic's action and Anand's portrayal of Lalu's "instantaneous resolution" convey the body reacting almost automatically to the situation. Questions that may raise productive conversation about the ways in which the bodies in these difficult scenes of violence reflect power differentials that can be tied to hierarchical, national, or racial considerations include:

- How do these scenes of killing demonstrate Frederic's and Lalu's different positions within armies of World War I? Who is killing whom, and how do you know this from the language used?
- What are the differences between the specific methods and weapons used here, and what do you make of the characters' immediate actions following the act—Frederic's reloading of an empty cartridge and Lalu's removal of the watch from the German? What kinds of meanings do these immediate responses have? Are these passages suggestive of war trauma?
- What possibilities for individual agency are open to Frederic and Lalu in these scenes—do they have a choice about what is happening? How does this relate to their military rank, and does this position relate in any way to their citizenship?

Beyond the similarity of the two protagonists engaged in the act of killing, these two passages include phrasing that evokes differing access to self-mastery and control. While Hemingway's dispassionate description of Frederic's gestures is tightly focused on a first-person perspective that seems cold and robotic, can we also understand Frederic's phrasing here as accepting responsibility for his actions? In Anand's writing, in contrast, we see indeterminate language (such as "the boy" and "the man") that makes it unclear who has the upper hand in the battle, a confusion that isn't clarified until "Lalu groped for his victim." Why does Anand create this confusion between Lalu and his enemy, and, in his initial descriptions of the combatants, why does he use the different terms *boy* and *man*? Moreover, the clarifying action "groped" still implies a clumsy desperation and a lack of control on Lalu's part. The horrifying physical interaction entailed in killing emerges full-force in Anand's description of the butt of Lalu's gun bouncing back into his own chest as his bayonet pierces the chest of his enemy, a clear illustration of the mutual pain involved in war, both physical and psychological.

Each text's description of killing also includes moments where characters' humanity drops from view, as with Hemingway's use of "dropped one" and Anand's use of the lion metaphor. Does blurring the lines of humanity here make the process of killing easier, or excuse it? In addition to questions of humanity, these actions also dismantle easy applications of the terms *hero* and *villain* in war. The question of whether Frederic acted wrongfully in killing the sergeant is given more emphasis when we consider his last action of reloading the empty clip of his gun. On a symbolic level, the gesture conveys a host of meanings related to Frederic's feelings of emptiness and powerlessness. Particularly in light of Hemingway's iceberg theory of writing, actions like this can significantly inflect our readings of characterization. As for Lalu, his seemingly heroic bravery in grappling with the German soldier is thrown into an odd dissonance by his action of removing the watch from the fallen soldier. This act immediately calls up the stark economic conditions of his home village and, on a more symbolic level, gestures toward his desperation around matters of time and his own life span.

These two scenes powerfully convey the ultimate bodily stakes of war, but other moments from these two texts would work equally well to further an understanding of the larger topic of the body in battle. Another possibility for close examination would be the two scenes where Frederic and Lalu are injured.

## II. Women, Gender, and War

> But she hung on his arm now with a pride and childish affection that he knew would certainly be constructed as a breach of the unwritten law that no sepoy was to be seen on familiar terms with the women in this country. And yet he felt the panic of abandon at the touch of her arm, and the pride of walking along next to her coursed in his veins, blinding him to the military and social prohibitions and weakening the defences which he had built up against the mire that had been stirred in India because he had dared to look at the landlord's daughter fondly. (Anand 193)

> I looked in her eyes and put my arm around her as I had before and kissed her. I kissed her hard and held her tight and tried to open her lips; they were closed tight. I was still angry and as I held her suddenly she shivered. I held her close against me and could feel her heart beating and her lips opened and her head went back against my hand and then she was crying on my shoulder. (Hemingway, *FTA* 27)

*Across the Black Waters* and *A Farewell to Arms* both detail the presence of women near the fronts of World War I, and the interaction between the military men and the female characters provides insight into the gendered dimensions of war. While Anand and Hemingway ultimately resist the traditional romance plot of the adventures of love in war, their depictions of female characters do largely reinforce gendered codes of women serving as saintly sisters who serve as the ultimate witnesses to war or as the sexualized objects of men's heightened passion in war. It's important to note that as a character of great depth, Catherine from *A Farewell to Arms,* does challenge these codes, but her inseparability from Frederic and her ultimate death (when read as a substitute for soldiers' deaths in the novel) largely reinscribe her as a character who functions to further our understanding of men's wartime suffering. Lalu's reaction to the women in France, specifically his consistent sexual fixation on women's bodies, likewise reproduces these problematic gender codes: "Lalu could not keep his eyes off the smiling, pretty-frocked girls with breasts half showing, bright and gleaming with a happiness that he wanted to think was all for him" (Anand 13). Though Lalu stands at an uncomfortable remove from the other Indian men during a scene at a French brothel, Anand positions most of Lalu's reactions to women in the novel in these sexualized terms.

In the scenes presented above, the authors portray early scenes of physical contact between the main characters and their love interests. The scene from *Across the Black Waters* depicts Lalu and a young French girl named Marie, whose family lives in a village near the front and regularly interacts with the men of the Lahore Division. In the scene from *A Farewell to Arms,* Catherine has just slapped Frederic for his untoward advances, and now yields to him. Prominent in both scenes is the way that the sexual danger that women present mirrors—and becomes a part of—the dangers of war. However, this sexual danger arises from very different considerations of nationality and power in each context. Questions that may help to unpack the loaded sexual danger in these scenes include:

- Pay attention in these scenes to the words used to describe the actions and bodily positions of each character. In these sexual(ized) encounters, which characters are passive or aggressive, advancing or retreating, on the offensive or defensive?
- What is the extent of the danger that can result from the two interactions? Do the consequences of the behavior in each scene relate to gender, racial, or national power differentials?

Lalu's reaction to Marie is refracted not only through racial policing and military rank but also through his experience of the caste system in colonial India. Interestingly, both Marie and Lalu feel "pride" as they walk through the French village arm in arm, yet while Marie's pride is "childish," Lalu's takes on a more decidedly sexual tone: he remarks that "the pride of walking along next to her coursed in his veins." The public nature of this gesture of walking arm in arm down the street is what simultaneously creates for Lalu both the danger and the thrill, and we see a triangulation of desire taking shape where it is the prospect of spectators that gives Lalu this thrill. However, the moment of connection is also a moment of resistance, as "he felt the panic of abandon at the touch of her arm." This moment marks the height of the couple's physical contact, and we can perhaps also read the gestures here as the transformative power of touch and acknowledgment, as Marie treats Lalu as a human and not, as Lalu previously describes, "as so much cattle in India" (Anand 27).

The tension between thrill and danger seen in *Across the Black Waters* plays out in the scene between Frederic and Catherine as well, as the language signals Frederic both tightening around and prying open Catherine's body. The movement between tenderness and force comes through in the alternation in the lines, as the first line ("I looked in her eyes and put my arm around her as I had before and kissed her") can be read as tender, while the second line ("I kissed her hard and held her tight and tried to open her lips; they were closed tight") has a much more forceful tone. This love scene undoubtedly creates discomfort in the reader, and this language of force can open important discussions in the classroom about the intersections between sexual violence and war. The violence embedded in this scene takes on a different tinge as Catherine's shiver seems to restore her to life somehow, and she goes from stasis to movement with "her heart beating and her lips opened and her head went back against my hand and then she was crying on my shoulder." Catherine, who has suffered the loss of her fiancé in one of the Somme battles just months before, could be read here as awakening bodily from her grief; her transformation or redemption in Frederic's hands, however, retains the problematically gendered subtext of her powerlessness.

### III. Relationships among the Men

> And [the French officer] solemnly shook hands with all the three Indians and then continued with appropriate gestures. . . . Lalu and Kirpu laughed mirthlessly at the mockery which his pantomime made of the war. And they lifted their heads to Babu Khushi Ram, as much as to say, "Did you hear that; that is war, it is a joke . . ."
> 
> The drinks came.

The officer began to pay for them, but Khushi Ram wouldn't have it and insisted on paying and there was a war of courtesies, in the midst of which arrived a Lieutenant of the Connaughts who spontaneously stretched his hands to the Indians without any formality and complimented them, "*Bahadur* sepoys!" as he drifted away. (Anand 164–65)

The major said he had heard a report that I could drink. I denied this. He said it was true and by the corpse of Bacchus we would test whether it was true or not. . . . I should drink cup for cup and glass for glass with Bassi, Fillipo Vincenza. . . . I said let the best man win, Bacchus barred, and the major started us with red wine in mugs. Half-way through the wine I didn't want any more. I remembered where I was going. (Hemingway, *FTA* 40)

Another theme shared by Hemingway's and Anand's novels is that of masculinity and war; both books detail the strong bonds formed between men serving in World War I. While some scenes in the novels depict stereotypical, swaggering aspects of masculinity, others reveal more tender displays of masculinity that testify to the deep bonds formed between the male characters, such as the brotherly love shared by Frederic and Rinaldi in *A Farewell to Arms* and the father-son relationship of Uncle Kirpu and Lalu in *Across the Black Waters*. In a more collective social context, *Across the Black Waters* and *A Farewell to Arms* contain scenes of male socialization across national and cultural lines in barroom scenes of raucous drinking. The specific scenes quoted above chart boozy rituals among the men that both express and relax the social and cultural restrictions within war.

In the quoted scene from *Across the Black Waters,* Lalu and his Indian friends transgress their cultural prohibition against drinking alcohol and their fear of socializing with white people by entering a bar in the French village in which they are stationed. While they are initially greeted with silent stares, the encounter becomes friendlier as the French officer attempts to bond with the Indians by using hand gestures to communicate their shared experience of the recent battles. Hemingway's *A Farewell to Arms* likewise describes male bonding over alcohol. In the quoted scene, occurring early in that novel, Frederic misses a meeting with Catherine when he stays too long with his Italian comrades at dinner, making the excuse to himself that "tonight we were not all brothers unless I drank a little" (38). This scene also marks the first time Frederic is identified as "Frederico Enrico or Enrico Federico" (40), a significant sign (however muddled) of his friendship with the Italian men with whom he works. The night culminates in one of the Italian members of the ambulance corps challenging Frederic to a drinking match. In untangling the complicated vectors of affiliation in these two scenes, the following questions may be useful:

- What function does drinking play in each scene? Why do you think alcohol specifically becomes a part of these wartime spaces? Does it allow for forms of behavior that wouldn't be acceptable under other conditions?
- These scenes of drinking include forms of social ritual like the drinking game and paying for another's drinks. What is the significance of these rituals, and how do they relate to concepts such as nation and gender?
- Both social encounters entail a certain degree of challenge and risk. What are the consequences of these risks for Lalu and Frederic? Do their nationally informed consciences play a part in their acceptance of these risks and their consequences?

The presence of drinking in these texts signals the way men cope with the overwhelming experiences of war, a point that can open into further classroom conversations about the role of drugs and alcohol as a significant feature in other representations of war. Making a link to war trauma can also add depth to these scenes, which may initially appear to be shallow descriptions of drinking. The scene from *Across the Black Waters* contains several levels of camaraderie conditioned by the men's national affiliations. The French officer's platitudinal gestures—shaking the men's hands, communicating about the battles, and trying to pay for their drinks—are only partially successful in dismantling cultural barriers; Lalu, Khushi Ram, and Uncle Kirpu exchange looks among themselves that cast judgment on the man's pantomime, and, in "a war of courtesies," Khushi Ram refuses to let the Frenchman buy their drinks. Rather than respecting the Frenchman's authority, Lalu and Uncle Kirpu "look up to Khushi Ram," who is of higher rank in their own Indian division, thus enacting a refusal to cross racial and national lines despite their shared battle lines in the context of World War I. Further, the scene from Anand includes the salute to the Indians from a member of the Connaught Rangers, which is an Irish regiment of the British Army that had been stationed in India at the outbreak of World War I. This encounter highlights the fact that both the Indians and the Irishman are British colonial subjects, perhaps suggesting a shared resentment of British power. (This resentment also links to Helen Ferguson, who, early in *A Farewell to Arms*, identifies herself as "Scotch" and informs Rinaldi that Scottish citizens "do not like the English" [21].)

The scene from *A Farewell to Arms* marks Frederic as an American and stages the Italian group's competition with him. Despite his closeness with Rinaldi, the dynamics of this scene indicate that Frederic remains an outsider in the group (as they are not even sure of his name). They stage the ritual of the drinking game to determine "the best man," a competitive performance of masculinity that in this case is drawn along the lines of nationality; the Italian major's humorous assertion that "by the corpse of Bacchus we would test whether it was true or not" that Frederic could drink bears the subtle trace of Frederic's American challenge to their Old World superiority. Frederic's decision to stop the drinking match "half-way through the wine" may signal his wavering commitment to the Italian cause, which ultimately breaks down in his "separate peace" later in the text. Frederic abandons the performance of his masculinity here in order to go to Catherine at the British hospital, and, significantly, Rinaldi decides not to cross over into the British space, leaving Frederic at "the gate of the driveway that led up to the British villa" (40). As his comments about wishing he'd joined the British Red Cross also indicate, Frederic's surrender during this drinking game may signal more than the onset of drunkenness and also point to the more significant waning of his alliance with the Italians.

Other possible scenes for inclusion within this category would be those depicting Frederic's and Lalu's unexpected brushes with the "enemy": the scene in Milan where the Italian barber mistakes Frederic for an Austrian and nearly slits his throat, and the important scene toward the end of *Across the Black Waters* where Lalu looks on in wonderment at the friendly interaction between British, German, and Indian soldiers in no-man's land on Christmas Day.

Conclusion: Global Modernisms and Global Realities

What also comes into fuller view from comparisons of works like *Across the Black Waters* and *A Farewell to Arms* is the diversity of modernisms that World War I engenders. Through such a connective project we can introduce our students to the field of global modernisms, thinking through how geopolitical structures affect the form that literature takes. Rather than thinking about modernism only as rooted in the metropoles of Europe and the United States, this approach alerts us to the ways in which works like *Across the Black Waters* develop a distinctive style of modernism that travels from their specific national context (in this case, Indo-Anglian) to reshape our understanding of war—and modernism—in Europe. By drawing on what students have learned about Hemingway's and Anand's national/imperial, cultural, and social contexts, we can ask them, "Why do you think Hemingway and Anand chose to write about the same world conflict with such different writing styles?" While both authors emphasize the chaos of battle, for example, Hemingway's iceberg theory of writing presupposes a particular worldview, while Anand's novel painstakingly casts Lalu in psychological detail and depth for an English-speaking audience. A valuable question to consider in our literature classrooms, then, is: How does literary form itself express the stakes or goals of a work of fiction? This question inevitably leads us back to the challenges of war representation and prompts students to think about how an author's act of literary creation always arises from its particular national, imperial, cultural, racial, and gendered contexts—but in its creativity is never fully determined by these contexts and can teach us something new.

This type of transnational viewpoint uncovers war fiction's entanglement in national power, enabling us as teachers and scholars to confront questions about nationalistic boundaries within our own disciplines. This approach opens provocative questions for students to consider, such as: Why can't we reimagine American war literature as *any* literary work written by an author of *any* nationality, combatant or not, that details the effects of a war in which the United States took part? In a transnational reappraisal of Hemingway's fiction, this kind of question is vital to widening the generic boundaries and thus the ethical implications of American war fiction in an increasingly violent, globalized world. Furthermore, asking such questions about war in our classrooms has gained heightened relevance in light of the end of the U.S. involvement in Iraq and the scaling back of U.S. involvement in Afghanistan, which have returned young veterans to the United States in large numbers. As a 2013 article in the *Chronicle of Higher Education* reported, these young veterans face a host of challenges in accessing higher education, particularly on campuses lacking awareness about war, peace, and veterans' issues today (Sander). In my aim to teach war literature transnationally, I hope for the spirit of the classroom to become "glocal"—prompting students' meaningful apprehension of global wars of the past while inviting them to take a fresh look at the worlds and wars around them.

Suggested Reading for Upper-Level Courses

*On the Challenges of War Writing*
McLoughlin, Kate. "War and Words." In *The Cambridge Companion to War Writing*. Ed. Kate McLoughlin. New York: Cambridge UP, 2009. 15–24.

*On The Link Between the Transnational, Language, Literature, and Identity*
Clingman, Stephen. "Introduction: The Grammar of Identity." In his *The Grammar of Identity: Transnational Fiction and the Nature of the Boundary*. New York: Oxford UP, 2009. 1–33.

*On the Social and Intellectual History of Trauma in the West*
Fassin, Didier, and Richard Rechtman. "A Dual Genealogy." In their *The Empire of Trauma: An Inquiry into the Condition of Victimhood*. Princeton, NJ: Princeton UP, 2009. 25–39.

*On the Body, Power, and Discipline*
Foucault, Michel. "'Panopticism,' 1975." In *The Routledge Critical and Cultural Theory Reader*. Ed. Badmington, Neil, and Julia Thomas. New York: Routledge, 2008. 178–201.

*On the Representation of Women in Colonial Contexts*
Mohanty, Chandra Talpade. "'Under Western Eyes: Feminist Scholarship and Colonial Discourses,' 1991." In *The Routledge Critical and Cultural Theory Reader*. Ed. Badmington, Neil, and Julia Thomas. New York: Routledge, 2008. 381–405.

# Character Construction and Agency

Teaching Hemingway's "A Way You'll Never Be"

Peter Messent

Students, unsurprisingly, often feel overwhelmed when faced with the task of writing a critical essay on a well-known author or text. They lack confidence in the practice of literary criticism and may not entirely see its point. Moreover, as they start to explore the past reception and interpretations of a writer's work, they can be quickly overwhelmed and disheartened by what they find. Books on Hemingway and his work continue to pour from the presses; at the time of writing, the latest, *Ernest Hemingway in Context* (2012), edited by Debra Moddelmog and Suzanne del Gizzo, weighed in at close to five hundred pages. A student glancing at the sheer amount of commentary in books and critical essays on just one Hemingway story—"Big Two-Hearted River," for example—might feel that the very idea of writing anything original or fresh about it is impossible. The amount written on such texts, most of it by academic scholars who have a sophisticated knowledge both of Hemingway and of the tools of literary criticism, is enough to lead a college or university student to throw up her or his hands in despair when asked for any fresh response. "What," that student might ask, "can I possibly say that James Nagel, Robert Scholes, Paul Smith, Linda Wagner-Martin, Philip Young, and all those countless others who have written on Hemingway have not already said a hundred times more effectively?" Indeed, there are many established teachers and critics who feel exactly the same way.

It is here that a structuralist methodology can prove an accessible and effective tool, even for relative beginners in literary studies. There is not the space here to explain the full workings and ramifications of this approach, nor how it has been challenged and modified by its critical successors (and especially by the poststructuralist turn). It may be enough, however, simply to say that the underlying premise of structuralist criticism is that all narrative fiction is part of a general *system* and, accordingly, subject to a set of basic rules or laws. Thus, we can take any one such fiction, however complex, and isolate and define some of the (shared) laws by which it gains its artistic effects. The various tools of narrative construction (the way character is built, the points of view represented, the chronological effects created, and so on) come together to form the complex and often densely patterned aesthetic whole that is the finished novel or story. And these basic tools can be discovered, described, and explained. The *mechanics* of this narrative process, then, are readily accessible once the literary work is seen as artificially *constructed* and, accordingly, subject to a type of "scientific" analysis. Such a focus allows any committed reader to "carry out structuralist analyses with enthusiasm and skill and . . . arrive at independent observations surprising in their scope. . . . The 'magically' acquired (class restricted?) 'feel' for literature [is replaced by] a sophisticated handling of texts. . . . The supposedly scientific grid can be applied without complexes, yet inevitably leads to the heart of the complicated narrative strategies that may well be the secret of the text's 'mystique' in the first place" (Tallack et al. 15). This type of approach can be liberating to any student, replacing apprehension of the "mastery" and "insight" of the (superior) professional literary critic with her or his own careful unpacking of specific textual effects and the way that these work. This way of examining and analysing a text builds critical self-confidence. It can also help to uncover the meanings and workings of a text in unexpected and sometimes illuminating ways.[1]

To illustrate such an approach in a highly selective way, let us examine one aspect of Schlomith Rimmon-Kenan's work on the construction of character in *Narrative Fiction: Contemporary Poetics* (1983) and see how it might apply to perhaps the least-known of Hemingway's Nick Adams war stories, "A Way You'll Never Be" (1933). I focus on the matter of personal agency (the ability to act meaningfully, to control one's destiny, in the social and historical world), a crucial issue for Hemingway and for his (and our) contemporaries.

Rimmon-Kenan distinguishes between direct definition and indirect presentation of character. In direct definition, a character trait is named: so, in *The Sun Also Rises* (1926), Jake Barnes speaks of Robert Cohn's "nice, boyish, sort of cheerfulness that had never been trained out of him" (*SAR* 52). Immediately, though, we have to bring in certain qualifications—for direct definition of character counts only if it comes from a reliable and authoritative textual voice (say, for instance, the narrator of a traditional nineteenth-century realist novel).

In Hemingway's modernist texts, such reliability is rare, so, as readers, we must proceed with caution. When we read the above description of character, therefore, we need to keep well in mind that this is a first-person narrative and that Jake's descriptions of Robert are informed by what David Wyatt calls "gratuitous bile" (57). Direct definition of character, then, can be heavily distorting depending on the voice used to express it, and any reading of character on such a basis should be highly tentative. Thus, while we do get some fragmentary examples of direct definition of character in Hemingway's "A Way You'll Never Be"—as, for example, when Paravicini remarks to Nick, "You seem in top-hole shape" (*CSS* 310)—such indicators are rarely reliable. In this case, Nick's immediate response—a direct definition of his own character, though through the eyes of the medical profession: "It's a hell of a nuisance once they've had you certified as nutty"—immediately throws the previous words into doubt. We quickly realize that Paravicini is looking to bolster Nick's fragile sensibility.

The more subtle approach of indirect presentation of character is, by and large, the dominant method used by Hemingway and most of his modernist literary contemporaries. In this method, character traits are not directly named but are instead "display[ed] and exemplifie[d] . . . in various ways," leaving the reader—who is given a more active role here—"the task of inferring the quality they imply" (Rimmon-Kenan 60). Character can be indicated in many different ways, and Rimmon-Kenan offers a helpful method of systematizing them. Her categorizations allow the reader to identify and compile combinations of attributes pragmatically and effectively as he or she struggles to name specific characters. The first indicator she names is that of action, central both to the construction of character and to its function in the narrative progression of the text. It is this field on which I concentrate. But the other indicators she names provide further useful approaches: speech, external appearance, environment, and what she calls "reinforcement by analogy" (70). Further explanation of these categories can be found in the third chapter of my *New Readings of the American Novel*. (Students might consider how such indicators work in the particular Hemingway text—or, indeed, any other text—that interests them.)

Rimmon-Kenan divides action into two sorts, one-time action and habitual or repeated action. The former she associates with "the dynamic aspects of character, often playing a part in a turning point in the narrative" (61). Habitual or repetitious actions illustrate the more static and constant aspects of character. Since habitual actions tend to have a less significant impact on the course of the narrative than one-time actions, the character traits the former reveal are, in her view, usually less significant than those revealed by actions occurring only once. Rimmon-Kenan divides both types of action into classes: acts of commission (actions performed by a character); acts of omission (acts which should be performed but are not); and contemplated acts (planned or intended actions that remain unperformed).

To illustrate the use of Rimmon-Kenan's categorizations, I use *A Farewell to Arms* (1929). Frederic Henry's most significant one-time act of commission comes near the end of Book 3, when he faces questioning by a group of Italian soldiers during the disorganized retreat from Caporetto. Knowing that his life was at risk ("I was obviously a German in Italian uniform. I saw how their minds worked; . . . They were all young men and they were saving their country"), Frederic decides to "make a break" for it (224), plunging into the Tagliamento River (the incident occurs at a wooden bridge crossing the flooded river) to pull himself ashore some distance downstream. He then cuts the identifying officer's insignia ("the cloth stars") from his coat sleeves, and sets out to make his clandestine way to Mestre, then Milan, where he hopes to connect up with his lover, Catherine (224–27). It is Frederic's plunge into the river that serves as a crucial narrative turning point in the book. Recollecting his action, on the flatcar of the train onto which he later jumps, Frederic initially uses the metaphor of a floorwalker in department store fire, going on to think, "You were out of it now. You had no more obligation. . . . I was not against them. I was through. . . . That life was over" (232). It is at the bridge and river crossing that Frederic, in one dramatic action, shifts worlds, moves from the arms of war toward the arms of love, gives up his institutional affiliations to enter a universe of two, "alone against the others" (249). Later, again reflecting on his situation, Frederic uses the now-famous words, "I had made a separate peace" (243). The book takes on a very different narrative trajectory once Frederic has acted in this way.

We must not, however, overplay the significance of Frederic Henry's action in terms of his personal agency, for this is not quite the dynamic one-time act of commission it might initially seem. We remember here that he initially plunges into the water as a forced evasion, an escape from the army's (mad) disciplinary processes. His move into the arms of Catherine becomes accordingly—and however much he loves her—something of a forced response to a situation where he has few other options. And when he lies in bed on first reuniting with her, "feeling that we had come home, feeling no longer alone" (263), he then unexpectedly shifts perspective, signalling the tragedy to come at the end of the book with the passage commencing, "If people bring so much courage to this world, the world has to kill them to break them, so of course it kills them" (264). We get here that strong sense of determinism that, from this point on, hangs over the whole text, the knowledge that some kind of "trap" is waiting to spring closed (336), to shape Frederic and Catherine's fate with nothing they can do to prevent it. The very idea of Frederic's agency and autonomy, then, is radically queried by such a narrative move, where evasion is so closely associated with a doomed entrapment. I return to this tension between individual action and a type of passive determinism when I examine "A Way You'll Never Be."

First, though, I return to the notion of habitual or repetitious actions. Hemingway's prose is full of such instances (or, rather, series of instances). Nick's actions in "Big Two-Hearted River" (1925) provide many examples: hiking over country that he has hiked over before; ritualistically making his camp, cooking his meal, boiling his coffee—all, clearly, according to past formula; collecting grasshoppers, baiting his line, and fishing for trout—all again long-repeated practices. Such careful repetitions serve here as acts of therapy, signaling in part Nick's status as a mentally and physically damaged victim of war and helping him to recover at least some sense of balance as he seeks the coherence and meaning that the world of public history (Nick's role as a soldier) denies him.

The taxi scenes in *The Sun Also Rises* provide further instances of repetitious actions: just two in a whole series of repetitious actions that frame Jake Barnes and Brett Ashley's relationship. Just after Brett has entered a taxi with Jake after the early nightclub scene, she says, "Oh, darling, . . . I'm so miserable." He responds: "I had that feeling of going through something that has all happened before" (70). This sense of endless circularity in their relationship operates on several levels. When they are "jolted close together" by the taxi's movements, we see both Jake and Brett associated with the same habitual physical actions. Their emotional need for one another is triggered by this physical contact, which they then (at least initially) actively prolong. But that physical contact results in a swift pulling-apart by Brett in a renewed realization of the hopelessness of their position, where the sexual satisfaction to which their emotional desire should lead is necessarily denied (for Jake is another figure wounded—rendered impotent—in the war). The sense of repetition without resolution is figured (in this first taxi scene) when they kiss and then separate:

> I kissed her. Our lips were tight together and then she turned away. . . .
> "Don't touch me," she said, "Please don't touch me."
> "What's the matter?"
> "I can't stand it." . . .
> "Don't you love me?"
> "Love you? I simply turn all to jelly when you touch me."
> "Isn't there anything we can do about it?" (33–34)

The nightmarish sense of circularity that marks this emotional routine is later repeated, and indeed it is exactly this that signals the ending of the first part of the novel. Jake's repetitions, a sign of his lack of emotional equilibrium, are evident in his words (speech here reinforcing action), the way his repeated act of physical intimacy and retreat is echoed in his repeated words, as his "there's not a damn thing we could do" shifts to "Couldn't we live together, Brett. Couldn't we just live together?" (34, 62); his "We'd better keep away from each other" to "I love you so much" (34, 61). These patterns of physical and verbal advance and retreat suggest the highly unstable nature of both Jake's and Brett's emotional states in the first half of the novel, where such habitual actions are concentrated.

The book, though, returns to Jake and Brett together in a taxi at its conclusion. Brett is again pressed against Jake as the taxi suddenly slows, a physical action that comes between Brett's words, "Oh, Jake . . . we could have had such a damn good time together," and his reply, "Yes. . . . Isn't it pretty to think so?" (251). There is a certain tension here between actions and words, for the habitual action (pressing close together) is again caused by what we might call external force, but this time is actually at odds with Jake's response—both his actions and his words. For this time he does not physically react to Brett's intimate presence (an act of omission? a contemplated act?), responding only verbally and with an apparent dismissive irony—his use of that word "pretty."[2] The novel ends inconclusively, with Jake once more (habitual action) metaphorically running to Brett's aid as soon as she needs him, but apparently finally refusing to be pulled yet again into the circular emotional patterning of an impossible relationship.

How, then, do such one-time and habitual actions work in "A Way You'll Never Be"? I am immediately confronted by a series of problems here. This challenge, while initially somewhat disconcerting, does not prevent me pursuing this type of analysis but, rather, makes me ask the question as to why such problems arise, for what strikes me here is the difficulty of attributing any significant one-time action (linked to the dynamic aspect of character) or indeed any significant habitual action to Nick Adams in a short story particularly lacking in any sense of important movement or drama. But I need to explain this, and do so by being pedestrian.

The story starts, in a somewhat disorienting manner, with Nick's view of the aftermath of a military defeat by Italian troops of an Austrian attack, somewhere near Fornaci, the place from which Nick has just cycled.[3] His journey may, for all we know, be a one-time action (he may never have cycled that road before) but it is also a type of repetition, for Nick is returning to the battle front, where the brigade to which he had previously been attached is stationed. (He will, moreover, reverse his journey at the story's end.) Nevertheless, the making of the journey does indicate some kind of turning point, although this turning point—again, a little oddly, given my remarks to this point—has in fact already taken place, *before* the narrative commences. Nick has come back to the front after being wounded (of which more later). But this time he comes not, as previously, to fight alongside the Italians (*CSS* 309). Rather, he has now been directed to wear an American military uniform, and—rather than serving with Paravicini's regiment—to "move around" the Italian front lines as a propagandist token, to assure the troops that other Americans are on their way. "If they see one American uniform," Nick explains, "that is supposed to make them think that others are coming" (308). When Paravicini asks him what he is doing in this uniform he now wears, Nick answers, "They've put me in it" (308). So if there is a (just-completed) one-time action with which the story starts—cycling to the front to assume a new role—any notion that this might reveal a dynamic aspect of Nick's character is denied, both by the absurdity of the task he is now to undertake (an absurdity of which he is fully aware), and by the fact that he is merely passively carrying out the orders of others. That vague pronoun reference *they* suggests an unknowable and impersonal force steamrolling any sense of personal agency on Nick's part out of consideration. It also reminds the reader of that sense of an overarching fatalism in *A Farewell to Arms*, when Frederic speaks of how one "never had time to learn [how life works].... [T]he first time *they* caught you off base *they* killed you" (327; emphasis added).

If this one-time action I associate with Nick (cycling to the front) is already under way as the narrative begins, the habitual actions that form his new role are yet to properly commence. If he has already put on his new uniform, with his presence at the front intended to signal other Americans to come, he is not yet acting in the way he is supposed to: moving from group to group and place to place with "pockets full" of chocolates, cigarettes, and postcards for the troops he meets (*CSS* 309). If Nick is, in Paravicini's words, "circulating around to no purpose" (313), as his supplies have not arrived, the assumption is that the same will be more or less true even when they have. What, then, does the habitual role that Nick is meant to be assuming reveal about the constant side of his character? Just, it would seem, that Nick's military life has become pointless; that he has become a type of absurdist figure, figuring promises of military reinforcement and handing out small material comforts in a role that stands at absolute odds with the reality of the general situation of ransacked bodies, terrified soldiers, operational blunders—everything, in Nick's expressive phrase, "a bloody balls" (310). Any sense of positive agency, in other words, has completely disappeared from Nick Adams's life.

This connects to the most significant incident in Nick's past army life, and one again where it is *what is done to him* rather than what he does that is crucial: Nick's previous wounding at the front. If this has occurred before the present narrative begins, it nonetheless affects that narrative's entire trajectory and meaning. If anything has been a turning point in Nick's life, this has. And it is this, too, that explains his new minor—indeed, more or less pointless—role. The trauma of Nick's head wound is signaled by his memory of both the event itself ("the white flash and clublike impact" of the rifle shot) and the "long yellow house with a low stable" beside the canal that he seems, in an act of transference (perhaps of psychological damage limitation), to have substituted for the shooting itself (314).[4] This trauma, moreover, has damaged him mentally as well as physically, producing the shell shock or post-traumatic stress that is so evident in the narrative. Such mental damage is especially marked by the several passages where Nick's mind spins out of control in fragmentary streams-of-consciousness, and where he seeks (presumably) to prevent this happening in his disquisitions on subjects (e.g., "the American locust") with little connection to the external reality around him (314).[5] Nick's words, "I can tell when I'm going to have one because I talk so much" (314), indicate his knowledge of the fragility of his own psychological state—"one" here referring perhaps to the distressing memory of the originating event itself, perhaps to a panic attack or sense of mental dislocation (still) caused by it, or perhaps to the two occurring simultaneously.

I find myself needing to modify Rimmon-Kenan's schema here to account for the particular effects of Hemingway's fiction, for I have switched my attention from any one-time action performed by Nick—and signalling his agency—to an action that has been done *to* him and that confirms his status as a victim of war, as one unable to determine his own fate in this context. (We remember Frederic Henry, in *A Farewell to Arms,* blown up in a dugout while eating a piece of cheese.) In "A Way You'll Never Be," Nick is, in fact, no capable agent of his own fate but a passive subject, whose sense of his own identity has been radically affected by the "clublike impact" of that bullet. If we had to identify the agent(s) whose actions had affected him in this way, it would be the Austrian soldier and the bullet he fires. More widely, though, it would be the series of determining forces that shape Nick's life—that unknowable *they*—both during the war and (to take into consideration the larger sequence of Nick Adams stories) before and after it, too.

Nick's own habitual acts, then, that follow on from this rifle shot, and the heightened sense of personal vulnerability caused by it, are all associated with his traumatized response. He is unable to sleep without a light (309), responds to others in an unbalanced and disturbing manner (the "American locust" monologue), and repeatedly has to try to "hold . . . in" feelings of panic and disorientation (314). The very role he has now been given (wearing the American uniform, handing out chocolate), consisting of repeated day-to-day activities on the periphery of meaningful military action, follows from this wounding and from the shared knowledge that Nick is not yet right in his head. Again, though, I am having trouble with that word *action* (and the agency it signals), for speaking (his conversations and monologue) is not acting—not, at least, in Rimmon-Kenan's sense of physical movement; of actually "doing" something that might affect the course of a narrative.[6] It functions, rather, as a verbal indicator of character. What is more, neither being unable to sleep nor looking to contain feelings of panic or mental collapse is an indicator of positive agency. Both are, rather, psychological states of being caused by trauma, by Nick's status as wounded victim.

So what actions does Nick actually perform within the textual space and time of this short story, and how else does he respond to his environment? He cycles to the front—and is about to cycle back from it at the narrative end point. He sees the corpses resulting from recent military action. (We should always note the verbal repetitions in Hemingway, thus here: "Nicholas Adams saw," "Nick noticed," "Nick Adams had seen," and another "Nick noticed," on the first two pages of the story, as Hemingway insists on his protagonist's spectatorial role.)[7] Nick here, then, is mainly one who observes—as he so often does in the series of short stories about him—rather than acts; indeed, he is one who may have been rendered incapable of meaningful action both by what he has seen and by the damage done to him. We do see him acting, though: showing the jittery second lieutenant his tesserae (an unusual word, apparently the *tessera sanitaria*, or Italian health insurance card, but clearly here meaning identification papers). This may seem an insignificant one-time action, but, as Paul S. Quick shows, it introduces the theme of identity, and how one can prove it, into the narrative—a theme of major significance to the Nick whose sense of his own identity and personal autonomy has been shattered by what has been done to him. So, although it is not a turning point in the narrative, this action and what follows from it (the conversations about false or lost papers) are nonetheless of some considerable importance. That slightly unusual sentence later in the story—"Let's not talk about how I am" (*CSS* 309)—has, then, a lingering resonance.

Next, Nick goes to the battalion and meets up again with his old friend Paravicini. If this is a one-time action within the text, it bears no huge weight, being (in the larger scheme of things) entirely routine—keying into a series of repeated actions in the past, when Nick and Paravicini were army colleagues. This meeting does bring Nick pleasure and does allow him to reveal something of his feelings and present condition. He is disappointed, though, that Paravicini sees through his partial pretence of being "perfectly all right" to the truth beneath (309): that he should in no way, and whatever his role, be back in active service. The two men's conversation about their past military history is also significant in terms of Nick's past habitual actions and response to battle conditions: "I was stinking [drunk] in every attack" (309).

Nick's next action is to lie down and "take a nap," following Paravicini's suggestion (310). This, something that might at first seem specific and one-time, nonetheless shades into the habitual—for not only does Nick revert temporarily here to an earlier horizontal and hospitalized state but we will also soon see him lie down again. Moreover, this single action again confirms a generally passive and damaged condition. He next—following the various jumps of his mind between past and recent present, from time spent in Paris to his wartime activity and to the yellow house and the injury and trauma it signifies—swings his damaged legs (presumably also wounded) to the ground, puts on his helmet, offers his hand to the adjutant with whom he is conversing (and to whom he will then launch his disquisition about locusts), takes off his helmet, puts it on again, and leaves the dugout. He then once more removes the helmet, a repeated action which is a physical symptom (overheating) of his inner turbulence, and starts up a bank toward the river to wet the helmet. But, immediately following, he changes his mind to come back down the slope. Again, whether these actions are one-time or repeated makes little difference here, as they work as a series to confirm static aspects of Nick's character, clearly indicative of a man who does not quite know what he is doing, has not quite got a hold on things, is in some kind of distressed state.

Nick then goes back inside the dugout, again at Paravicini's suggestion, and sits down, where, unable any longer to "hold it in" (314), has what we assume to be renewed feelings of panic, of being out of control, of being unable to hold the past at bay. And on Paravicini's advice once more, he lies down again. It is at this point that he shuts his eyes, a minimal physical action that brings the time of his wounding, now fully realized, back to him again: the "man with the beard" who shot him, his own response "on his knees, hot-sweet choking, coughing it onto a rock," the vision of the "long, yellow house" (314). It is this pressing memory of his traumatic wounding that makes the reader understand why he can sleep only with a light on (see both "Now I Lay Me" and "A Clean,

Well-Lighted Place"). Then, realising that there is not much point in remaining where and as he is, Nick stands up and starts back on the road toward his bicycle. At this almost-final point, he remembers a past scene that he initially (but wrongly) associates with this same road—an Italian cavalry unit riding in the snow, bearing lances, the horses steaming the air with their breath. This image forms a fine conclusion to the story, reminding the reader of the way heroic conceptions of war (men fighting one-to-one in a traditional chivalric way) have been absolutely and finally shattered by the conditions of the First World War: as Hemingway would later say, "the most colossal, murderous, mismanaged butchery that has ever taken place on earth" (*MAW* xiii). The story then ends with Nick saying to himself that he must get to his "damned bicycle," as he does not "want to lose the way to Fornaci" (*CSS* 315). He has, after all, as the story has revealed, lost his way in almost every other sense possible.

When we look at Nick's actions in this story, then, both one-time and habitual, we find a degree of confusion between the two. We find, too, that the very word *action* does not take us very far in a story without any kind of climax and in which Nick's actions appear insignificant, as he looks at things, meets various people, goes in and out of a dugout, lies down, take his helmet on and off, and so on. Such actions, though, crucially serve to reveal Nick's present damaged state, his lack of real agency. Indeed, the fact that he is "circulating around to no purpose," war-damaged goods whose very subjectivity is at risk, only confirms the far greater significance of the action done to him, the "clublike impact" of that wounding. All this emerges as we look carefully at the actions associated with the protagonist of what is a very typical Nick Adams story and one that belongs in loose sequence with "Now I Lay Me" and "Big Two-Hearted River."

Paul Goodman makes one of the most astute critical comments on Hemingway when he suggests that, when his characters act, those actions have a disturbing quality, for "though the characters [may] come on with a heavy preponderance of active verbs . . . the effect is passive." Even when these characters initiate actions, "they influence nothing; events happen to them" (181). We see exactly what Goodman means when we look at "Big Two-Hearted River." Nick does this (builds a camp), does that (cooks his meal), but these actions only serve to disguise the fact that he is, in reality, just a later version of the Nick we see in "A Way You'll Never Be." This latter, chronologically earlier, Nick does not initiate much action at all. Both, however, are versions of the one man: a wounded protagonist, damaged by life, and particularly by the impact of war, who feels himself more or less powerless in the face of the various forces that have affected him (whether a result of family, social, or historical circumstance).

In "A Way You'll Never Be," though, there is no preponderance of active verbs. This Nick is more tentative, less sure of himself and his ability to act with any positive outcome at all, more passive, than his later version. The more we look at his actions here, whether one-time or habitual, the more we realize how traumatized he is: how provisional and uncertain his life has become.

As a coda to all I say here, I would draw my reader's attention to the novel Hemingway published seventeen years later, *Across the River and into the Trees* (1950). Its protagonist, Colonel Cantwell, is—in one way, at least—a later version of this Nick Adams, for Cantwell returns to the same place (Fossalta) and the same river (the Piave) beside which he, too, had earlier been wounded. Although the color of the house has been changed from yellow to red, other details (a road below the river level, willow trees) are the same (*ARIT* 20–22). Returning to this place, Cantwell surveys the ground, then squats and "relieve[s] himself in the exact place where he had determined, by triangulation, that he had been badly wounded thirty years before" (*ARIT* 18).[8] Cantwell substitutes for his fictional predecessor here, the Nick Adams who was wounded in that same geographical place. This is both a highly significant one-time act within the novel itself and an act of constructive repetition (when one takes "A Way You'll Never Be" into account)—a return to the site of injury and a deliberate excremental voiding performed there. Such an act signals the move from bodily vulnerability to authority, a deliberate act of exorcism with which the Hemingway protagonist metaphorically (but also effectively) leaves trauma once and for all behind him.

In this essay, then, I show how a student might start to apply just one aspect of Rimmon-Kenan's work on character construction to a text. While I recognize the problems that arise when we look to apply her scheme to "A Way You'll Never Be," I see these as enabling rather than a reason to stop a critic in her or his tracks. Moreover, I have not hesitated to follow additional—though relevant—chains of critical thought as they have been stimulated by this initial process, a willingness to follow the evidence that I see as a positive counter to any overly mechanical application of Rimmon-Kenan's structuralist approach. Were space available, I would go on to look more closely at other aspects of Nick's character, and especially how it is indicated here by his speech, both to others and in the inner conversation he holds with himself. I also would explore in much more detail how repetition works within the text. The more any student is able to move between such analytic tactics, the more, I contend, she or he will realize just how liberating the type of methodology I bring to this essay can be, allowing the student to build up a whole range of patternings to open up texts in ways that are often surprising and rewarding.

As I have tried to suggest, the approach I use here does not finally treat the text only as an independent entity, something standing outside its sociohistorical context; instead I have begun to indicate the historical resonances of this narrative, how it fits into the larger story of American masculinity and male selfhood in the period. What we see here is suggestive of a larger picture, both in literary and sociohistorical terms—and, indeed, in terms of the connections between them—for if modernism is associated with the representation of inner consciousness, with an alienated subject (often an artist) operating at one remove from, and out of joint with, the larger world within which he or she must move, we see in Nick Adams's experiences (and particularly in the relationship between agency and passivity in the stories about him) some of the reasons for such a dislocation. It is often said that a structuralist approach is disabling in terms of sociohistorical criticism. I strongly disagree. I see it as inevitably leading to the consideration of larger cultural and ideological issues of the type to which I have just alluded. Thus, in this story and in Hemingway's other Nick Adams stories, any understanding of what Georg Lukacs would call "historical sequence," a sequence in which the individual might play a meaningful part, has been replaced by the overwhelming conditions of modernity: a world in which the "dynamic interaction" between the individual character and "objects and events" has broken down (Lukacs 144, 13).[9] Here, the human subject stands in anxious and passive relation to his (or her) surrounding world, totally unable to influence it significantly.

I have spoken about notions of character and subjectivity in a relatively schematic way in this essay. In a final warning note, I would add that such a discussion is not necessarily intended to endorse a sense of character as "essential," stable, and one-dimensional, for this is exactly what Nick is not. Different aspects of Nick's character (and of those of Hemingway's related protagonists) appear in other texts—and, indeed, most of the Nick Adams stories are not about his war experiences. The approach I take fully recognizes the broader range of character indicators that can be found (especially in any longer text), and recognizes, too, that *identity* remains a fragile term, a slippery and multiform thing that can never be pinned down too firmly.

## Notes

1. The present essay condenses theoretical material from my book, *New Readings of the American Novel: Narrative Theory and its Application* (Houndmills, Basingstoke: Macmillan, 1990), and initially borrows from my essay, "Character and Agency: Teaching Mark Twain's 'A True Story'" (*Eureka Studies in Teaching Short Fiction* 4.1 [2003]: 20–31).

2. In both taxi scenes, the fact that the two come together through external force, the jolting vehicle, blurs the boundary between external force and subjective agency, and it is noticeable that Jake in fact does nothing, does *not* act in this final example: we can speculate that either he remains passively beside Brett or actively moves away. I recognize that my exploration of habitual action is thus muddied here, but see that fact as useful to us as critics, since it highlights the tension implied between agency and passive determinism, and between emotional weakness and self-control, lying at the larger heart of the novel (and of so much of Hemingway's early work). Students might look at Jake's drinking and bar-hopping, or at the way he acts as an intermediary for Brett's romance with Romero, as other examples of habitual action in the novel.

3. Hemingway himself was wounded at Fossalta di Piave in July 1918, about seven kilometers from the village of Fornaci. The river location of the story, together with its "deserted" town with its "houses ... broken by the shelling" (*CSS* 307), implies that the immediate story is set in and around Fossalta. For more information on the military references in this story, see Paul S. Quick's very useful "Hemingway's 'A Way You'll Never Be' and Nick Adams's Search for Identity," <http://www.thefreelibrary.com/Hemingway's+%22A+Way+You'll+Never+Be%22+and+Nick+Adams's+search+for . . . -a0105518230>.

4. See also *CSS* 310–11.

5. See also *CSS* 310–11 and 312–13.

6. Rimmon-Kenan separates action from speech: the way "[a] character's speech, whether in conversation or as a silent activity of the mind, can be indicative of a (character) trait or traits both through its content and through its form" (63). However, critics such as J. L. Austin, in *How to do Things with Words* (Cambridge, MA.: Harvard UP, 1962), associate "speech acts" with intentional action. While accepting that latter connection, I choose, too, to keep the difference between word and physical action distinct. See my section on speech in *The Sun Also Rises* in *New Readings of the American Novel* (109–11, 125–29).

7. For other material on Hemingway and repetition, perhaps the most crucial technique in his stylistic armory, see the chapter on style in Messent, *Ernest Hemingway* (Houndmills, Basingstoke: Macmillan, 1992). See, too, Messent, "Liminality, Repetition, and Trauma in Hemingway's 'Big Two-Hearted River' and Other Nick Adams Stories," in *Mapping Liminalities: Thresholds in Cultural and Literary Texts,* ed. Lucy Kay et al. (Bern: Peter Lang, 2007), 136–65.

8. Directly anticipating here the work of the contemporary author who perhaps most resembles him, Tim O'Brien. See "Field Trip" in O'Brien's *The Things They Carried* (1990).

9. Hemingway's use, here and elsewhere, of the first-person perspective, subjective impression received through the data of the senses, reminds us of Fredric Jameson's

comment on impressionist painting: "A style like Impressionism . . . discards even the operative fiction of some interest in the constituted objects of the natural world, and offers the exercise of perception and the perceptual recombination of sense data as an end in itself" (Fredric Jameson, *The Political Unconscious: Narrative as a Socially Symbolic Act* [1981; rpt., London: Methuen, 1983], 229–30). In Hemingway's case, however, the world of external reality never loses its importance. Indeed, it is in the very disparity between the one and the other that his fiction operates to its most powerful effect.

# Part Two

# The Spanish Civil War

# Seeing Through Fracture

*In Our Time, For Whom the Bell Tolls,* and Picasso's *Guernica*

Thomas Strychacz

Like Poland in Sylvia Plath's famous poem "Daddy," the world in the twentieth century was "Scraped flat by the roller / Of wars, wars, wars." Total war. Guerilla war. Blitzkrieg. Cold war. World war. Great War. Even a war to end war (World War I, supposedly). There was war by proxy (the United States in Vietnam, the Soviet Union in Afghanistan) and domino wars (World War I segueing into the Greco-Turkish war; the Spanish Civil War into World War II, World War II into the Korean War). Twentieth-century wars renamed peoples and erased and rewrote national borders, sometimes over and over; the case of Poland, as Plath recognized, was characteristic. Twentieth-century warfare invented new technologies of slaughter (tanks, planes, nuclear weapons) and newly efficient procedures for using them (killing fields, carpet-bombing, concentration camps, satellite surveillance). The potential for war so lethal that its consequences could barely be imagined drove its strategists to this jaw-dropping euphemism: M.A.D. (mutually assured destruction). Ezra Pound's famous elegy, in "Hugh Selwyn Mauberley" (1920), for the soldiers enmeshed in the trench warfare of World War I—they "walked eye-deep in hell"—perhaps proves an apt epitaph for the entire twentieth century. At the very least, that nightmarish experience was to become mundane.

For this reason, if for no other, Hemingway's work is worth studying. He experienced two world wars and was wounded in the first, reported on the Greco-Turkish war, reported on the Spanish Civil War and gave his support to the Republican side in it, and lived to see the start of the cold war. More importantly, he wrote compellingly and movingly about the experience of war—its logic, its madness, its brutal consequences, its effects on women and, in particular, on men. But his strategies for depicting war changed dramatically over time. This essay traces the shift in style between two war fictions—*In Our Time* (1925) and *For Whom the Bell Tolls* (1940)—and provides new ways to think about Hemingway's important shift in attitudes during the crucial period between the two world wars, as his experience in the Spanish Civil War and his awareness of the rise of fascism reshaped his opinions of what war was *for*. There is some truth to the popular conception that *For Whom the Bell Tolls* restores to acts of war a sense of moral purpose. If *In Our Time* and *A Farewell to Arms* (1929) represent war as a meaningless horror—the "sacrifices were like the stockyards at Chicago if nothing was done with the meat except to bury it," says Frederic Henry of soldiers dying in *A Farewell to Arms* (185)—*For Whom the Bell Tolls* seems to argue that war is a horror that must be endured if fascism is to be defeated. From that perspective, sacrifices carry a profound significance; they are not absurd at all. But this is not the only way to understand how warfare becomes newly meaningful in the later novel. The problem Hemingway confronts in *For Whom the Bell Tolls* is not simply one of strategy—how to oppose fascists who command superior military forces—but also one of principle: the fact that the fascists' most successful strategies make formidable military sense and, at the same time, embody terrifying totalitarian principles. Fascism must be opposed. But what sort of resistance is possible when effective resistance might mean duplicating fascist tactics on the grounds that they are necessary for military success?

The broad and intricate relationship between war and Hemingway (and other modernist writers, for that matter) poses a special problem to the educator: Where does one begin? I like to use the visual arts to frame the big issues. Along with its innovative military technologies, the twentieth century saw the development of numerous ways to record the carnage that ensued. Students' command of twentieth-century political and military history is usually weak, but they seem to have little trouble recalling touchstone images: herky-jerky movie footage of soldiers leaving the trenches in the First World War; soldiers raising flags over captured terrain; a screaming girl fleeing napalm attacks; mushroom clouds. The power of images over the memory is why I like to begin by studying one of century's most famous and harrowing paintings: Pablo Picasso's *Guernica* (1937), which he painted to commemorate Nazi Germany's devastating bombing of the village of Guernica in northern Spain during the Spanish Civil War. The attack was spearheaded by Hitler's Luftwaffe. Although there were clearly political affinities between Nazi Germany and the fascist forces in Spain, Germany seems to have intervened partly to test the efficacy of aerial bombardments, given Nazi plans for future conflicts. Whatever the political or military reasoning, perhaps 1,600 people died during the two to three hours of bombing.

Picasso's *Guernica* is justly acclaimed for its emotional impact. Its subdued palate, somber shades of white, black, and blue, evokes still photos of the destruction of Guernica, while its monumental dimensions (3.5 meters by 7.8 meters, or 11 feet by 25 feet) seem to dispute its possible function as a mere record or document. It is epic, designed to convey something of the scale of the carnage and raising a once-insignificant village to iconic status. Yet one difference from epics of old is noticeable straight away: there are no heroes. This is total war; civilians and soldiers go down together. Its images are prosaic—a bull, a horse, a bird, a lamp, a section of tiled roof—and its human (or human-like) figures are bowed, staggering, and broken. The soldier (and/or toreador) at bottom left holds a sword, but it is shattered, and he, like the figures to his left and right, gazes shrieking up at the sky, where the enigmatic eye of a jagged light bulb replaces whatever providential, or nurturing, or even just minimally responsive gaze one might wish to have from the heavens. Also absent, perhaps oddly, is any obvious sign of an enemy. Perhaps the oval light bulb hints at the shape of a bomb; perhaps the radiance just right of center reminds us of a bomb blast glaring through an open door. But the painting omits the political machinations and military decisions, the aircraft and pilots, the falling bombs. The painting places us definitively on the ground, in the aftermath, facing the awful tangle left behind when a bomb has done its indiscriminate work. Consequences replace motivation; shards replace things that might once have been whole.

Picasso's tactic of placing viewers completely amidst chaos is clearly crucial to the effect of the painting, and I try in class to reproduce it by, at first, just showing the image. A statement such as "Look at the painting for a few minutes and jot down your responses" is as much as I offer, on the principle that it is important to feel the power of a terrain without clear contextual markers—to know what it is like to *not* understand something. And that first glimpse of the painting for those who have not seen or studied it before tends to be one of complete incomprehension. The eye wanders, trying and failing to see it whole (even more so if faced with the vast original), trying to disentangle the fractured shapes, trying and failing to relate one enigmatic shape with another. Everywhere, boundaries are erased. The bull's tail at far left twists into a plume of smoke. The body of the soldier/matador at bottom left merges into the horse, and the patterns layered on this composite body remind us of still other superimposed

realms: parallel rows of little lines that look like newsprint, and what appear to be lines of latitude and longitude, putting us in mind of the global issues at stake or perhaps of the navigational mechanisms that brought the planes to their target. But opening up to confusion need not lead to the global. It can help move students toward a much more intimate effect: apprehension that the figures in the painting are terribly vulnerable. They seem defenseless because we cannot see the sources of their terror and therefore cannot rationalize any possible escape. A moment spent looking at the figure of the mother holding the dead child at far left demonstrates this quickly: the inordinately long line of her exposed throat as she throws her head back to scream implies helplessness, as does her left hand, outsized, imploring, but grasping nothing. Other weirdly

Pablo Picasso, *Guernica*. Paris, June 4, 1937. Oil on canvas, 349.3 x 776.6 cm. Museo Nacional Centro de Arte Reina Sofia. © 2014 Estate of Pablo Picasso/Artists Rights Society (ARS), New York. (Photo Credit: Erich Lessing/Art Resource, NY.)

disorienting effects of the painting intensify this disquieting sense of being lost, of not knowing our way around this world anymore. Everyone is shrieking, but in complete silence. Everyone is looking, but we cannot interpret their gazes: they are looking up at nothing we can perceive, and in any case their eyes are literally askew. They cannot "see straight," and neither can we.

The question of why Picasso paints in this style of fractured lines, odd juxtapositions, and frightening omissions, is clearly crucial to this entire discussion. One purpose of cubism—originating a quarter of a century before *Guernica*—was to disassemble what passed for reality. Why not respect, for example, the reality—the two-dimensionality—of the canvas? Instead of using realist strategies for creating the illusion of three-dimensional objects in two dimensions (e.g., linear perspective), why should one not strive to represent a fourth dimension, time, as if one painted all that could be seen by walking around the object? Why not paint two eyes in two different positions as if one were observing a face from separate perspectives? Instead of building up from a few geometric shapes and regular proportions sketched on a canvas, why not build down *to* those shapes and thus recompose a guitar or human figure into the flat planes and simple shapes that "really" are there? Cubism disorients, and then *re*orients, what we think of and perceive as the real.

In *Guernica*, however, Picasso directs the project of modernist art along political lines. The actual attack on Guernica governs the painting's aesthetic, and the result is a painting that makes explicit the synergy between war and a modernist idiom of fragmentation, juxtaposition, and omission. There is a sort of literalism to Picasso's style here that students respond to very quickly. Bombs violently wrench apart a mundane world; indiscriminately, they blow bodies and things together. A village destroyed in such a manner has no coherence—no paths, no communications, no voice, no intact families, no distinctions—and the villagers have no way of understanding the relationship between devastation and the politics of terror. No wonder, then, that the grieving mother's and the soldier's eyes are set at such haphazard angles. And no wonder if one's first glance at the painting tends to create a sense of bewilderment. Refusing the harmonious unity of bodies and things, fracturing bodies under tremendous physical and emotional pressure, and drawing viewers into the same vortex of confusion, Picasso's style observes the logic—and horror—of total war.

*Guernica* and *For Whom the Bell Tolls* arise out of the same set of historical circumstances, the complicated and vicious civil war in Spain staging a conflict between fascism (the Nationalists) and its opponents (the Republicans) as a prelude to the Second World War. But *Guernica* provides a particularly rich frame for the earlier *In Our Time*, Hemingway's first major work, a collection of short stories interspersed with even shorter vignettes, some of them only a few sentences long. Only the impressionistic vignettes bring us directly into the action of World War I, but the war appears everywhere as a concussion still being felt in the psyches and relationships of people even after it has technically ended. Like *Guernica*, *In Our Time* deals with consequences, and in Hemingway's work, like the painting, those consequences seem to demand a fractured style heavy on omission and bewildering leaps.

Turning to *In Our Time* from *Guernica*, I like to begin with the same sort of very simple questions—"What is your general response to the opening stories? What difficulties are you encountering?"—on the principle, once again, that confusion, and the subsequent process of trying to account for that confusion, is productive. And students are generally perplexed. Why does the action leap back and forth between the war and Nick Adams's youth, between Europe and the United States, between prewar and war? Where is Smyrna [now Izmir], and what is happening in "On the Quai at Smyrna"? Where is the lake in "Indian Camp"? What is the time frame of the early stories? (It is not even really evident until chapter 6, when Nick himself is wounded, that the first stories are prewar.) Why are these stories shuffled together in such a strange way? I always find it worth jotting down these confusions on the board, partly because it usually makes for quite a list—visual testimony to a shared response—and partly because I try to move slowly, by way of a few careful close readings, toward some provisional responses to these conundrums. The point, I think, is not to provide answers but to try to grasp the terms of the dilemma; and it is not to make students feel silly for not "getting it" but to see "not getting it" as a functional device for representing conflict in general and war in particular.

I find "On the Quai at Smyrna" a perfect starting place: it is the first story (added to the collection in 1930), the key ("quai") to it all, and a master class in confusion. After reading the whole vignette to get the full flavor of it, we turn to the opening lines: "The strange thing was, he said, how they screamed every night at midnight. I do not know why they screamed at that time. We were in the harbor and they were all on the pier and at midnight they started screaming" (*CSS* 63). After four sentences we are lost. We are presented with a welter of pronouns (he, I, they, we) before the nouns appear; indeed, the referents never do appear. There is a confusion of speakers too: "he said," but who is "he" and whom is he addressing? Does the "he" of the first sentence become the "I" of the second, his words now being reported directly by a silent interlocutor? Or is "I" a different speaker who picks up his acquaintance's conversational thread? Are "we" the two speakers here (he and I together) or some other group? Who are "they" who scream, and how shall we know why they are screaming when the speaker himself does not understand?

There are several ways of dealing with this confusion, and it is worth pausing for a moment to consider the implications of each, since they create very different dynamics. One way, of course, is to bring in historical information from outside the story: "Smyrna" helps us to identify the situation as the evacuation of Greek civilians from Smyrna [Izmir] during the Greco-Turkish war in 1922, one of those domino wars so frequent in the twentieth century, which the young Hemingway covered as a journalist. Most students expect this sort of explanation. They want it: they (like anyone else) do not do well with confusion. And, having received it, they tend to consider the interpretive job done: now that the story can be located in time and space, its mysteries have been cleared up. There are two important reasons for deferring this sort of revelation. First, a slew of riddles in the story cannot be resolved by any amount of historical information. We never learn the identities of "I" or "he" except in a nonspecific way (i.e., that they are British officers); we cannot know why the Turkish officer is raging or whether the speaker actually saw what a doctor considers "impossible" (*CSS* 64); we never know why "they" scream at midnight even after we have identified them as refugees. This points to the second problem: Why was the material omitted in the first place? What does this omission give readers? What does it do to readers? What experience does it grant us? It is possible—some students, I find, react this way to modernism generally—that withholding information grants the author authority over the reader, so that it feels like a power play. Or perhaps we are shut out for other reasons: the participants in the conversation know the subject so well they need not speak it, or the story pays tribute to a specific type of laconic, stiff-upper-lip heroism, or it tries to capture the "fog of war."

However, the image of *Guernica* and the discussion of its effects allow a different approach to the story's disorienting omissions. The mother grieving for the dead child and her unheard screaming in Picasso's painting also figure in "On the Quai." The story, like the painting, shows us voicelessness. The refugees' screaming can be heard, but not understood. Or does the speaker not *want* to interpret it? And is that because of the mothers who will not let go of their dead babies (something the speaker describes twice, the second time after admitting that it was the only time in his life he "dreamed about things")? Is it because the speaker feels helpless, or in some way complicit? Or is it because the fog of war is so pervasive that even the main players cannot tell who is doing what to whom? After all, the speaker says he will punish the gunner's mate (though he will not) for offending a Turkish officer (though he did not) for being insulting (though the officer could not understand what the mate was saying). And the speaker tries to stay on amiable terms with this officer, even though he later contemplates shelling the Turkish forces for their aggressive posture—even though their aggression appears to be an error! At least the Turkish commander gets sacked for exceeding his authority "or some such thing" (*CSS* 64). The speaker's brilliant assessment of this bewildering tangle—"or some such thing"—invites us to see that the contexts we might supply so blithely a hundred years later ("well, what's happening is the Greco-Turkish war") were unavailable to the people struggling in the conflict. They are subject *to*, not in charge *of*, their experience. As in *Guernica*, figures remain incomplete, events blurry, and place unreadable, when all familiar landmarks have been rearranged by bombs or evacuations. The voiceless stay unvoiced, their stories related piecemeal—and that includes the narrator, even though, since he is there in a position of relative power, one would think him ideally placed to translate to us and mediate for us the nature of the conflict. No detached perspective seems possible in either story or painting. As the title of the story unobtrusively implies, the narrator(s) and we readers are all *on the quai*, herded alongside the baffled refugees.

Reading "On the Quai" by way of *Guernica* suggests that both works set out to find a new language to address traumatic experiences so intense that they cannot be "spoken" in conventional terms. "On the Quai" may be a classic example of what is now called post-traumatic stress disorder (PTSD). Trauma studies in literature since the mid-1990s have emphasized that the response to traumatic injuries is often marked by a refusal to articulate their meaning and emotional impact. A simple catalog of events—this happened, then this—substitutes for what is too painful to think about or feel. This helps to explain the lack of affect in the narrator's laconic descriptions. And it helps to explain the fractured nature of the narrative: if dislocation characterizes the experience of war, perhaps the refusal to examine it too deeply is a way to deal with the psychic shock it causes. Though the narrator cannot help but return to the scene of trauma, perhaps he does not *want* to know the connection between screaming and midnight or to pursue the reasons why mothers hold on to their dead babies for six days. They exist, after all, in the darkest part of the hold, the place of nightmare.

As readers, we undergo another disorienting leap when we turn to "Indian Camp" and "The Doctor and the Doctor's Wife." We might spot thematic continuities—a baby gets born in "Indian Camp" amid great difficulties, for example, like the babies on the pier at Smyrna—without perceiving the relevance of the early Nick Adams stories to war. Yet they advance and deepen that conversation in unexpected ways. One way to read "Indian Camp" is to see it as an echo of a centuries-long history of whites expropriating and colonizing Native American lands. The doctor, "fathering" the Indian child and in so doing reenacting the role of "Great White Father," justifies his incursion into Native American space by taking a page from the Manifest Destiny playbook: he introduces superior (medical) knowledge to the waiting "Indians." "The Doctor and the Doctor's Wife" makes that subtext still more evident as Dick Boulton draws attention to the logs on the doctor's property—"You know they're stolen as well as I do" (*CSS* 74)—and the doctor, after his humiliation, cradles his rifle, sign of the technological superiority that gave colonists the edge in centuries of conflict. Armed incursions into and bloody conflicts over North American land appear phantomlike in these stories. And so, crucially, does a long, tragic history of consequences. There is "no end and no beginning" to the sufferings of the refugees streaming away from Adrianopolis in chapter 2 (*CSS* 71), and certainly there is no end of historical precedents for forced relocations of civilian populations on the North American continent. "Indian Camp" and "The Doctor and the Doctor's Wife" urge us to recall, for example, what we now call the Long Walk (of the Navajo) and the Trail of Tears (undergone by the Cherokee and Choctaw, among others) in the nineteenth century. We begin to see now why the referent of "they" in "On the Quai at Smyrna" never appears in the story itself. "They" are the refugees at Smyrna—but also those fleeing Adrianopolis and those herded by the U.S. military, and potentially many more displaced populations besides. Like *Guernica*, the opening stories of *In Our Time* have the capacity to represent a time and locale very specifically while picking up the reverberations of wars, wars, and more wars across a huge span of history.

Published fifteen years after *In Our Time*, *For Whom the Bell Tolls* develops a very different way of representing war. It therefore presents a different set of challenges to the teacher. Gone is the lurid confusion of "On the Quai at Smyrna." Within the first few pages of *For Whom the Bell Tolls* we know a great deal about Robert Jordan, his mission, his guide, and the locale. The narrator secures the bulk of the story in Jordan's consciousness, a self-described "windy bastard" (*FWBT* 43), and one consequence is that the narrative replaces *Time*'s sharp fractures with a detailed exposition of just about everything. Moreover, the narrator proves quite capable of seamlessly shifting to the consciousness of other characters and omnisciently relating events Jordan does not experience. We are therefore never exposed to the terrifying disorientations of "On the Quai at Smyrna" and *Guernica*. One recognizes this fact quite simply from the differing teaching tempos demanded by these works. Elucidating missing contexts and accounting for the problem of having to elucidate them mean that "On the Quai at Smyrna" could easily occupy an entire class period. The slowly unwinding narrative form of *For Whom the Bell Tolls* imposes a different constraint: students must assimilate a large swathe of the novel before its dimensions begin to come clear.

In part, this measured narrative pacing captures Jordan's increasing preoccupation with cramming in the sights and sounds of this world in an effort to slow down the remorseless clock, every tick of which takes him closer to the fateful blowing of the bridge. (Jordan is always looking at his watch, counting and hoarding the moments left.) In part, the narrator's ability to take different points of view implies Hemingway's desire to move beyond polemical support for the Republican side and see a single country at war with itself as a whole. Pilar's harrowing account of Pablo's slaughter of the fascists in their hometown counterbalances tales of Nationalist atrocities (Maria's story, for example). Chapter 15, famously, alternates perspectives between Anselmo, who is observing a fascist sentry post for Jordan, and the sentries themselves, who long for home. This tactic cannot help but increase sympathy for the fascist soldiers when they are later killed during the blowing of the bridge. Still more strikingly, Hemingway draws attention to the capacities of the narrative to "see things whole." In the second paragraph of chapter 15, for instance, we are told that though Anselmo looks at a passing car and an officer inside looks out, "neither of them saw the other" (*FWBT* 191). But the narrator, knowing what they cannot know, sees both. In this sense, the experience of reading *For Whom the Bell Tolls* is quite different from reading "On the Quai at Smyrna" or viewing *Guernica*. Here, an omniscient narrator stands apart from the limited perspectives of the characters, orienting us to the sort of broad contexts—the strategies, the forces involved, the political motives, the historical figures behind the scenes—that the physically and psychically broken eyewitnesses at Smyrna [Izmir] and Guernica could not provide, and whose shock and bewilderment Picasso and the younger Hemingway strive so hard to emulate. Put another way, it would seem imperative to frame students' entry into the world of *For Whom the Bell Tolls* with a clear and detailed synopsis of the circumstances of the Spanish Civil War. *Guernica* here can be used effectively to illuminate the historical record.

Any consideration of history in the late 1930s must include an account of totalitarianism, insofar as it informed fascist thinking in Spain, in Mussolini's Italy, and—most evidently by the time the novel was published—in Nazi Germany. Hemingway's approach to totalitarianism in *For Whom the Bell Tolls* is very much bound up with the fascists' ability to exercise what I call *super-vision*—the desire to see everything, know everything, and therefore supervise or control everything. In the novel, the fascists are not literally omniscient, but they know about the forthcoming assault to which Jordan's bridge-blowing is a prelude, just as, he admits, they have known about every other major move of the Republican armies. And the Nationalists' planes offer more than air superiority; they represent a near-total exercise of power. "We are nothing against such machines," says Pilar after Jordan and the guerillas watch waves of planes pass overhead (*FWBT* 89); they are the new gods of the heavens, like Thor, "hammering the sky apart" (75). Jordan's response to the first planes is telling: he "knew they would not see him, and that it did not matter if they did" (75). Jordan means, of course, that the planes are too intent on their own military business to bother with him. But he implies more: they are motivated by a form of power that is indifferent to individuals on the ground and even, since his "they" refers quite specifically to the planes, to the pilots as well. Individuals are simply inconsequential—it does not "matter" whether they are visible or not—to what Jordan calls the planes' "mechanized doom" (87). One of the fascist soldiers in the sentry post in fact echoes the guerrillas' fear, confessing to being terrified of the Republican bombers "when they were a horror to endure" (196).

Picasso's *Guernica*—in particular the electric light bulb (off-center to the left, at top), which invokes both an eye and an exploding bomb—can help us understand the sort of power that the novel associates with the planes. Like some technologically mediated eye of God, the light bulb/eye/bomb seems to have the power to see all and destroy all simultaneously. It presides over the carnage of broken bodies with the same sort of indifference that the planes in *For Whom the Bell Tolls* display to individuals on the ground. Most importantly, it makes the human sources of that power invisible by erasing from the canvas the political and military circumstances and the decision-makers who were behind the attack. Picasso's painting seems to grasp its historical moment as one where real power can no longer be identified with the motivations of individual humans. This sort of power is inscrutable. It dominates through surveillance, through disciplining human lives to accept its stark, indifferent supervision, through being largely invisible and therefore impervious to resistance. (Possibly the figure whose foot extends into the bottom right corner does discern the power of the bulb/eye/bomb; if so, it seems to be creeping helplessly in terror.) It therefore implies totalitarianism—the development of systems for the total domination of human populations. And these systems are abstract, disembodied, and pervasive. Planes (and spies and cavalry) mediate this power, but it is omnipresent, as Jordan and the guerillas are aware: there is never a moment when they can *not* hide.

One major question Hemingway poses in *For Whom the Bell Tolls* is whether the Republicans should adopt the same strategies. The novel is carefully constructed to associate totalitarian power with the fascists. The guerillas do spy on the Nationalist forces, but they lack planes; they are dedicated, but they lack discipline—Pablo even steals Jordan's detonators the day before the attack. But Jordan understands the allure, perhaps the necessity, of total "super-vision." When he observes that he "knew [the planes] would not see him, and that it did not matter if they did" (*FWBT* 75), he is simultaneously looking up at the planes and looking down from their perspective. He knows what it means to exercise "super-vision" over the ground below. He also knows how to implement it. He sees in his mind's eye the operations required to blow the bridge many times before he actually swings into action. The first page of the novel shows Jordan surveying the bridge by eye, map, and binoculars. Later, Jordan explains how to deploy the machine gun strategically so as to "command" the territory in front of the gun (276): "See?" Jordan tells Agustín, "All that is dominated" (272). It would appear that the only way to counter the fascists' strategic advantage is by extending Jordan's lesson in machine-gun placement to the entire Republican army and state—to put the whole of Spain under the sights of the Republican gun, as it were. Jordan's strategy makes perfect military sense: to see more than the near-total gaze of the fascists would seem to be the only way in which, as Jordan tells Pilar about the planes, "we can beat them" (89). But would not this route to military success transform the Republicans into a mirror-image of the oppressive system they are fighting?

For Jordan and the guerillas in the novel, this vexed issue never comes fully into play. They are behind enemy lines, and victory of any sort seems increasingly illusory. But it is relevant to wonder whether Hemingway falls into a fantasy of total power—or at least omniscience—in a novel that sometimes seems to document every instant of Jordan's last days and to know every last circumstance and key player of the war. In this sense, the narrative behaves like Picasso's electric light bulb, promising to bring every thought and action under a watchful eye. The narrative does admittedly sacrifice its own power to know everything. We see inside the sentry post in chapter 15, but we do not witness its destruction. Other crucial events also happen offstage: We learn afterward about Pablo's stealing of the detonators and El Sordo's tragic error of stealing horses during the snowstorm. We never know Lieutenant Berrendo's fate or learn what happens to Pablo's band. Nonetheless, the fundamental issue that distinguishes *For Whom the Bell Tolls* from the fractured experiences of *In Our Time* and *Guernica* is the novel's ability to bring order to and exert control over its narrative materials. Examining the function of the light bulb/eye/bomb in Picasso's painting is one way to draw attention to the important question of whether Hemingway himself longs to impose a sort of military command-and-control structure on soldiers and civilian populations.

At Mills College, the liberal arts college for women where I teach at the time of writing this essay, students are generally more impressed with Hemingway's earlier work on war. These students are responding, I think, to two main issues. First, the female students in my classes often experience the disorientations of *In Our Time* as an awakening to the power of Hemingway's fiction. Always alert to problems of masculinity and power, Mills students find it hard to square their suspicions of a notoriously he-man writer with what they find here: the anxieties over masculinity, the sensitivity to the plight of women, the deeply felt experience of trauma in specific encounters and across a tremendous sweep of history. Second, these students are reading *For Whom the Bell Tolls* after more than a decade—the very decade during which they matured into adults—of deeply unpopular U.S. wars of choice. The case can be made that the morality of a war against fascism should be distinguished from the morality of a war against terror, but my students, at least, seem disposed to look more favorably on stories registering the horrific consequences of conflict without seeming, as does *For Whom the Bell Tolls,* to justify acts of war.

One of my goals in teaching *For Whom the Bell Tolls* is to argue that it in fact raises questions of profound concern to today's students. The novel does permit a complicated discussion about the morality of warfare. But just as interesting is the frightening prospect that the maintenance of an orderly state may be shaped by, may even require, the military logic of the warplane's eye-in-the-sky: systems for managing human lives, within which those lives do not really matter. Students grasp immediately the fact that we live in an era of unprecedented technological surveillance. There are military aspects to this. American drone strikes launched by controllers thousands of miles from their target introduce ethical questions not just about transgressing national boundaries (in Pakistan, for example) but about war trivialized, sanitized, pursued as a sort of video game. The invisible surveillance of citizens by the state in an effort to secure the homeland against terrorist attacks causes more consternation among my students. This may be because these operations are more immediately threatening to their liberal sensibilities while also seeming to be the result of an impeccable logic—Jordan's logic, that is to say: the notion that winning wars requires perfect knowledge and total supervision. Still more perplexing to my students are the new non-military tactics of surveillance produced by the pervasive use of new electronic technologies. In the tracking programs that deliver personalized ads to one's computer, for example, individuals are of no more consequence than functions in an algorithm. My students are hyperaware of the extent and implications of their interconnectivity. Children of the web, they can give dozens of examples of how the web works its data-mining magic. They do not like it, yet by and large they accept it. Such surveillance, after all, exercises a merely impersonal power over their lives. It takes an effort to realize that a system for collecting, organizing, and redistributing data, which, like Picasso's electric light bulb, observes them all the time without ever really "seeing" them, can be considered coercive.

This is not by any means to claim that we live in a totalitarian society. Most of my students are aware that living in a liberal state (and under market capitalism) requires trade-offs; they do not equate internet supervision with Big Brother. They continue to believe in personal agency; they want to believe that their individual voices are efficacious. But then, so does Robert Jordan as he advocates for more surveillance, more control over the terrain, and more discipline among the individuals under his command. This seems to me the central conundrum of the novel—and of *our* time. In *For Whom the Bell Tolls*, fascism cannot be defeated and individuals cannot be freed from totalitarianism without new strategies for dominating space and disciplining people; but those strategies lead inexorably toward impersonal and depersonalizing systems for controlling social relations. In its guise as a chronicle of the Spanish Civil War, *For Whom the Bell Tolls* does an end run around this issue: the Republicans have already lost when the novel appears. But in its efforts to investigate the logic of total control, which is both feared and desired, a military requirement and an ethical dilemma, *For Whom the Bell Tolls* confronts its readers with something that *Guernica* and *In Our Time*, for all their remarkable insights into the horror of war, cannot emulate: a foreboding of the all-but-invisible systems of social management that surround us all.

# Hemingway and the Spanish Civil War

The Writer's Maturing View

Milton A. Cohen

The Spanish Civil War

Though both sides in a war would have us believe otherwise, wars are seldom clear-cut matters of white and black, good guys and bad, right and wrong. Each side may well proclaim "God's on our side," but subsequent historians and students must sort out conflicting claims of justification, actions, and counteractions. Often, gray shades their conclusions. The Spanish Civil War is a good example. The war is typically remembered and taught as a clear-cut conflict between good and evil, democracy and fascism. In July 1936, fascist General Francisco Franco led a right-wing rebellion to overthrow the duly elected Republican coalition government (supporters of which were called Republicans or Loyalists). Backed by wealthy landowners, the military, and the Catholic Church, Franco's forces (called Nationalists or Rebels) were soon aided by Nazi Germany, which provided primarily planes and pilots, and fascist Italy, which provided primarily tanks and soldiers. The Republicans received military leadership and arms from the Soviet Union. Thus, the civil war quickly expanded into an international battleground, pitting fascism against a fragile democracy aided by communist Russia. Although other Western nations (including the United States) remained neutral and declared an arms embargo on Spain,[1] thousands of leftist idealists, concerned with the expansion of Nazism and fascism, volunteered to go to Spain to aid the Republicans. After the Nationalists prevailed in 1939, Spain became a dictatorship until Franco's death in 1975.

This summary, however, omits facts that complicate the cause of the "good guy" Republicans. First, extremist supporters of the Republican government—which had existed, shakily, only since 1931, Spain having previously been a monarchy—had sometimes committed atrocities against priests and royalists, which turned many deeply religious Spaniards against the Republicans. (Franco's Nationalists committed many more such atrocities when they took over towns; thus, the war's nature was ugly and brutal, and civilians on both sides suffered grievously.)[2]

Another ambiguity concerning the Loyalist cause was the involvement of the Soviet Union. Partly because the Republican coalition government, splintered among many leftist parties, was ineffectual in commanding Republican forces, the Soviet-organized Communist International (Comintern) quickly took over that role. But as the Stalinists had done in their own country, the Comintern leadership in Spain ruthlessly suppressed Republican socialists, anarchists, and anti-Stalinist communists, conducting numerous political executions. In addition, counterintelligence officers, both Russian and Spanish, arrested and executed thousands of civilians and Republican volunteers accused of being fascist spies. This repression clouds the "democracy vs. fascism" depiction of the war. Idealistic volunteers like George Orwell, W. H. Auden, and John Dos Passos left Spain thoroughly disillusioned with Russia's role in the civil war.[3] Dos Passos, for example, discovered through his own investigation that his close friend and literary translator, José Robles, had been executed by the Soviets for allegedly having been a spy.[4] When Dos Passos bitterly complained of this to Ernest Hemingway, the latter condescendingly lectured Dos Passos on the need to accept the communists' military discipline for the good of the cause—the same logic Robert Jordan uses to justify similar brutalities in *For Whom the Bell Tolls*. Hemingway's callous response ended their friendship. But for Dos Passos, the Robles murder also destroyed any remaining sympathy he had for the pro-Soviet Left and intensified his distrust of absolutes in political partisanship. As he wrote a few years later, on 19 July 1939, in a letter to the *New Republic*, Robles's death "gives us a glimpse into the bloody tangle of ruined lives that underlay the hurray-for-our-side aspects. Understanding the personal histories of a few of the men, women and children really involved would, I think, free our minds somewhat from the black-is-black and white-is-white obsessions of partisanship" (625).

The motives of the international volunteers who fought in this war were still another source of ambiguity. What made them volunteer? Their foreigner status rules out patriotism. Political idealism? If so, idealism as practically determined by whom, the individual or the Soviet Cominern (which controlled the International Brigades)? Love of adventure? Money? Glory? The answers—when they could be determined—were often mixed.

Consider Ernest Hemingway's involvement. For Hemingway, the outbreak of the war in 1936 resolved a dilemma of his literary politics. In the preceding few years, he had struggled to redefine his relationship with the political Left in America, secretly wanting to gain the approval (or at least stop the carping) of leftist critics while maintaining his image as a staunch individualist.[5] He had already, in 1935, made a significant overture to the Left by publishing his diatribe, "Who Murdered the Vets?" in *New Masses*, the Communist Party-USA's literary magazine. But it wasn't until Franco's invasion of the Spanish mainland in July 1936 that Hemingway found a leftist issue to which he could commit himself fully without being accused of having abjectly buckled to the prevailing leftist pressure of writers, critics, and intellectuals. After all, from the beginning of his career, he was well known to have had a close affection for Spain in his life and work, and, like so many of his contemporaries, he was genuinely distressed to see Spain's shaky democracy now under attack.

In this sense, Hemingway's situation reflected that of leftist writers and intellectuals generally, for whom the Spanish Civil War provided a concrete cause for their growing concern about fascism since Hitler's rise to chancellor of Germany in 1933. Indeed, the Soviet Comintern, which set the Left's agenda in these years, spearheaded this concern in 1934–35 by reversing its earlier doctrine of implacable hostility to all noncommunist leftist groups and, instead, establishing the Popular Front against fascism, comprised of these very groups.[6] Before the outbreak of the Spanish Civil War, opposition to fascism took the usual forms of demonstrations and petitions, meetings and rallies—all patently ineffectual. Now, however, as both Germany and Italy quickly intervened on Franco's behalf, leftists worldwide found an antifascist cause in which they could actively participate. As Hemingway expressed it eloquently in *For Whom the Bell Tolls:* "It gave you a part in something that you could believe in wholly and completely and in which you felt an absolute brotherhood with the others who were engaged in it. . . . you gave such importance to it and the reasons for it that your own death seemed of complete unimportance; . . . But the best thing was there was something you could do about this feeling and this necessity too. You could fight" (251). The formation of the International Brigades, comprising volunteer battalions from England, Europe, the United States, and elsewhere, to fight alongside the Spanish Republicans, demonstrated that antifascist leftists were willing to do more than just talk. Thousands of volunteers fought in Spain, and many died for their idealistic beliefs.[7]

## Hemingway's Involvement

Hemingway, already in his mid-thirties, did not tote a rifle for the Republicans—though a photograph shows him on the front lines, unjamming a Republican soldier's rifle as the two lay side by side. Rather, he chose journalism—reporting the war for a consortium of news agencies and later for *Ken* and other magazines—as a means of getting close to the action, yet having the capacity to influence readers in the neutral United States. In all, he made four trips to Spain in 1937 and 1938 and, during the siege of Madrid, stayed in a Madrid hotel so close to the front lines that it was shelled several times.[8] Written from the Republican perspective, his dispatches made no pretense of objectivity and gave close-up descriptions of combat and the strategic importance of particular battles. But Hemingway's support of the Republicans went beyond journalism. Together with Dos Passos, Archibald MacLeish, Lillian Hellman, and Dutch film director Joris Ivens, Hemingway helped make a propaganda film, *The Spanish Earth,* to present the Republican side of the war and raise money in America for ambulances and medical supplies for the Republicans.[9] That Hemingway's participation in the war gave him new standing with the American Left was dramatically demonstrated when he gave the keynote speech at the Second American Writers Congress at Carnegie Hall in 1937. He brought down the house.

Though Hemingway still had to finish his Key West novel, *To Have and Have Not,* when the war broke out, his creative attention soon turned to the new war and took several forms over the next four years: five short stories, written mostly in 1938; the play *The Fifth Column,* written in the fall and early winter of 1937 and performed on Broadway in 1940; and finally the novel *For Whom the Bell Tolls,* published in 1940. When these works are compared, it becomes clear that Hemingway's treatment of the war matured significantly from the stories and play, written quickly and mostly while he was in Spain, to the novel, written slowly after he had returned for the last time and had time to consider the issues—historical and fictional—more fully.

## The Stories

None of the five stories about the Spanish Civil War represents Hemingway at his best. All but one reflect his relatively narrow perspective as a foreign journalist and filmmaker, living in Madrid among other foreigners, both civilian and International Brigade volunteers back from battle.[10] In fact, three of the stories—"The Denunciation," "The Butterfly and the Tank," and "Night Before Battle"—are wholly or partly set in his favorite Madrid bar, Chicotes, and capture its atmospheric tension, uncertainty about which of its patrons are true Republicans and which are fifth columnists,[11] and its buzz of rumors and loose talk, intermingled with the fear of being overhead. "Night Before Battle," by far the longest of the five stories, is even more autobiographical in being set partly in a hotel room exactly like Hemingway's at the Florida Hotel; moreover, just as Hemingway had done, the narrator, Henry, generously makes his room available to Brigade volunteers in need of a hot shower, sleep, liquor, good food, and Chopin recordings. Only one story, "Under the Ridge," is set on the battlefield, but its narrator-observer is a filmmaker, not a soldier. (In "Night Before Battle," the first-person narrator is also filming a nearby battle.)

The autobiographical basis of these stories, limited mostly to what Hemingway observed in and around Madrid, contributes to the feeling of authenticity for which the author is famous. In "Night Before Battle," for example, besides capturing the tense atmosphere at Chicotes, he effectively contrasts the moods of various International Brigade volunteers: the tank-driver Al's resigned fatalism at his probable death in the next day's battle; the pilot Baldy's drunken elation in having shot down a fascist plane; the crap-shooters' obliviousness to everything but their game. True to Hemingway's aesthetic of understatement, these juxtapositions receive little comment, and when Al and the narrator part, they don't talk about Al's slim chances in the morning.

This emphasis on close-up realism, conveyed through precise observation, dialogue, juxtaposition, and understatement, does not significantly distinguish these stories from Hemingway's World War I stories; only their Madrid settings, with their undercurrents of spying, fear, and denunciation, are distinctive. But the stories sidestep the larger causes and meaning of this atmosphere: not merely fifth-columnist spying, but the brutally repressive Russian and Spanish police tactics and leadership of a "democratic" cause. That Franco's fascists committed atrocities against civilians was a given; that the Republican government committed them was a profound contradiction that Hemingway did not want to deal with at the time.

One partial exception to this claim reveals Hemingway's political and moral ambivalence when he wrote these stories. In "The Denunciation," Mr. Edmunds, the writer-narrator, is approached by a waiter in Chicotes who has spotted a prominent fascist, an old-time customer whom they both know—Edmunds had once shot pigeons and gambled with him before the war. The fascist is sitting with new Republican pilots who don't know him; worse, he is wearing a Republican uniform. Should he be denounced, an action that will inevitably lead to his arrest and execution? And if so, by whom? The waiter expects the well-connected narrator to do the dirty work. Edmunds refuses, but, on being prodded, gives the waiter a phone number and tells him to ask for Pepé. The number is for Seguridad (security) headquarters, and Pepé is the head man.[12] The police soon arrive to arrest the fascist (which Mr. Edmunds safely observes from outside the bar). But he feels guilty about the denunciation, especially about having the waiter do the dirty work: it was "one of those excesses of impartiality, righteousness and Pontius Pilatry, and the always-dirty desire to see how people act under an emotional conflict, that makes writers such attractive friends" (FC 97). To make amends, he calls Pepé himself and asks that the prisoner be told that he, Mr. Edmunds, denounced him, not the waiter. Besides showing how well-connected Mr. Edmunds is (and, by extension, Hemingway is) to the counterintelligence apparatus of Madrid, the story conveys considerable moral ambivalence about the act of denouncing, even though the target in this case is an enemy spy in false uniform. What neither this story nor the others addresses are those thousands mistakenly arrested and executed as spies and those purged and executed by the Soviet NKVD because they belonged to the wrong leftist faction.[13]

## The Fifth Column

Other than a three-page story-drama entitled "Today is Friday" (1927), *The Fifth Column* was Hemingway's only play, and most Hemingway critics don't regret that fact, feeling that his true art was fiction. Indeed, the play's characters tend to be two-dimensional, the action melodramatic. In brief, the play presents a double conflict, political and romantic. The political-action story opposes Philip Rawlings, an American counterespionage agent for the Republicans, who poses as a journalist and is aided by his disfigured German comrade, Max, against the bad guys: fascist spies, assassins, and artillery observers in Madrid. The romantic story presents Philip's affair with journalist Dorothy Bridges; but, like the political action, this romance opposes, first, Philip's real counterespionage job with Dorothy's obtuse assumption that he is a lazy war correspondent and playboy, and, second, Dorothy's self-centered hedonism and political naïveté with Philip's commitment to the antifascist cause. In the latter conflict, Philip must overcome the temptations Dorothy holds out of a civilian life of pleasure (all the more tempting to Philip because he is tired of the brutalities his job requires). At the climax, he abandons her and the life she represents—"where I go now, I go alone" (*FC* 83)—and reaffirms his commitment to a long-term fight against fascism: "I've signed up for the duration" (80). Meanwhile, the political conflict resolves itself easily and melodramatically as Philip and Max alone overwhelm a fascist observation post and capture the civilian ringleaders.

Although the play consistently privileges Philip's political depth against Dorothy's naïve and obtuse shallowness, it avoids any serious analysis of the war itself and never questions the Republican cause. About the only rationale for fighting is expressed in Max's generically egalitarian speech (he is a Marxist), which sounds almost like a brief for the New Deal: "You [fight] so *every one* will have a good breakfast. . . . You do it so *no one* will ever be hungry. You do it so men will not have to fear ill health or old age; so they can live and work in dignity and not as slaves." When a child is wounded nearby by a fascist artillery shell, Max adds: "You do it to stop *that* forever" (*FC* 67–68; emphasis in original).

If he ignores the war's larger issues, Hemingway does confront the ugliness of one of its actions, namely gathering intelligence and dealing with spies. Philip's job requires him to interrogate fifth columnists, who are often tortured to elicit information.[14] They are usually executed, sometimes mistakenly (as Philip's superior admits); moreover, Philip and Max shoot one of the recalcitrant prisoners they've taken in their raid. But the play softens these brutalities by showing how burned out Philip has become because of them and how he intercedes on behalf of a Republican soldier who has fallen asleep on the job and is likely to be shot. Finally, the play depicts the recipients of these brutalities as fascist spies and assassins, not Republican political victims of the government.[15]

Philip's dramatic triumph is in resisting the comfortable life Dorothy offers and committing himself fully to the antifascist cause; but that cause is presented as essentially two-dimensional: good guys versus bad guys, right versus wrong. It is easy to read into Philip's dilemma Hemingway's own conflict between living the comfortable life in Key West, with his yacht and deep-sea fishing, and devoting himself to a strenuous and highly political cause. But his treatment of the war itself, and particularly its complicated political aspects, is shallow. At most, it recognizes the government's sometimes mistaken torture and execution of suspected spies. As in "The Denunciation," the protagonist is troubled by his role in these brutalities, but not enough to stop participating in them. In this respect, the play and story show a more aware and conflicted Hemingway than he publicly presented in his journalism or in his argument with Dos Passos. Nevertheless, except for one facetious reference,[16] the play makes no mention of the Soviet presence, much less its terror tactics, in Spain. Not surprisingly, once American interest in the Spanish Civil War faded as World War II intensified in 1940, the play, opening on Broadway that year, closed after three months.

*For Whom the Bell Tolls*

The plot premise of this novel is remarkably simple. Robert Jordan, an American volunteer for the Republicans, works independently behind enemy lines, primarily as a bridge blower. Assigned to blow a bridge for an upcoming Republican offensive, he requires the assistance of a group of Republican guerrillas, led by the formidable Pilar, and, in their few days together, gets to know them intimately, falling in love with a war victim they shelter, Maria. Unlike Philip Rawlings's simplistic devotion to the cause, Jordan's attitudes toward the war are complex, an unsettling fusion of a technician's pride in the skillful performance of his duties, an idealist's nebulous desire to support democracy, and an antifascist's belief that fascism must be stopped in Spain before it can spread further. He is not a communist (he tells Pilar), but he willingly takes orders from the Soviet leadership, about which he has very mixed feelings. Moreover, Jordan's attitudes about his role in the war and its larger meanings undergo significant change because of his involvement with Pilar's group and his love affair with Maria. Let us consider this last topic first.

Initially, Jordan sees himself as an independent technician, a bridge blower who believes primarily in his work and is happiest when working alone, when he need rely only on himself. Thus, he approaches the necessity of having to work with this group of partisans with considerable trepidation and skepticism. Hemingway is especially good at evoking the tension of Jordan's first meeting with the group as they size each other up, particularly his encounter with the dangerously unreliable and murderous Pablo and his dominating, idealistic spouse, Pilar.

As Jordan becomes intimately involved with the band—sexually and romantically with Maria, but also emotionally with the others—his sense of purpose subtly changes. His hazy idealism about supporting the Spanish people has clarified and gained meaning though his experience with this representative group. Importantly, Hemingway does not stereotype or idealize the group: it is a mixture of personalities, each a complex of attitudes and behaviors. Pablo, for instance, kills unhesitatingly but has largely lost his will to fight, partly from guilt over having led a massacre. He now prefers the alcoholic self-indulgence of doing nothing. Yet Jordan must rely on him, because Pablo knows the territory and the other guerrilla groups and is good at finding and stealing horses. Thus, even though Jordan realizes that in the bridge blowing Pablo will murder his own recruits for their horses, Jordan tacitly accepts these crimes so that the larger mission can succeed and the group escape. A good end justifies immoral means. By the end of the novel, Jordan's devotion is clearly to the group as much as to his mission: When he can no longer ride with the group after the bridge is blown, he sacrifices himself by fighting off the pursuing fascists to enable the group to escape.

Yet, as Pablo demonstrates, the group as Spanish microcosm is a complex mixture of good and evil, idealism and barbarism, courage and self-serving expediency, and shades between. Hemingway powerfully reinforces this moral complexity when Pilar recounts, in vivid and horrific detail, the Republican atrocity committed in her town: the villagers' murder of fascist sympathizers, landowners, and the village priest. Although Jordan had "always known about. . . . [w]hat we did to them at the start," Pilar's story "had made him see it in that town. . . . you heard the shots; and you saw the bodies" (*FWBT* 149). Again, the group's actions are a microcosm, representing many atrocities committed by the Republicans, just as Maria's rape and the murder of her parents and of Joaquin's represent fascist atrocities. Pilar's gruesome story does not diminish Jordan's sense of purpose, but it complicates his already mixed feelings about the Spanish people: "There is no finer and no worse people in the world. No kinder people and no crueler. And who understands them? Not me" (374). Likewise, the expediency of using Pilar's group, knowing some will die, runs counter to Jordan's former idealism: "You went into it knowing what you were fighting for. You were fighting against exactly what you were doing [using them] and being forced into doing to have any chance of winning" (177). Again, ends and means. The reader experiences this same contradiction in the depiction of Lieutenant Berrendo, the fascist officer pursuing Pilar's group. Rather than characterizing him as a beast, or simply as other, the novel presents him as intelligent, competent, sensitive, and sympathetic despite his fighting on the wrong side. Thus, the happenstance that he is the first man Jordan must kill to ensure the group's escape is richly ironic.

For his determination to paint the Republicans—and for that matter, the fascists—in morally ambiguous tones, Hemingway was severely criticized by Mike Gold, editor of *New Masses*, the literary magazine of the Communist Party-USA (see Gold, "Change the World"), and even by some American volunteers of the Abraham Lincoln Brigade. In the 20 November 1940 issue of *The Daily Worker*, the latter group submitted a letter, printed as "Open Letter to

Ernest Hemingway," claiming that Hemingway had "mutilated" the Republican cause and "misrepresented the attitude of the Soviet Union towards the Spanish Republic" (qtd. and paraphrased in Baker, *Life Story* 356). But these criticisms that Hemingway's ambivalent depictions undermined the Republican cause suggest why they are admirable as literature: they are not propaganda, and they realistically complicate the issues of the war.

Equally complex are Jordan's attitudes toward the Russians he serves. From his conversations with Karkov, a cynical Russian journalist with insider information, Jordan receives a completely different view of the war from the view he experiences with Pilar's group, namely, its political aspect: the Soviets' repressive control, their brutal campaigns against socialist and anarchist groups, and their murder of people (like José Robles) solely for ideological reasons. "'[Political assassination] is practiced very extensively,' Karkov said. 'Very, very extensively'" (*FWBT* 261). From this perspective, the Spanish "people" scarcely exist; the war is about power and control exerted ruthlessly from the top.

Jordan's responses to Karkov's revelations are disingenuous, ambivalent, and self-protective, sometimes amounting to flat-out denial. About the political assassinations themselves, he declares unconvincingly: "I don't mind them.... I do not like them but I do not mind them any more" (*FWBT* 261). As Hemingway himself did to Dos Passos, Jordan tries to justify Russian brutality with the argument that ruthless discipline is necessary in a war, particularly in *this* war, where so many splinter groups, with widely differing beliefs, fight on the Republican side. Jordan is willing to serve under Comintern leaders because they offer the best chance of winning: "He was under Communist discipline for the duration of the war.... in the conduct of the war, they were the only party whose program and whose discipline he could respect" (178). And winning is everything: once again, the end justifies the means. The human costs of that victory are matters he prefers not to contemplate.

Jordan also tries to compartmentalize this disillusioning knowledge, just as he does the Republicans' massacres, by focusing on his assignments and mentally segregating these larger issues. In this way, he can continue to "believe" in his small role in the war: "Today is only one day.... But what will happen in all the other days that ever come can depend on what you do today" (*FWBT* 454). His method of segregation echoes Scarlett O'Hara's perennial solution for dealing with unpleasant realities in *Gone with the Wind*: "I'll think about it tomorrow." Several times, Jordan thinks: "My mind is in suspension until we win the war," and "if he were going to form judgments he would form them afterwards" (261, 150). *After* the war, when he writes a "true" book about it, he will come to terms with these brutalities. Although Jordan's techniques of denial are convincing to his troubled character, they enable Hemingway to avoid dealing fully with the issues that he himself has raised in *his* supposedly "true" book about the war. While he certainly deserves credit for recognizing these issues, his refusal to take a stand on them (except to show their complexity) frustrates the reader.

One other aspect of Jordan's ambivalence toward the Russians needs comment. As a special operative, he is accorded "insider" privileges at Gaylord's Hotel, the Russians' headquarters in Madrid. Thus, besides receiving privileged information, he has access to good food and drink unavailable to the commoners. Like Hemingway himself, Jordan does not deny himself these luxuries so as to achieve an ascetic oneness with the people; in fact, he ruefully admits to himself that he "corrupted very easily" (*FWBT* 245). Jordan's characterization here is a threadbare cover for Hemingway's own self-criticism, but it prevents Jordan from being an idealized construct—in the way that Philip Rawlings becomes in *The Fifth Column* in rejecting Dorothy's enticements.

Finally, Jordan comes to question an important aspect of his own motives. From his earliest contact with Pilar's group, he has developed a special bond with the old man, Anselmo, who becomes his most reliable aide. Anselmo's literary function is to act as foil for Jordan on the subject of killing. For Anselmo, an unreconstructed Catholic, killing is an unambiguous sin. He accepts that he must kill in war time but hates to do so and prays for forgiveness. Jordan respects Anselmo's attitude and even echoes it: "Nobody [likes to kill men] except those who are disturbed in the head" (*FWBT* 48). But he also recognizes that he is not like Anselmo and—in a passage of remarkable candor—contradicts his earlier disclaimer and admits to himself that he has secretly enjoyed killing: "you have never been corrupted by it? . . . [A]dmit that you have liked to kill as all who are soldiers by choice have enjoyed it at some time" (287). Thus, even on this most personal level of his involvement with the war, Jordan cannot be sure of his real motives.

On every level of the novel, then—the depictions of Pilar's group, of the hijacked military and political leadership, of Robert Jordan's knowledge and feelings about both, and even of Jordan's own motives and attitudes toward his participation—Hemingway avoids a simplistic, two-dimensional contrast between good and evil, right and wrong. As Jordan himself understates the matter: "The things he had come to know in this war were not so simple" (*FWBT* 264). Instead, Hemingway presents a complex and ambiguous situation in which morality is equivocal, motives mixed, and seemingly good ends are undercut by immoral means. While the author refuses to let moral ambivalence fully disillusion and paralyze his protagonist—to do so, of course, would result in a very different, un-Hemingwayesque novel, a novel much closer to Dos Passos's *Adventures of a Young Man*—and although Hemingway, like his protagonist, sometimes ducks the thematic implications of the moral issues he raises, the novel still achieves a moral complexity that the author had scarcely imagined just a few years earlier.

## Pedagogical Challenges

Before teaching any of Hemingway's treatments of the Spanish Civil War, it is important to provide students with a clear understanding of the nature of the war—no easy matter considering its complexity and students' ignorance of the basic facts of its historical and political context. They need to know that by 1936, Spain's democracy was only five years old and in extremely fragile health.[17] In Europe, fascism, which repressed all facets of free expression in arts, ideas, and politics, was on the move. Nazi Germany had marched unopposed into the Rhineland. Italy had gone to war against Ethiopia. The nonfascist Western states seemed paralyzed to resist this expansion, and only the Soviet Union's Popular Front stood against fascism and Nazism. Thus, when Germany and Italy entered the Spanish Civil War on Franco's side, providing significant quantities of men and materiel, many leftists in the West grew convinced that spreading fascism had to be stopped now. They saw the fate of Spain as a harbinger for the fate of Europe. That's why so many young people from around the world volunteered to fight in Spain on the Republican side. Perhaps bringing in a history colleague to team-teach this background would enliven the process for students by providing a different voice.

At the same time, it's also important—yet tricky—to go beyond the oversimplified stereotype of bad-guy Nationalists versus good-guy Republicans, as Hemingway himself learned to do in his evolving treatments of the war. What makes this tricky is that, while this good-bad opposition is *essentially* true—virtually all historians, for example, not to mention the majority of Spaniards, feel that Franco's victory proved a disaster for Spanish civil liberties—several factors complicate it. As noted earlier, *both* sides committed atrocities and persecuted their opponents. In addition, when the Soviets entered the war on the Republican side, quickly asserting military control and secretly influencing civilian leadership, they persecuted and sometimes murdered *leftist* allies. To further complicate the picture, the Left in Spain was splintered into several parties whose agendas were frequently at odds. The Soviets thus provided a kind of brutal unification in asserting their form of leftism. The result was hardly a liberal state.

But it is also important not simply to equate leftist and rightist atrocities and persecutions. As many historians have pointed out, the Republican atrocities were fewer and more spontaneous; those committed by the fascists were far more numerous, widespread, and systematic. And although Soviet military leadership was brutal, Hemingway had a point when he asserted that unifying the squabbling factions on the left into an effective military opposition to Franco's forces required a kind of brutality from above. The question then becomes, how much and what kind of brutality?

Finally, students need to understand something of Hemingway's own political evolution, from being apolitical in the early 1930s, to being a proto-leftist in 1935, to becoming an enthusiastic supporter of Republican Spain and the Soviet-communist position there once he involved himself in the war as a journalist and propagandist, to finally (in *For Whom the Bell Tolls*) grappling with the complexities of the war. If this novel is taught to show how Hemingway deals with these complexities, rather than being presented as merely an adventure and love story, students should come away from the experience not only with greater knowledge of the war itself and of the ambiguities surrounding it but also with greater respect for a writer often demeaned as nonintellectual.

### Notes

1. The official neutrality of Western nations like the United States, influenced by anticommunism, isolationism, and the Catholic Church, did not prevent American companies from directly aiding Franco's fascists. The Texas Oil Company (later Texaco) supplied oil and gas on credit, while the Ford, General Motors, and Studebaker corporations provided numerous trucks (Beevor 138).

2. Discussion of atrocities on both sides and their comparative differences can be found in Vernon, *Hemingway's Second War* 153–54.

3. The best first-person account of Russian repression on the Republican side is in George Orwell's *Homage to Catalonia*. Recent research has revealed that the Soviets secretly manipulated the Republican government even more than previously thought; see Payne, *The Spanish Civil War, the Soviet Union, and Communism* (New Haven, CT: Yale UP, 2011). Nonetheless, it is important to recall that leftist volunteers initially *perceived* the war as a struggle between fascism and democracy.

4. Robles, who strongly supported the Republican cause, was executed in Spain in 1937, most likely by agents of the Russian secret police, the NKVD. The Russian claim that he was a fascist spy was patently false, but the real reason for Robles's execution

remains unclear. For a detailed discussion of the affair, see Stephen Koch, *The Breaking Point: Hemingway, Dos Passos, and the Murder of José Robles* (Cambridge, MA: Counterpoint, 2005).

5. For a discussion of Hemingway's shifting relationship with the American Left in these years, see Milton A. Cohen, "Beleaguered Modernists: Hemingway, Stevens, and the Left," in *Key West Hemingway: A Reassessment,* ed. Kirk Curnutt and Gail Sinclair (Tallahassee: U of Florida P, 2009).

6. Within Spain, however, as noted above, the Soviets did not apply a similar united approach to other leftist groups, ruthlessly suppressing them instead.

7. International volunteers who fought for Republican Spain numbered from 32,000 to 35,000 and came from more than fifty countries. Another 10,000 volunteered for noncombatant jobs, such as driving ambulances (some of which Hemingway personally paid for). Approximately 2,800 volunteers came from the United States and formed the Abraham Lincoln and George Washington Battalions (often miscalled the Abraham Lincoln Brigade). Casualty rates were very high: an estimated 10,000 were killed in action (including the English poet and critic Christopher Caudwell), while about 7,700 were wounded (including George Orwell, who was wounded in the throat). Seven hundred United States volunteers were killed in action or died from wounds or sickness, a death rate of 25 percent.

8. Although Hemingway's involvement in the war was certainly risky—as always, he enjoyed courting danger—it was also quite comfortable and hedonistic. In Madrid, he had an ongoing affair with journalist Martha Gellhorn, hoarded good food and drink that were unavailable to ordinary Madrid residents, and enjoyed his celebrity status by generously making his hotel room a hub and R&R center for other volunteers.

9. Of the coproducers, although MacLeish organized the project and Ivens directed it, Hemingway assumed major responsibility during the actual filming, scouting filming locations with the cameramen as close to the front lines as possible. He is credited with writing the narration, and even provided the voice-over when the original Orson Welles version was considered too elevated. Through Martha Gellhorn's friendship with Eleanor Roosevelt, Gellhorn and Hemingway presented the film at the White House, but it did not succeed in changing American policy. The film was later shown several times in Hollywood, where it did raise considerable money. See chapters 3 and 4 of Vernon, *Hemingway's Second War,* for a detailed discussion.

10. The exception is "The Old Man at the Bridge," a sketch set at the Ebro River during a retreat, which Hemingway published as one of his *Ken* pieces.

11. The phrase *fifth column* comes from Franco's boast, before his siege of Madrid, that he had four columns advancing on the city and a fifth column of informers and spies already within it.

12. Rather remarkably, Hemingway did not even change the first name of the real head of counterintelligence in Madrid, Pepé Quintinilla, known as the "chief executioner." Hemingway knew him well (Herbst 154).

13. For example, in June 1937, Andrés Nin, the head of the anti-Stalinist Marxist Party (POUM), was arrested by Soviet NKVD agents, tortured, and murdered on Stalin's express command (Payne 228).

14. Although the play is ambiguous about whether Philip himself tortures these fifth columnists, he has clearly been present during their torture. By contrast, Max cannot stand to watch their new captive being interrogated and leaves beforehand. Philip's conversations with his superior and with Max show that he is fed up with his counterespionage role, but he never criticizes the need for conducting this torture.

15. Nonetheless, as Michael K. Solow summarizes, the play has been sharply criticized for its "Machiavellian" ignoring of the systematic brutality of Comintern leadership (108–9).

16. During their raid, Philip answers Max with the Russian "Da," and Max sardonically explains to the prisoners: "You see. We are all Russians. Everybody is Russians in Madrid" (*FC* 74). Both here and in his journalism, Hemingway ridiculed charges (by Dos Passos and others) that Soviet agents were controlling Republican politics with terror tactics.

17. In 1933, for example, in response to the chaos and atrocities of the first two years of the republic, a rightist government was elected that sought to undo the reforms achieved by the leftist coalition. In 1936, the leftists took power again, prompting the Franco-led Nationalist rebellion.

# "What you were fighting for"

## Robert Jordan On Trial in the Classroom

Steven A. Nardi

Introduction: Confronting the Text

In the late spring of 2009, Robert Jordan, the main character of *For Whom the Bell Tolls,* was charged with crimes against the Spanish nation and people. The indictment asserted that because he refused to abandon his mission against the bridge, despite clear indications of its futility, Jordan displayed reckless indifference to the lives of his fellow soldiers and prolonged a war that he knew to be hopeless, all in the service of an ideology he knew to be bankrupt. Jordan was tried twice and, despite a vigorous defense, was both times convicted by a jury of his peers.

That trial was, of course, a fiction. The courtroom was my American Literature II classroom, and the jury, my students. Two weeks before the trial, I had assigned everyone a character to play (each student was responsible for researching his or her assigned role and for role-playing the character during cross-examination); some had also volunteered for either the prosecution or defense team. The prosecution articulated the charges, called witnesses to testify, and made opening and closing statements. The defense lawyers likewise made opening and closing statements, followed each testimony with a cross-examination, and called their own witnesses. There were various "objections" available to the lawyers, including accusing witnesses of textual inaccuracy. After closing statements, the entire class debated and then voted on Jordan's guilt or innocence. Following the verdict, we even staged our own version of the Academy Awards.

This experiment came out of my unease with a more conventional pedagogy. When teaching *For Whom the Bell Tolls* the semester before, I had found my students drawn into arguments about Hemingway the writer rather than about the complex moral world presented by his novel. This was particularly true of their essays; my prompts, as I will discuss, were channeling the students into polemics rather than critical inquiry. The results produced by the trial, in contrast, were much better. Not only was I happy with the students' writing, but the exercise produced a further, unexpected benefit. Forced to reimagine the entire process of teaching the novel, I had to rethink my learning goals from the ground up. In guiding me through that rethinking, the trial assignment helped me articulate to my students and myself why I found one of my favorite novels worth reading.

Even before coming up with the trial, I meant *For Whom the Bell Tolls* to shake up the course. My American Literature classes had begun to feel a bit tired. My approach to the writing assignments, especially, had become increasingly set, and as a result the responses were falling within increasingly predictable parameters of argument. I found that even though I introduced new prompts and new texts every year, the thematic coherence of my syllabus meant that I kept the basic structure of many of the essay questions—jumping off from the same critical sources, for example, or asking the students to relate the new text to the same core idea: Emerson's transparent eyeball, for example, was a favorite image in American Literature I. The result was that the class, while running quite smoothly, was starting to feel stale to me, which meant, of course, that it would soon feel stale to the students.

I had previously found teaching *For Whom the Bell Tolls* too daunting to attempt. The Spanish Civil War had seemed too remote, the novel too long. By 2007, however, I had come to see the book in a new and very different light. The war in Iraq had stalemated. In 2006, a spate of books had been published, including Thomas Ricks's *Fiasco*, Bob Woodward's *State of Denial*, and Rajiv Chandrasekaran's *Imperial Life in the Emerald City*, that as a group seemed to signify a shift in the national perception of the war. What many had regarded as a necessary crusade was suddenly being widely labeled a badly handled misadventure. The idealism with which the Bush administration had framed the invasion of Iraq was being called into question by voices from across the political spectrum. The moment seemed ripe for the element of *For Whom the Bell Tolls* that most appealed to me: its chronicling, according to the blurb on the back of my copy, of "the tragic death of an ideal."

When we actually started discussing the book, I found myself at an impasse. The students seemed bored as I struggled to communicate the novel's value, let alone its relevance. Part of the problem was an aspect I had anticipated—the remoteness of the war—but even after I had compensated for this (by showing clips from a documentary, giving a mini-lecture about leftist intellectuals and politicians of the thirties, and showing the course of the war with a time lapse map of Spain), the students were unmoved.

By the second class, I knew that I had a deeper problem than student indifference. While the students quickly recognized the analogy to current events, they did not see how that analogy was relevant to them and their world. To my surprise, I realized that I didn't have much to say about the novel's relevance to the Iraq war either. Certainly Hemingway's portrayal of the disorganization and petty infighting within Spain's Second Republic echoed the chaos in the Bush administration that Chandrasekaran, Ricks, and Woodward described, but Hemingway's targets are so specifically historical that criticizing them offers little insight into bigger issues. Further, although the protagonist, Jordan, feels himself drawn into the cynicism that surrounds the war and acknowledges the bankruptcy of his own idealism, the novel does not expressly draw any wider social significance from that personal crisis. Instead, it confines itself to exploring the inner experiences of the characters. As Allen Josephs has said, in *For Whom the Bell Tolls* Hemingway was "inventing a world where politics were but a remembrance of nights past at Gaylord's"—not writing a political novel (Josephs, "Volatile Mixture" 183).

In drawing parallels with contemporary politics, therefore, I was left with a rather mundane point—that wars tend to play havoc with ideological preconceptions—but with no sense that reading Hemingway's novel revealed anything deeper. Standing in front of my students, I even started to wonder why I had bothered to assign this difficult text. I realized that if I were going to keep teaching the novel (and intuitively I wanted to), I needed to clarify to myself what I found so compelling about the book in the first place.

At the time, as coordinator of the campus Writing across the Curriculum Program, I had been experimenting with different types of graded and ungraded writing. Even more importantly, I had fallen under the influence of James Gee's *What Video Games Have to Teach Us About Learning and Literacy*. Gee argues that video games incorporate a marvelously successful pedagogy from which educational professionals could learn a great deal. In order to sell, a video game must persuade players to invest the time to learn the intricacies of its particular fantasy world. Games that are successful lead their players to spend countless hours mastering a virtual world. Those same gamers often go even further, writing Internet guides and programming mods and arguing online about strategy and tactics. Moreover, games succeed with an audience that is mostly young and generally male—a demographic higher education often has difficulty reaching.

What can higher education learn, Gee asks, from the methods video games use? How do games produce behaviors that most professors would love to induce? Gee answers these questions by exploring the pedagogy the games employ. A gamer doesn't learn by studying a book; he or she is continually trying out new strategies—even absurd ones—the vast majority of which end in failure. To encourage this kind of learning, in most video games the penalty for failure is kept very low: a player can always hit the reset button. Games that set that penalty too high are often criticized as boring and frustrating. The players, therefore, can become very adventurous learners, exploring and experimenting for themselves. Committed players test every premise, challenge every limitation. Since such games impose a substantial penalty for conventional thinking—the player will get stuck—gamers must think creatively. Games wouldn't be entertaining if repeating the same strategy every time was a successful gambit.

In contrast to such tactics, Gee notes, stakes in the classroom are typically pitched very high: few students can afford to be adventurous on a midterm exam! Consequently, students have scant opportunity to try out radical ideas and great incentive to repeat formulas that have been successful. Small wonder that most college essays are dull. As one of my graduate school professors once said, "Students are too often afraid not to bore you." In staging the trial, therefore, I sought to introduce an element of risk into the classroom—but that risk would have to work both ways. The students, of course, would have to surrender their reflexive moral judgments and step out of their safe habits of essay writing, but I would likewise have to leave behind my own safe habits of teaching.

### The Moral Problem at the Heart of the Novel

At root, the problem I was having is that, for all of the cynicism in *For Whom the Bell Tolls*, it is by no means an antiwar book. To the contrary, many core critical commentaries have read the novel as a defense of war, and Jordan as an exemplary military hero. Allen Josephs, for example, in For Whom the Bell Tolls: *Ernest Hemingway's Undiscovered Country*, recounts an anecdote from a conference in Russia. When his hosts suggested that Jordan's sacrifice might have been in vain, Josephs responded hotly: "If Robert Jordan had died in vain—if the fate of humanity had not swung on that bridge and on all such bridges and all such Robert Jordans—we would not be discussing this novel freely here in Moscow today." Jordan's actions, in other words, represent the interests of all humanity.

Josephs is specifically referring to one of the most optimistic moments of the novel. On his first day in the mountains, Jordan, torn by misgivings at the brutal necessity of his orders, searches for a rationale to go through with the mission. His answer is to equate his own personal trial with the largest possible framework of meaning: "You are instruments to do your duty," Jordan tells himself. "There are necessary orders that are no fault of yours and there is a bridge and that bridge can be the point on which the future of the human race can turn" (Hemingway, *FWBT* 43). Carlos Baker, in his glowing account of the novel in *Hemingway: The Writer as Artist* (1952), also takes Jordan's words at face value. Jordan, Baker argues, stands apart from the sordid politics of the Spanish Civil War and remains engaged in the good fight. Even if the cause he is fighting for is undermined by political opportunists and ideologues, Jordan "will remain as an essential nonconformist, a free man not taken in, though doing his part in the perennial attempts which free men must make if the concept of freedom is to last" (245).

And yet, elsewhere in his work, Hemingway has been celebrated for challenging exactly this species of overinflated rhetoric. In a frequently quoted passage from *A Farewell to Arms*, Frederic Henry disavows the romantic vocabulary of war: "I was always embarrassed by the words sacred, glorious, and sacrifice and the expression in vain.... There were many words that you could not stand to hear and finally only the names of places had dignity.... Abstract words such as glory, honor, courage, or hallow were obscene beside the concrete names of villages" (184–85). It would seem that Henry is also offering a critique of a later Hemingway. Certainly, if the "obscenity" Henry rails against is the ideologue's habit of ignoring the fate of real people in real places in the name of abstract meaning, Robert Jordan is guilty of it. Jordan goes ahead with the attack even though he knows it is no longer a military necessity, and he does so because he believes that there is a pure good in following through with orders, even at the cost of lives. Necessarily, he is sometimes indifferent to the pain he inflicts. As he sums up the casualties, Jordan can't even remember Eladio's name (*FWBT* 455). Jordan is, as Pilar says, a "cold boy" (91).

Even before *For Whom the Bell Tolls*, Hemingway was on both sides of this controversy. As Delmore Schwartz pointed out in a 1938 essay, "it is ... precisely glory, honor, and courage which constitute the ideals of conduct in all of Hemingway's writing" (248). More recent criticism has interpreted Jordan as a more complex examination of military values. According to Alex Vernon, although *For Whom the Bell Tolls* at first glance "turns Hemingway's anti-heroic novel *A*

*Farewell to Arms* on its head," on closer examination that opposition unravels (*Hemingway's Second War* 199). Among other things, Vernon views the novel as a meditation on political killing that compares Jordan's decisions with those of a range of other characters—Pablo and Andre Marty, for example (155).

Perhaps the most damning evidence against Jordan is the collapse of the ethical distinction that he uses to distinguish himself from Pablo. In the early scenes, Pablo's rigid refusal to risk the group was viewed by Pilar and others as cowardice and lack of vision. In Anselmo's words, Pablo puts his "fox-hole before the interests of humanity" (*FWBT* 11). But when Pablo returns, it is with a new gravitas. He can no longer be dismissed as merely defending his horses. He returns because, as he says, "I believe if we finish we must finish together" (390). The band will live or die together: the bonds that tie them outweigh their individual interests. This is in sharp contrast to Jordan, who sends Maria away with exactly the opposite argument: "What I do now I do alone. I could not do it well with thee" (463). Pablo's insight, in fact, is rather similar to Henry's. It is the local that provides value, not the grand perspective to which Jordan retreats. As a result, Jordan's attempts to reestablish a distinction between himself and Pablo gradually wither. When he allows Pablo to go ahead and murder the new men without interference, Jordan must reluctantly shelve his ethical repugnance. "I wonder what the bastard is planning now," he thinks to himself, "But I am pretty sure I know. Well, that is his, not mine" (404). Later, when Pablo claims that he and Jordan "understand one another," it is surely this silent agreement that he has in mind, and for all that Jordan claims moral disgust, he also feels strongly the new comradeship between himself and Pablo. "Thank God I do not know these new men," he says to himself, which is no ethical defense at all if one is to believe that no man is an island (404).[1]

At the heart of Hemingway's novel, therefore, is a tension between the impulse to idealize war and the impulse to critique that idealization. Hemingway himself was ambivalent as to how effective *For Whom the Bell Tolls* would be as propaganda. While he spoke about the film version as if it were to function as antifascist war propaganda (Carroll, "Hemingway, Screenwriter" 282), he also understood that the brutal honesty of the novel, particularly Pilar's account of the massacre of fascists in her village, would undercut the Republican cause.

Hemingway's pessimism is especially evident in the narration of Jordan's thoughts. Jordan is often the most telling witness against himself, undercutting the grandiosity of his most optimistic musings with much more pessimistic afterthoughts. The soaring optimism in the lines that Josephs cites, for example, are followed closely by a much more cynical caveat: if the bridge can be the pivot point for the future of the human race, so it "can turn on everything that happens in this war," Jordan corrects himself, adding, "Stop worrying, you windy bastard" (*FWBT* 43). Despite his proclivity for windiness, a side of Jordan is as uncomfortable with inflated rhetoric as is Frederic Henry.

On reflection, I realized that it was Jordan's habit of critiquing himself that drew me to the story. Habitually wishing to speak to others—Golz, and especially Karkov, but also his grandfather—Jordan clearly regards his own education as incomplete. He is particularly aware that his ideas about the war, his own role, and the justification for killing, are still naïve. When Jordan reads over the letters and personal papers of the cavalry officer that he has just killed, it is in order to confront his own conscience with the humanity of the man whose life he has taken (*FWBT* 302). He needs to expose himself to the full cost of his actions. One of his regrets as he dies is that he dies just as he was starting to make sense of Spain: "Christ, I was learning fast there at the end. I'd like to talk to Karkov" (467).

The shifting point of view of the novel likewise corroborates Jordan's self-doubt. By allowing us to enter into the minds of the Nationalist soldiers, particularly that of the officer, Lieutenant Berrendo, the novel humanizes their deaths. As Jordan guesses, the enemy soldiers are from Navarra and have little intellectual connection to the political ideology for which they are fighting (*FWBT* 318). Through such insights, the reader is confronted with the concrete costs of abstract ideals. Despite the atrocities committed on the bodies of El Sordo and his comrades, Berrendo, in particular, is portrayed sympathetically.[2] Within the terms Jordan understands, he is even a good soldier.

The complexity of Jordan's internal voices adds most dramatically to the interpretation of the ending. Jordan's sacrifice, he knows well, will not change the outcome of the battle—that has already been decided. He also knows that it will not halt the flow of weapons up the road—they have already passed. In fact, although he holds on to the hope that he can slow down the pursuit of Pablo's band, this, too, is not so. Lieutenant Berrendo, as he rides into sight, reflects that the horses are "wet and blown" from the long detour and "have to be urged into the trot" (*FWBT* 471). With or without Jordan, there will be no immediate pursuit. Surely Jordan, who knows horses well, sees this immediately. Yet, in his dying moments, Jordan once more reverts to his most grandiose, most optimistic vision of the war. "I have fought for what I believed in for a year now," he says to himself. "If we win here we will win everywhere." Then he adds, "There's no *one* thing that's true. It's all true" (467; emphasis added). This moment seems a resolution of the search for something true that has haunted

Jordan through the entire book. Like Pilar, who, Maria says, once told her that "nothing is done to oneself that one does not accept and that if I loved some one it would take it all away" (73), Jordan elevates intensity of experience over all other ways of being.

But even here there is a correction. Jordan once again catches himself going too far. After reflecting that "it's all true" and elaborating, "the way the planes are beautiful whether they are ours or theirs," he quickly corrects himself: "The hell they are, he thought" (*FWBT* 467). There is obviously something wrong with concluding that war itself, particularly in its most mechanical and inhuman manifestation, is beautiful. But despite his internal reprimand, Jordan goes no further. Although he disapproves of the opinion he finds himself holding, he clearly still holds it. And isn't this slip particularly damning? In his reverie, Jordan finds the very weapon that is at that moment killing Golz's soldiers—his friends—beautiful, without regard to how it is being used. Isn't this apolitical aestheticism destructive of the cause in the name of which Jordan is fighting? Embracing intensified experience becomes deeply problematic when it renders someone insensitive to killing or to putting one's friends in danger.

If Jordan's life has made up in intensity for what it lacked in duration, the price of that accelerated life has fallen on other people as well. This is particularly true of Maria, who desperately wants to join Jordan in his heroic end but is dissuaded when Jordan fills her ears with what he regards as romantic blather in order to persuade her to go. If embracing experience is good for Jordan, why not for Maria? Rather than being a hero, is Jordan not merely a selfish lout, sacrificing his friends to boost his own sense of adventure?[3] Instead of an account of "the tragic death of an ideal," the novel seems to show how ideals refuse to die. Jordan can't give up his belief in glory, honor, and the righteousness of the cause, even as his refusal to relinquish those ideals begins to have disastrous consequences for the people around him. "If a thing is right fundamentally the lying was not supposed to matter," Jordan muses, distastefully paraphrasing the attitude of the Comintern (*FWBT* 229). But Jordan, too, allows convenience and ideology to trump truth.

Alternatively, is it even accurate to say that Jordan stands for an ideal? It could just as easily be said that Jordan is simply too eager to play soldier. He refuses to deviate from orders that he knows are too narrowly contrived and, in context, purposeless. Of course, to disobey is to risk being shot, but although this reality surfaces in Jordan's mind, it bears little weight. For Jordan, obedience is good in and of itself. When Anselmo remains on his watch through the snowstorm, his constancy overjoys Jordan, despite the element of foolishness in it. To return without relief "would have been the intelligent and correct thing to have done under the circumstances," Jordan reflects (*FWBT* 191). But he is ecstatic that Anselmo stayed anyway. In contrast, even Berrendo can make the distinction between honorable service and foolish submission to wasteful orders. When asked to charge El Sordo's position, Barrendo agrees to do so only if ordered, and then only under protest (318). For him, there is no honor in a futile act, only foolish waste. Lieutenant Berrendo confirms this distinction when the captain, confronted by the sniper's reluctance to follow orders, turns to him for support. Berrendo refuses to simply affirm a soldier's obligation to obey, answering instead that the soldier "has the right to say he is afraid" (317). For Berrendo, in other words, orders do not supersede a man's humanity.

Again, the case against Jordan is best made by Jordan himself. The doubts that creep into his mind lead to one of his most pessimistic moments in the novel. Immediately after Jordan has had sex with Maria in the field, his mind leaves her and starts to wander. Drifting, he confronts himself with the contradictions of his idealism: "You went into it knowing what you were fighting for. You were fighting against exactly what you were doing and being forced into doing to have any chance of winning" (*FWBT* 162). Jordan knows, unequivocally, that he is on both sides of this battle—his own worst enemy as well as his own best friend.

Framing an Assignment

Looking at examples of essay prompts on the Internet, I found nothing that would encourage students to explore the ambiguity of Jordan's character. As in the major criticism, the standard writing prompts tend to take Jordan's nobility for granted and invite students to either embrace or attack his idealism. If the paper topics suggested by the website Sparknotes.com, for example, can be taken as representative, the complexity of Jordan's representation is less interesting than the polemics centered around Hemingway's personality and political leanings. Of the five suggested essay topics on the website, two focus on aesthetic aspects of the novel (the effect of the ending and the role of memory) and two invite students to attack Hemingway (either for a poor portrayal of women or a fetishistic attitude toward the Spanish peasantry). The one question that addresses Jordan's ethics asks students to decide whether Jordan is a cynic or an idealist. While this is not a bad question, it underscores a problem inherent in the form of the persuasive essay itself. By asking the student to decide between polar opposites, the essay question represses consideration of Hemingway's refusal to depict Jordan as one or the other. Jordan, of course, is both.

The most revealing of the essay questions posed on the Sparknotes website raises the issue of gender. The question reads, "One of the most frequent criticisms of *For Whom the Bell Tolls* is that Hemingway portrays Maria as too submissive and eager to please to be a believable character. Do you agree with this critique? What is the role of women in the novel?" The invitation to polemicize here is so irresistible that it hides another truth: that the question is impossible to answer *without* polemics. On what textual grounds would a student dispute that Maria is "too submissive" or "too eager to please"? There is certainly room for productive analytical essay prompts on Hemingway and gender, but, as posed, this question is little more than throwing raw meat to lions.

The first time I taught the novel, I assigned a paper topic on Maria nearly identical to the Sparknotes gender question, although phrased even more polemically. It will surprise no one that the students overwhelmingly chose this option, I suspect because it gave them free reign to maximize indignation and to short-shrift textual analysis. Although I had used a deliberately provocative tone, I was unprepared for the vitriol of the responses. Given permission, the students vented, attacking Hemingway as sexist and dismissing the book as a failed attempt to impose a masculinist hegemony. Many of these essays were quite persuasive and well written, but in the heat of the rant the students took the book as a springboard to launch into diatribes rather than to entertain sets of ideas. In offering the students a question that rewarded, even required, a brutal attack, I had chosen a writing prompt that made it even more difficult for the students to see the novel as morally complex. If Hemingway was sexist and had failed to present a realistic female character, what student would bother fishing around in the novel for ethical depth? Who wants to take sides with a misogynist, particularly when one's grade depends on it?

The more I thought about it, the more I realized that what I wanted the students to do was to put aside easy answers. I wanted them to step into the shoes of the characters of the novel, to face the same sets of choices confronting them and weigh the same options and dangers. I wanted them to risk setting aside their own moral perspectives and adopt another's. I wanted an assignment that challenged the students to flesh out these people within the novel's own terms. Putting Jordan on trial came to me as a means of reaching some of these objectives. The students would have to think the novel through from a different viewpoint. Even better, a trial would hold Jordan accountable to his own ideals. What if he were forced to answer his own sharpest criticism? In moving too far toward a pragmatic utility of violence, had he really become his own enemy?

The omniscient narration of *For Whom the Bell Tolls* never offers a moral evaluation of Robert Jordan, as it does of, for example, Andre Marty (422–23). Instead, the novel presents the different characters' perspectives on his actions and leaves judgment to the reader. Rather than asking the students to repress the conflicting voices in the novel, a trial would invite students to explore those disparate voices, to hear them out. And instead of asking the students to synthesize the divergent characters' perspectives into one master truth, it would offer them the chance to explore those characters as unexpected and alien points of view, with the only incentive being to better understand, so as to better enter the role.

Staging the Trial

The first step was to find something with which to charge Jordan. While nothing that he does is a war crime under the Nuremberg definition, the Nuremberg Principles do make a relevant distinction between following orders and exercising the moral sensibility expected of basic humanity. Principle IV states: "The fact that a person acted pursuant to order of his Government or of a superior does not relieve him from responsibility under international law, provided a moral choice was in fact possible to him" (United Nations 375). Because Jordan puts the lives of those under him at risk to follow through with an attack that *he knows very well* is pointless, he does seem vulnerable to the charge that his actions violate his basic humanitarian obligation to weigh the benefit of following orders against his responsibility as a human being to avoid needless death. By following through with empty orders, and so needlessly causing death, isn't Jordan morally equivalent to Comrade Marty, who orders pointless attacks on valueless targets? (*FWBT* 422–23). Even when he does not have the numbers or equipment necessary, Jordan, commits himself to going forward. "You have to go and make a plan that you know is impossible to carry out," he accuses himself (385). He even conceals important details from the others to ensure they carry on. After Pablo deserts, for example, the only one to whom Jordan confides that the attack's odds of success have become abysmal is Maria—who is asleep at the time (371).

To articulate this as a case, I wrote up an indictment that left the specific "law" broken couched in vaguely legalistic language:

> Pursuant to the authority of the International Court of Human Rights of University X, being duly empowered to act in defense of basic human rights and decency, the court calls Robert Jordan to answer for the following actions taken during the events related in the novel *For Whom the Bell Tolls:*
>
> Whereas Robert Jordan did display callous indifference to the lives of the people under his command and did needlessly endanger the lives of the rest

of his compatriots and cause his own death as well as the deaths of Anselmo, Fernando, Eladio, and the new men from Elias's band,

And whereas Robert Jordan, in the service of a empty ideal and his own personal glory, proceeded with his mission in the full knowledge that the mission undertaken no longer had any reasonable expectation of military necessity,

And whereas Robert Jordan's choice to proceed with the mission, despite being presented with reasonable alternatives, showed a rigid adherence to orders without regard for the lives of his subordinates that can be called criminal,

Thereby Robert Jordan is charged with becoming the very enemy that he claims he came to Spain to fight, and so should be treated accordingly—as an enemy not only of the Spanish people but of the international community.

To give the indictment an air of authority I printed the handouts on fake letterhead and sealed them in envelopes decorated with impressive looking stamps I had bought in Japan (luckily none of my students could read Japanese or they would have known that those stamps were designed for grade school kids' homework).

The next step was to create a witness list. I picked the most relevant characters and printed out the list of names on stickers. Each indictment envelope got a sticker. There were eighteen students in the class the first semester, so I opted for two trials, each with eight characters to be called as witnesses. That gave me room to double up on the characters whom I considered bore the most important testimony—we had three Robert Jordans and three Pablos. For the other characters, I appointed either two students (for Pilar, Anselmo, Augustin, and El Sordo), or one (for Golz, the gypsy Rafael, Barrientos, and Maria).

We spent six class periods total on *For Whom the Bell Tolls*. The first week covered the historical background, Hemingway's style, and other more "literary" topics, but the second week focused on the scenes most relevant to the trial, particularly where the characters debate killing Pablo and the ethics of war—Anselmo's meditations on killing, for example. I also included an option to write about the trial on the list of prompts for the course's final paper—the students could write closing arguments for either the prosecution or defense.

I introduced the trial during the second class meeting on the novel. Just before the end of the period, I had the students pick one of the prepared envelopes out of a paper bag and then explained the outlines of what we were going to do. I let the students know that reading the indictment would spoil the ending, and so I invited them to open the envelopes as they finished the book. Since they already knew which character they were going to play (it was stickered on the outside of the envelope), they could pay particular attention to those scenes. To get them started, I passed out a cheat sheet with special scenes for each of the characters I posted (see Appendix A). They were allowed to trade characters, but they had to keep me posted.

To cast the prosecution and defense, I asked for volunteers. The list was kept as first-come, first-serve, and the parts filled quickly. The students worked in teams of two, both to foster teamwork and to mitigate the risk of the students disappearing at the crucial time. These students were also allowed to play a character, but not in the same trial they lawyered. The jury would be the class at large, and the verdicts would be decided by majority vote after a short debate.

In all, there was space for up to six witnesses at each trial—three for the defense and three for the prosecution. Hoping to encourage competition among the teams for the best witnesses, I allowed each student to testify only once; if a student was called as a witness by more than one team, he or she could choose in which trial and for which side to testify. Even if none of the lawyers testified, the numbers meant that there would not be enough slots for every student to directly participate. Initially, the students reacted to this with relief, but after the trial some of them seemed disappointed not to have been called.

Finally, in the week of the trial, the first class meeting was set aside for practice. This allowed the students time to decide which witnesses to call and which actor they would use for the characters. That day in class, the prosecutors and defense teams interviewed the various students who were playing characters, rehearsing what they would ask and developing questions and answers. (There was no penalty for coaching the witnesses.) This ended up being a quite wonderful day of conversations about the book. Watching the students huddled over copies of the novel, flipping through the pages and arguing how each character would respond to a specific question, was enormously satisfying.

On the day of the trial, I gave the legal teams five more minutes of prep time to account for absences and make last-minute adjustments. While the teams worked, I passed out a pair of handouts to the other students. The first consisted of the jury ballots that they would use to render a verdict in each case. The second was what I called the Academy Awards ballot—which was a chance to vote for various categories of best actor. There was absolutely no grade incentive for this second round of balloting, but it ended up being the part of the trial that was most controversial and most grabbed the students' attention.

After the last-minute preparation, we ran though the two trials with a five-minute pause in between them. In those five minutes, I asked the students to fill out a verdict sheet, but we did not count the votes until both trials were finished. I hoped in this way to open the possibility for students to split their verdict—voting guilty in one trial and innocent in the other—but in practice this didn't happen. In both trials, the consensus ran heavily toward guilty one year and toward innocent the next. The verdict was decided by a simple show of hands.

Finally, in the last minute, I collected the Academy Awards handouts. I did the tabulation at home purely for reasons of time, but this proved to be a fortunate delay. It ended the whole experiment on a note of anticipation; the students were genuinely passionate about who should win these awards. When we began the next class by announcing the winners, it capped the whole event nicely.

Surprisingly, I found that the Academy Award ballot was enough of an incentive to get the students to embrace their roles. I think they also warmed up to the project because, in the spirit of Gee, I made the entire trial low stakes. Other than a flat mark for participation, which was simply a check mark, the only grade I offered was to promise that the winning lawyers wouldn't have to write the final paper. Even this incentive was very weak, however, because the students who volunteered for the lawyering were among the more motivated students and could have written the essay with much less effort than they put into the trial.

Among the students who had struggled through the rest of the semester, several shone during the trial. These were students who had difficulty writing but were extremely capable speakers. The rest were effectively getting the chance to write the final paper collectively by following the trial closely, since the paper topic was being modeled by each of the lawyer teams.

For reference, see the three handouts that I used in addition to the indictment, appearing here as Appendixes A, B, and C. The first, Appendix A: Character List, with Pertinent Scenes, is a list of the "playable" characters, with suggestions for helpful scenes and some thoughts about what perspective each might offer. The intention was to frame some of the debates for the students as they started "researching" their roles. Of course, these suggestions are not meant to be exclusive.

The other two handouts, Appendixes B and C, are both intended to clarify the structure of the trial. Appendix B: Trial Day Schedule of Events showed the order of speaking and inquiry and the amount of time allotted to each section. I toyed with this over three semesters, finally settling on a format that seemed to fit my students. Because they all knew each other very well, they were very comfortable staging cross-examinations. This might work less well with a different class dynamic.

Appendix C: Valid Objections in the Trial Process contained the grounds upon which an objection could be claimed. In brief, I allowed the students to challenge the witnesses if their testimony misrepresented the text or if they made up something that seemed out of character for the role they were playing. I played the part of judge and ruled immediately on the objections—although in practice there were very few. One question I was left with was whether I myself should actively object to testimony that was either wrong or speculative, or if it wasn't better to put the onus on the students to keep each other accurate. At the end of the day, I didn't need to worry about this. The students handled it quite well by themselves.

Notes

1. In this exchange, Jordan also perhaps speaks for an earlier Hemingway, now undergoing self-critique. Stephen Koch, in *The Breaking Point*, relates a conversation that John Dos Passos claims he had with Hemingway in Spain: "The question I keep putting to myself," Dos Passos reports asking, "is what's the use of fighting a war for civil liberties, if you destroy civil liberties in the process?" According to Dos Passos, Hemingway's reply was "Civil liberties, *shit*. Are you *with* us or are you *against* us?" (qtd. in Koch 216; emphasis in original).

2. See Vernon, *Hemingway's Second War,* 154.

3. Hemingway himself was similarly criticized by Stephen Spender, to whom he reportedly confessed that he was in Spain to find out "whether he had lost his nerve under conditions of warfare" (Wilson 504).

# Teaching *The Spanish Earth* in a War Film Seminar

Alex Vernon

I

When the college's sole film studies professor took leave, I had the opportunity to teach a film course for the first time in my career. An upper-level war film seminar made perfect sense. My knowledge of war literature and the seniors' knowledge of the cinematic arts, I reasoned, would fruitfully combine.

The course took advantage of the parallel development of cinema and modern warfare by focusing on representations of armed conflict and its consequences in the twentieth and twenty-first centuries. We began with *Saving Private Ryan* (1998) in order to complicate and enliven a text dulled by the students' familiarity with it. The film self-consciously constructs itself on earlier war films. Its narrative frame gives us an aged veteran recalling a mission he can only imagine, as he was not there for most of the film's happenings—his visual recall relies on cinematic portrayals of his own war to supply the imagery. The film thus constitutes an explicit argument for studying the tradition. We then returned to the Great War and proceeded chronologically by conflict rather than by film. The course surveyed broadly in terms of nationality and genre (though it included more American than foreign films). Each film and accompanying readings occupied a week of the schedule.

1. *Saving Private Ryan* (1998)
2. *The Big Parade* (1926)
3. *All Quiet on the Western Front* (1930)
4. *The Spanish Earth* (1937)
5. *The Devil's Backbone* (2001)

6. *The Thin Red Line* (1998)
7. *The Best Years of our Lives* (1946)
8. *The Battle of Algiers* (1956)
9. *Apocalypse Now* (1979)
10. *Waltz with Bashir* (2008)
11. *Lebanon* (2009)
12. *The Hurt Locker* (2009)
13. *Restrepo* (2010)

I wanted to include *War Witch* and *The Act of Killing*, but these 2013 films were not yet available on DVD or through a streaming service. I would have bumped *Restrepo* for either of these films in an instant.

Joris Ivens and Ernest Hemingway's film, *The Spanish Earth*, served the course as the documentary version of "committed journalism." As some of the students had not studied nonfiction film history, the film introduced them to the genre's deep roots in subjectivity. I also hoped it would make for a nice foundation for our later explorations of the semidocumentary *The Battle of Algiers*, the animated documentary *Waltz with Bashir*, and the embedded documentary *Restrepo*. My own scholarship on *The Spanish Earth* granted me a relatively light preparation, as I could talk off the cuff about its production and its hidden historical facts—in other words, about its propaganda moves.[1] I also included it as a transition between *All Quiet on the Western Front* and *The Devil's Backbone*. The 1937 documentary seems visually indebted to, or in the same vein as, *All Quiet on the Western Front*, Lewis Milestone's film on the Great War (four years later, Milestone and Ivens would work together on the 1941 *Our Russian Front*), and it provides the necessary background for watching *The Devil's Backbone*, Guillermo del Toro's first Spanish Civil War film.

The accompanying readings included Cary Nelson's short online piece, "The Spanish Civil War: An Overview," and Vivian Sobchack's "Inscribing Ethical Space: Ten Propositions on Death, Representation, and Documentary." I also asked the students to review one of the readings for *All Quiet*, Bernd Hüppauf's "Experiences of Modern Warfare and the Crisis of Representation," which begins with the American Civil War but turns its attention primarily to *All Quiet* and *The Spanish Earth*. The Hüppauf piece engaged the students more than the Sobchack, and was unexpectedly joined by the other *All Quiet* reading, Santanu Das's introduction to his *Touch and Intimacy in First World War Literature*.

The seventy-five-minute class period ended the conversation prematurely. In my inexperience at teaching this particular course, uncertain as to which readings would be most consistently productive, I assigned too much reading for most films. In teaching *The Spanish Earth,* the need to lecture on the background to the film and to reveal the extent of its creative license took too much class time away from discussion. Moreover, my expertise on the subject became something of an impediment. The question raised in connection with Das's *Touch and Intimacy* came in the final minute of class. While I usually enjoy ending the class with a compelling question, especially one new to me as well as the students, this class meeting suffered from surfeit. Having too much material to process left no time for unhurried collaborative discovery.

In the weeks after that class meeting, however, I used the conversation to draft my own reflection on the connections between *The Spanish Earth* and our readings. This inquiry led me to other texts—from class, from research, and from suggestions by Kristi McKim, my brilliant and generous film studies colleague. The ideas that follow are a bit too raw to publish as an act of interpretation, reading like a hybrid of an article and my in-class riffing. I present the next section as a representation of that creative if messy space where teaching and scholarship meet as full partners in curiosity and mutual germination. I also present it as the foundation for class preparation, if I ever again have the opportunity to teach the course or the film. If not teaching a war cinema course, for example, I could share the block quotations below in class without requiring the lengthy readings. We teach to learn how to teach.

II

Bernd Hüppauf's important 1993 essay, "Experiences of Modern Warfare and the Crisis of Representation," analyzes visual representations of the Great War, complaining that they employ "obsolete, traditional metaphors" in order to

> maintain a language that is morally justified but largely incapable of reflecting the structural modernity of the war experience.... By placing on the screen images of increasingly brutal war conditions and juxtaposing them with the human face, [the framers of these images] establish a visual code defined by political and humanist commitment. It seems beyond doubt that this emotionally powerful iconography differed from previous representations of wars in which violence and destruction were embedded in images of heroism and purpose. Yet the moral framework within which these images were created and are received largely excludes representation of the structurally inhuman battlefield of modern warfare.

> In [such] anti-war iconography, the camera lens has adopted the position of the suffering soldier as a victim of violence rather than exposing the structure of violence and presenting soldiers as elements of it. (62–63)

In other words, films must not encourage us to mistake *a* human face in *a* war as the Face of War—as truly representing the totalizing phenomenon of modern war.[2] They must not encourage us to see soldiers as sufferers rather than perpetrators.

Following his critique of Lewis Milestone's 1930 adaptation of *All Quiet on the Western Front,* Hüppauf concludes by discussing documentary representations of the Spanish Civil War, "a war of modern technology" as well as "the last war of heroic imagery," which caught pro-Republic photographers and filmmakers "between a moral commitment and the aesthetic requirements of representing a technological war" (64). *The Spanish Earth* serves as his example of visual narratives that falsely "preserve an image of man outside of the war machine, an image that makes him either the victim or the master of modern destructiveness but not an element in or a product of its technological structure" (68).

For Hüppauf, Hemingway's failure in the film lies in his preference for the individual experience: "Since for him the reality of the war is identical with individual experiences, he aims to make visible on the screen the memories imprinted on his body" (67). This preference leads the film to commit the larger moral crime of failing to depict War. Oddly, Hüppauf quotes Hemingway's own 1938 article "The Heat and the Cold" as evidence of his recognition of the film's failure: "Although it is *his* film on *his* war, ... in watching the film he cannot help realize that he has lost both" (66). Hüppauf presumes, then, that Hemingway expected the film to communicate the war's *feltness.* He also presumes that Hemingway imagined the film as an outlet of self-expression, like his fiction.

I read "The Heat and the Cold" differently: not as a postscript recognition of failure but as a postscript reminder to viewers and readers of what he already knew about the film medium's inherent haptic—that is, tactile and sensory—challenge. As Hüppauf quotes Hemingway's article: "Afterwards when it is all over, you have a *picture.* You *see* it on the screen; you *hear* the noises and the music. . . . But what you *see* in motion on the screen is not what you remember.—The first thing you remember is how cold it was; how early you got up in the morning; how you were always so tired. . . . and how we were always hungry. . . . Nothing of that *shows* on the screen. . . ." (66; emphasis added). Hemingway remembers the cold, he remembers the onions he could feel in his pockets but that the viewer could never see, he remembers the heat, he remembers the dust in his nose and hair and eyes, and the thirst and the dry-mouth (67). The article succeeds where the film does not because cinema cannot render embodied experience as print can—so, at any rate, Hemingway's article implicitly argues. A movie like *Saving Private Ryan*, with its strenuous visual and aural verisimilitude, overcompensates for this intrinsic deficiency of the medium, either distracting us from the problem or pushing past it to get after what it cannot achieve by employing sight and sound as objective correlative. As Tom Hanks—that movie's star actor, who was never soldier—offers in an interview, "It's not hard to imagine what it must have *looked* like; what it must have *felt* like, however, is something that guys like myself will never know—never—never in a million years" (qtd. in "Into the Breach").[3] I am tempted to propose that modernist writers like Hemingway and Stein intensified the haptic in writing in reaction to the specular new narrative medium of cinema.[4]

Santanu Das's excellent study, *Touch and Intimacy in First World War Literature*, in its introductory discussion on Wilfred Owen's correspondence from the front, draws attention to the poet's "repetition of the word 'felt'" because of its import throughout the book: "'felt' gathers its full significance in relation to the emotional world it contains, hovering at the threshold between the sensory and the psychic, bringing together the body and the mind" (8). Here is Owen: "Can you photograph the crimson-hot iron as it cools from the smelting? This is what Jones's blood looked like, and felt like. My senses are charred" (qtd. in Das 7). Though Das's afterword would have us think otherwise in its two pages on cinema (230–31),[5] the book's unstated argument—for this reader, if not for Das himself—matches Hemingway's from "The Heat and the Cold": Written expression achieves the sensorily and psychically haptic more naturally than motion pictures do. Because how can you photograph the warmth of seeping blood?[6]

We might surmise the mechanics here. Holding a book in the hands and lap literally touches us, as watching a distant screen does not. Imagining sights and sounds, imagining what we can't actually see or hear when reading, enables imagining what we can't feel. The mind's eye and ear become conduits for the mind's skin. I am reminded of Kate McLoughlin's assertion about the "adynaton or impossibility trope" in war writing, in that "absence conjures up presence" as "a reader informed that a battle is too shocking to be described is likely to envision horrors exceeding anything that straightforward description could invoke" (22–23). Visual cues to the tactile are bricks of the fourth wall, sometimes responsible for a pining response. Like maps that appear in film, they situate *and* absent us.⁷ And they can lie: a character in a hot climate glistening with sweat, while sensually appealing to the viewer, probably feels only suffocating, miserable, sticky heat, wanting touch only from a breeze. Music in cinema can stir the spectator by misdirection from what the bodies on the screen would actually feel. Italics in prose, on the other hand, function as *somatic* qualifiers of the semantic.

Had the book version of *The Spanish Earth* been the photo-essay Hemingway and its editor, Jasper Wood, wanted, rather than a printing of a voiceover script draft, I suspect it could have surpassed the film's sensory engagement. Though only a film still, the call to the hand of a static image approaches that of a painting whose unnaturally immobilized incompleteness demands active imagination (Das devotes the first five pages of his book to John Singer Sargent's *Gassed*). A photo object, even one in blurred motion, is graspable as a moving image is not—especially one in a book in your hands and lap. As my collaborator and filmmaker friend Peter Davis has said, many images from *The Mexican Suitcase,* the collection of lost Spanish Civil War photos by Robert Capa, Gerda Taro, and David Seymour, "make the brain reel" as the moving images of *The Spanish Earth* do not.

Wood's inclusion of "The Heat and the Cold" as the afternote in the book version of *The Spanish Earth* unintentionally reinforces the article's argument. Hemingway's voiceover script studiously declines the very physical and sensory depictions that the article exploits in allowing the soldiers' *feltness* to travel through the writer's to the reader. He avoids it because he knows better than to try, and because he understands his role as propagandist. Hemingway would save his humanist commitment to what Hüppauf deems "highly individual sensations" for his own prose (67). Contra Hüppauf, *The Spanish Earth* does not fail because Hemingway and Ivens focused on the individual and the experiential. In its own biased and terse way, the narration of the film does attempt to explain something of that war's larger dynamics even as it grossly simplifies and polarizes: "For fifty years we've wanted to irrigate, but *they* held us back."⁸

Hüppauf's critique productively reminds us to proceed with caution when watching war films to avoid the delusion that we understand War because we've watched Milestone's Paul Bäumer killed reaching for a butterfly. Yet I sometimes wonder if a cinematic war drama could ever satisfy him. Bäumer's death by a French sniper echoes an earlier shot of his fellow German sniper potting French soldiers in the trench opposite, thus deconstructing Hüppauf's own binary of "the suffering soldier as victim of war" and "soldiers as elements of it" (63). The film also strives against what Hüppauf sees as a false distinction between home and the front (63) through its many deep-focus shots, in which borders between interiors and exteriors violently collapse, and through the absent bodies of soon-to-be-dead Bäumer and his French lover of one night as they talk in bed, a visual synecdoche, perhaps, for the invisible connections between warscape and domesticity as well as an adumbration that she, like he, might not survive the war. In the end, Hüppauf's critique resembles the old charge about the impossibility of antiwar narratives. Do antiwar novels really argue for pacifism, or only against the waging of the specific war (a difference Dalton Trumbo poignantly attests to in his 1959 introduction to *Johnny Got His Gun*)? Does antiwar cinema inevitably become war porn?

Indeed, one way *The Spanish Earth* might have satisfied is by more fully embracing the individual experience, with human stories indicating the full complexity of that war's political dynamics. But that was not what *The Spanish Earth* was supposed to be, or what any film from that time and place could ever have been.

## Notes

1. For my work on this film, see Alex Vernon, "*The Spanish Earth* and the Non-Nonfiction War Film," *Hemingway Review* 34.1 (Fall 2014): 30-46; and Vernon, *Hemingway's Second War*, chs. 3 and 4.

2. What Jan Mieszkowski, following Rousseau, calls the "invisible forces" of war that "[need] to be revealed." These processes make war an "effect" or "product," not a cause (1650). That she follows Rousseau and focuses her study on the Napoleonic era provides a point of contention with Hüppauf's potentially nostalgic, Luddite critique of modern war.

3. This line appeared as the epigraph on the course description for my course.

4. Abbie Garrington's *Haptic Modernism: Touch and the Tactile in Modernist Writing* (Edinburgh UP, 2013), while almost entirely a study of literary effects, sees the literary and the cinematic as both working toward the same sensorily evocative end but does not concern itself with differences between the two media (48, 142–47).

5. Garrington and Das would seem to be in agreement.

6. Generally what I'm suggesting rather sophomorically and absurdly briefly butts against several sophisticated studies devoted to insisting on cinema's evocation of the touch sense. See Laura Marks, *The Skin of the Film: Intercultural Cinema, Embodiment, and the Senses* (2000); Vivian Sobchack, *Carnal Thoughts: Embodiment and Moving Image Culture* (2004); David Trotter, "Lynne Ramsay's Ratcatcher: Towards a Theory of Haptic Narrative" (*Paragraph* 31.2, 2008); Jennifer M. Barker, *The Tactile Eye: Touch and the Cinematic Experience* (2009); and Laura McMahon, *Cinema and Contact: The Withdrawal of Touch in Nancy, Bresson, Duras and Denis* (2012). McMahon addresses the effect of the distance between spectator's body and the image.

7. "A map in a film prompts every spectator to consider *bilocation,* which may indeed be cause for the resurgence of debates in which film is treated in terms of issues concerning identity. Identity can be defined in a narrow sense as the consciousness of belonging (or longing to belong) to a place and of being at a distance from it. When a map in a film locates the geography of its narrative, it also tells us that we are not where it says it is taking place. The story that is said to be there is nowhere" (Conley 3–4; emphasis in original).

8. In addition to writing the commentary, Hemingway was the narrator for the English-language version of *The Spanish Earth.*

# Part Three

# Trauma Tales

# Hemingway, PTSD, and Clinical Depression

Peter L. Hays

When I teach Hemingway, I usually start with the interchapter for chapter 3 of *In Our Time,* where British troops kill advancing German soldiers in a garden near Mons. I point out the irony of killing in a garden, with its associations of flowers and peacefulness, perhaps even of the Garden of Eden, and point out also the British slang term *potted,* here meaning "killed" but also appropriate for gardening. Then I ask my students why the narrator displays no emotion over the killings. Some students suggest necessary control over emotions in order to perform efficiently, much like Dr. Adams in "Indian Camp." Others suggest a soldier drained of emotion, numb over killings seen and done, a symptom of post-traumatic stress disorder.

We've come a long way from World War I accounts of shell shock (that war's label for those suffering from war-related psychological damage) and now have acronyms to describe the same or related conditions: PTSD (post-traumatic stress disorder) and TBI (traumatic brain injury), the latter referring not just to shrapnel or bullet wounds in the brain but also to severe concussions. These conditions, PTSD and TBI, can present and be treated almost identically, making distinguishing them both challenging and somewhat moot. And, of course, we now know that such physical injuries as TBIs can also cause subsequent psychological disorders, such as PTSD. Even what Dr. Jonathan Shay calls moral injuries, such as witnessing the death of innocent civilians in barbaric ways, being present at the brutal deaths of one's comrades, simply finding oneself participating in collective, sanctioned violence, and suffering the guilt of the survivor, can cause PTSD.

We know that Hemingway inherited bipolar disorder from his father and that he was diagnosed as severely depressed at the Mayo Clinic in 1960. (The doctors there mistakenly believed that his depression had been caused by the medicine he had been taking to control his blood pressure and that he would recover once off that medicine and after shock therapy [Nuffer 122, 124]. He didn't.) Like his father, his sister Ursula, his brother Leicester, and one granddaughter, Hemingway committed suicide. Two of his sons also underwent shock therapy.[1] We now know that bipolar disorder can be transmitted genetically.

But in addition to the inherited disease, which often starts in one's early twenties, Hemingway had undergone an earlier, traumatic war experience while serving in the Red Cross at Fossalta, Italy during World War I. A trench mortar shell had exploded a few feet from him, killing the man between him and the explosion, knocking him out, and leaving him with 227 shell fragments in his right leg alone (Reynolds, *Young Hemingway* 19). Since it knocked him out, the force of the blast was definitely concussive. Phillip Young, as early as 1952, labeled Hemingway's nonphysical wound as "traumatic neurosis" and discussed its psychological ramifications (Young 162). To the extent that we can conclude that Hemingway's fiction has autobiographical elements, the characters' war experiences certainly have psychological consequences. Nick Adams and Frederic Henry, in "Now I Lay Me" and *A Farewell to Arms* respectively, are both blown up at night as Hemingway was. The two fictional characters felt their souls leave their bodies and then return; as a result, both have difficulty sleeping when it's dark, doing so more easily when there's a light, as Jake Barnes did (Hemingway, *SAR* 152), and as Hemingway also did (Young 137; Villard and Nagel 214). Nick also undergoes visible symptoms of mental instability in "A Way You'll Never Be": He discourses volubly about locusts and acts in such a disturbed manner that his friend Paravicini tells Nick he must go back behind the lines because he is frightening the Italian troops, to whom he has been sent in an American uniform as a morale booster. Nick also feels something "coming on" that he tries to control (*CSS* 313); Hemingway does not explain what "it" is—trembling, mild hysteria—but it is visible and hastens Paravicini's decision. This behavior does not seem autobiographical, but it certainly fulfills Bugs's prophecy in "The Battler." When Ad says of an adolescent Nick, "He says he's never been crazy," Bugs's reply is, "He's got a lot coming to him" (100). Nick climbs the railway embankment at story's end, only to discover that he has a ham sandwich in his hand (104), the encounter with Ad having been so traumatic that he underwent a temporary dissociation of mind and body.

Hemingway's first mission in Italy was to remove the dead from a munitions plant outside Milan that had exploded. Many of the victims were women, war casualties also, and moving them was a gruesome task for an eighteen-year-old to handle (Baker, *Life Story* 41). Despite his own wounds at Fossalta, he is reported to have carried an injured man back to an aid station, but the man had died by the time they arrived. If the account is true, then it adds to the number of dead that Hemingway dealt with, including the wounded we can speculate he transported, some of whom could have died in his ambulance.

"Soldier's Home" is taken by several critics to be Hemingway's first war trauma story. Joe DeFalco and Paul Smith say that it deals with shell shock, while Milton Cohen calls it PTSD (DeFalco 144; P. Smith 70; Cohen 163). Although the protagonist is named Krebs, after Hemingway's friend Krebs Friend, who also suffered shell shock (Reynolds, *Paris Years* 189), the similarity between the story's setting of Oklahoma and Hemingway's birthplace, Oak Park, and between Harold's and Ernest's mothers, is impossible to ignore.[2] The title could be read multiple ways. The word *soldier's* in the title could be a contraction stating that the soldier is home or a possessive indicating that he is back at his home, but the title could also be a reference to Soldiers' Homes, the federally funded hospitals, nursing homes, or retirement homes for war-damaged veterans that used to exist. That is, the author may be indicating in the story's very title Krebs's state of impairment.

The narrator says of the girls that Krebs watches, "the world they were in was not the world he was in" (*CSS* 113); so removed is he, after killing and watching killings, that "he did not want consequences ever again" (113). The frequent repetition of the word *like* in the story is often attributed to the influence of Gertrude Stein, but in Hemingway's use of free indirect discourse, Krebs's repetition of *like* could be an confused expression of his desire for a relationship with one of the "girls" he sees, in conflict with his never wanting any consequences again, the inchoate result being nothing more defined than a simple, inarticulate "like." His fear of entanglements and emotional involvement are symptoms of PTSD, which both the National Institute of Mental Health (NIMH) and the American Psychiatric Association's *DSM-4* (the medical handbook that defines psychiatric disorders) describe as characterized by, in part:

- feeling emotionally numb; and
- losing interest in activities that were enjoyable in the past (NIMH; American Psychiatric Association 428).[3]

Another symptom of PTSD is that of reexperiencing the triggering event, reliving the trauma, over and over—as Hemingway did in his writing and possibly in his nightmares.

In "Big Two-Hearted River," Nick Adams comes to Seney to fish. Seney, burned to the ground, looks like a war zone—as my students recognize—an indication of what Nick is leaving behind; he is a psychically wounded war veteran, still wearing a khaki shirt (CSS 174). Beyond the town, Nick looks at the black grasshoppers, changed from their usual color, wondering "how long they would stay that way" (165), and he looks at the trout, holding themselves steady in the current (163), as he must learn to do for himself, and he does so through what amounts to occupational therapy. The American Occupational Therapy Association (AOTA) recognizes that victims of traumatic brain injury need help in adjusting to normal life. Among the therapies for victims of TBI that AOTA seeks to help the person minimize overstimulation and confusion in his or her environment while performing simple, meaningful tasks. Hemingway knew that also. I ask my students how many have fished, then, how many have lost a fish. Of these latter, I ask if they ever felt nauseous after losing a fish. None has ever said yes. But when Nick loses his big fish, he loses his composure as well: "The thrill had been too much. He felt, vaguely, a little sick, as though it would be better to sit down" (CSS 177). Nick's whole regimen in preparing camp in familiar terrain—controlling his hunger so as to not burn his tongue, using a pine chip to turn his pancake over in the pan so as to avoid the risk of trying to flip the pan and losing the pancake into the fire—is intended to minimize overstimulation, as are his attempts to tire himself so that he can sleep without lying awake thinking and remembering. For Nick, to fish is to perform a task meaningful in his life. The story is based on a fishing trip Hemingway took in 1919. He rode on a train that ordinarily only slowed at Seney to let fishermen jump off, but this time, when Hemingway prepared to get off, the brakeman told the engineer to stop the train because "there's a cripple and he needs time to get his stuff down" (Baker, *Life Story* 63). Hemingway may have received physical therapy in Milan, but in "Big Two-Hearted River," he prescribes for Nick a form of occupational therapy that he also used. In "Soldier's Home," Krebs, too, tries to control his environment by performing enjoyable tasks that risk little chance of major disappointment: playing pool and practicing his clarinet. And Hemingway repeats that Helen, Krebs's sister, plays indoor baseball (i.e., softball), a game in which she is indoors, sheltered, away from the life-changing environment that Krebs endured, and thus part of the unchanged, still-uniform existence Krebs no longer feels part of.

I have previously written about Hemingway's bipolar disorder, but I did not think to relate it at the time—before the Iraq war—to his war injury.[4] Depression (part of the cycle of mood shifts in bipolar disorder) and PTSD can overlap, sharing similar symptoms. Thus in my article I note as shared symptoms identified in the *DSM-4* a "markedly diminished interest or participation in significant activities" and "difficulty falling or staying asleep" (American Psychiatric Association 428). We've already seen the "diminished interest" evinced by Krebs, a symptom not evinced by Hemingway in his life. In "A Clean, Well-Lighted Place," the old customer has attempted suicide; we do not know why, except that he is old and has lost his wife. But the older waiter empathizes, having experienced nothingness—nada—in his life as well. And, like Nick Adams, he needs light to go to sleep: "He would lie in bed and finally, with daylight, he would go to sleep. After all, he said to himself, it is probably only insomnia. Many must have it" (*CSS* 291).

Is this, too, autobiographical? We know that Hemingway suffered from insomnia (Hemingway, *SL* 96), and Mike Reynolds ties it to both the depressive disorder he inherited from his father and his wartime wounding (*Young Hemingway* 85–86). Having difficulty sleeping is a PTSD symptom (NIMH; American Psychiatric Association 428), and the Nick Adams of "Now I Lay Me" is clearly an insomniac. In *For Whom the Bell Tolls*, Pilar complains of periods of deep sadness: "All my life I have had this sadness at intervals. . . . It may be it is like the times of a woman" (90), but of course, Hemingway is not describing PMS (premenstrual syndrome) but depressive episodes, such as those he himself had undergone. He wrote to Robert McAlmon in 1924 about "having a period of not being able to do anything worth a shit" (*Letters 1* 135), and to John Dos Passos about his "gigantic bloody emptiness and nothingness like couldn't ever fuck, fight write, and was all for death" (qtd. in Beegel 65). Billy Campbell in "A Pursuit Race" has come to a similar conclusion. He has withdrawn from the world, using heroin as his escape method (much as Hemingway self-medicated his depression with alcohol). But Billy's reason for doing so no doubt preceded his addiction, much as that of the old man in "Clean Well-Lighted Place" preceded his suicide attempt. As Campbell explains to Billy Turner, "You're called 'Sliding Billy.' That's because you can slide. I'm just called Billy. That's because I never could slide at all. I can't slide, Billy. I can't slide. It just catches. Every time I try it, it catches" (*CSS* 269). He cannot proceed smoothly; he cannot catch a break. Instead, the world catches at him. And so he gives up, like Bartleby (another depressed individual with no interest in daily activities), and medicates himself with heroin.

Did Hemingway indeed suffer from PTSD? Nagel writes that Hemingway's nurse in Milan, Agnes von Kurowsky, and the patient in the next room, Henry Villard, "saw no sign of shell shock whatever. Indeed they remember him as being almost incessantly cheerful" (Villard and Nagel 214). Which leads to the question, when does PTSD set in? Many soldiers serve valiantly in combat, suffering only on their return home; in addition, Hemingway was trying to impress Agnes, his first love, with his stability and his manliness, as he was eight years her junior. His letters home after his wounding are quite cheerful. On 21 July 1918, he wrote, "This is a peach of a hospital here. . . . [I have] a wonderful lot of souvenirs[:] . . . Austrian carbine and ammunition, German and Austrian medals, officer's automatic pistols, [etc.]" (*Letters 1* 12). His next letter, of 18 August, seems full of joy: "There certainly has been a lot of [newspaper] burbles about my being shot up! . . . It's the next best thing to being killed and reading your own obituary. . . . Well I can now hold up my hand and say I've been shelled by high explosive, shrapnel and gas. Shot at by trench mortars, snipers and machine guns, and as an added attraction an aeroplane machine gunning the lines" (13–14). There's no historic documentation of poison gas at Fossalta, nor of aircraft strafing; both seem displays of Hemingway's gift for heroic exaggeration. Those lines, together with his claim in another letter, written 18 October, that "I've looked at death, and really I know, If [sic] I should have died it would hve [sic] been very easy for me. Quite the easiest thing I ever did" (14), smack of Henry Fleming's reaction at the end of Stephen Crane's *Red Badge of Courage:* "He had been to touch the great death and found, after all, it was but the great death. He was a man" (Crane 266)—that is to say, his reaction is one of youthful bravado, much like that of a shell-shocked soldier insisting that he is fine because he does not want to be hospitalized, leave his buddies behind, or, even worse, be judged mentally unstable and thus less than a man. Other boasts by Hemingway of the same stripe include his inflation of his linguistic ability in French and Italian, and more pertinently, his claim, in the letter of 18 October 1918, that "wounds don't matter. I wouldn't mind being wounded again so much because I know just what it is like" (*Letters 1* 147). More youthful bravado is his inflating the reason for which he got the *Medaglia d'Argento al Valore Militare* (Silver Medal of Military Valor). Says the boastful young Hemingway to his parents on 4 August 1918, "The silver medal is next to the highest Decoration that any man can receive. . . . The silver valour medal is corresponding to the Victoria Cross. It is higher than the French Croix D'Guerre and Medaille Militaire and ranks with the Legion of Honor." In fact, as Baker's footnote on the next page states, "the silver medal was awarded to all soldiers who were wounded in action, and the war cross, like U.S. Army campaign ribbons, to all who were engaged in action" (*Letters 1* 124, 125). Nagel says, "The official records of the American Red Cross Hospital in Milan list no shell-shock victims, nor could Agnes later recall that they ever had such a patient" (Villard and Nagel 214)—which suggests they never looked for it or did not recognize it when they saw it. Hemingway, on the other hand, reports on 18 November 1918 that the hospital's doctor, presumably Italian, describes his patient saying that "I'm all shot to pieces, figuratively as well as literally.... [A]nd he says that I won't be any good for a year" (*Letters 1* 154).

In 1919, Hemingway saw Dr. Guy Conklin in Boyne City, Michigan, for his insomnia. Dr. Conklin told Constance Montgomery forty-one years later that "Ernest was badly shell-shocked" (qtd. in Reynolds, *Young Hemingway*, 69), although Reynolds dismisses the claim, saying that if Conklin thought that Ernest was shell-shocked, it was because Ernest wanted him to think so. Why could he not equally well have made von Kurosky and Villard think he was cheerful? In a telephone conversation with me on 30 September 2011, Dr. Jack Downhill, psychiatrist at the Valley Division Sacramento VA Medical Center, suggested that Hemingway's behavior could also have been a compensatory response for feelings of inadequacy—being wounded not as a soldier, but while delivering chocolate and cigarettes for the Red Cross—as well as a compensatory response driven by his need to seem heroic to Agnes Von Kurowsky. Hemingway's letters to his parents do address such feelings of inadequacy as an ambulance driver, protesting their vital service and the dangers they are exposed to. In a letter dated 18 October 1918, he wrote: "I will stay here just as long as I can hobble and there is a war to hobble to. And the ambulance is no slackers job. we [sic] lost one man killed and one wounded in the last two weeks, And when you are holding down a front line canteen job, you know you have just the same chances as the other men in the trenches and so my conscience doesnt [sic] bother me about staying" (*Letters 1* 147). More pertinent, however, the *DSM-4* states that while "symptoms usually begin within the first 3 months after the trauma, ... there may be a delay of months, or even years" (American Psychiatric Association 426)—that is, after Hemingway had left Italy.

Carl Eby also dismisses PTSD as an illness of Hemingway's, basing his argument on Nagel's, asserting instead that Hemingway's first depressive episode occurred months later, on receiving Agnes's rejection letter, an occasion of loss linked to his wound and threats of castration (61). The *DSM-4* says that PTSD is deemed to have a delayed onset if it first occurs at least six months after the event (American Psychiatric Association 429); Eby dates its first occurrence in

March 1918, nine months after Hemingway's wounding. Milton Cohen rejects PTSD for Krebs in "Soldier's Home" based on Krebs's reading of war histories: "No one suffering from PTSD would look forward 'eagerly' to reading about battles he was in" (163). Interestingly, his argument against Krebs's having PTSD does not diminish the possibility that Hemingway's suffered from it. We know that he read G. M. Trevelyan's history of the British ambulance service in order to write *A Farewell to Arms* (Cecchin 42ff.), and that his library contained numerous volumes, histories, biographies, and fiction about Roman wars, the Revolutionary War, the Civil War, Custer, and both world wars, but other than Trevelyan's ambulance history, which is not listed, of the eighty-six books in Hemingway's library dealing with the First World War, Michael Reynolds cites only three that focus on Italy: *The War in Italy*, number 18 in the serial *Arms and Ammunition* (Sept. 1918); Amedeo Tosti's *L'Italie dans la Guerre Mondiale (1915–1918)* (1933); and Charles Bakewell's *The Story of the American Red Cross in Italy* (1920) (Reynolds, *Hemingway's Reading*), which Cecchin also cites. That is, he read only those accounts of World War I in Italy that he felt necessary to write *A Farewell to Arms*.

The most detailed argument for PTSD in Hemingway's fiction comes from a veteran of Vietnam. Ronald Smith finds Nick Adams, as depicted in "A Way You'll Never Be" and "Big Two-Hearted River," to be suffering from PTSD, basing his conclusion on the *DSM-4*, criteria that include exposure to a traumatic event which threatened death and elicited a response of intense fear, helplessness, or horror, and recurrent and intrusive distressing recollections of the past (American Psychiatric Association 427). Both are quite apparent in "A Way You'll Never Be," and their repetitions there and in *A Farewell to Arms* suggest they recurred to Hemingway as well. As Smith says, seeing PTSD in "A Way You'll Never Be" and "Big Two-Hearted River" "might also shed light on other Hemingway characters and perhaps even Hemingway himself" (R. Smith 45).

How can we possibly separate clinical depression from PTSD, especially since they share major symptoms, without having the live patient before us? In a phone conversation with me on 5 May 2011, Dr. Captane Thomson, former president of California Psychiatric Association, explained that PTSD may not show initially and that the symptoms of PTSD and clinical depression may well overlap. The current diagnostic list for PTSD symptoms include: (a) exposure to a traumatic event and a response involving intense fear, helplessness, or horror; (b) persistent reexperience of the traumatic event; (c) persistent avoidance of stimuli associated with the trauma and numbing of general responsiveness; and (d) persistent symptoms of increased arousal, such as insomnia or irritability.

Krebs shows only numbing of general responsiveness; Nick in "A Way You'll Never Be," all of the symptoms. Hemingway experienced trauma, reexperienced it in his writing, and was an irritable insomniac. If all four symptoms must be present, then Nagel and Eby are right: Hemingway did not have PTSD. What the *DSM-4* also says, however, is "if the symptom response pattern . . . meets criteria for another mental disorder (e.g., . . . Major Depressive Disorder), these diagnoses should be given instead of, or in addition to, Posttraumatic Stress Disorder" (American Psychiatric Association 427).

Hemingway's depression was not severe in the 1920s; I concluded that he had a milder form of bipolar disease, cyclothymia.[5] He had depressed moods and feelings of worthlessness, as the letters above indicate; he had insomnia and thoughts of suicide, as other letters indicate (*SL* 94); and he had weight changes indicative of bipolar disorder. But he also had hypomanic episodes—periods of great energy and great productivity. Before he had published much, he was able to convince Ezra Pound, Gertrude Stein, James Joyce, Ford Madox Ford, and Archibald MacLeish that he was a writer of amazing talent and worth their respect. As Dr. Ronald Fieve writes, "Manic grandiosity, when associated with people like Hemingway, Roosevelt, or Churchill, is grandiosity with a basis in fact. They are the biggest, bravest, most powerful men in the world. For these few a delusion of grandeur coincides with the actual state of things" (59). It is possible that manic upswings could mask "numbing of general responsiveness" and thus hide PTSD. Werner Gottlieb, a clinical social worker who has dealt with veterans with PTSD, told me in a phone conversation on 8 June 2011 that, the *DSM-4* notwithstanding, a numbing of general responsiveness is not always present. We may never know in full Hemingway's early mental condition, although the release of his medical files and the notes of psychiatrist Harold Rome at the Mayo Clinic would surely provide pertinent information.

In class discussions of Hemingway's short stories, particularly "Soldier's Home," "Big Two-Hearted River," "Now I Lay Me," and "A Way You'll Never Be," and the interchapters in *In Our Time*, the subject of PTSD often arises. There is psychological trauma, too, in "Indian Camp," as young Nick watches his father cut open a screaming woman held down by three men, and in "The Battler." Thus I think his stories describe a likely combination of PTSD, caused at least by traumatic brain injury and possibly by moral injury as well, and a depressive disorder within himself, the two illnesses overlapping each other. "Soldier's Home" may be our first PTSD story in American fiction. As in so much else, Hemingway was a pioneer (Was *Green Hills of Africa* the first nonfiction novel?). He did not cure himself through his scriptotherapy, but he created marvelous fiction, and he did so heroically, while struggling with a debilitating inherited disease and wartime injuries.

## Notes

1. Patrick's is recorded by Jeffrey Meyers in his book *Hemingway: A Biography* (422); Gregory's, by Valerie Hemingway in her memoir *Running with the Bulls* (235, 241–42, 264).

2. Cf. Baker, *Life Story* 132.

3. Among the symptoms of PTSD, as described in the *DSM-4*, are a "markedly diminished interest or participation in significant activities" and a "feeling of detachment or estrangement from others" (428).

4. See Peter Hays, "Hemingway's Clinical Depression: A Speculation," *The Hemingway Review* 14.2 (Spring 1995): 50–63.

5. Again, see Hays, "Hemingway's Clinical Depression."

# "Shot . . . crippled and gotten away"

## Animals and War Trauma in Hemingway

Ryan Hediger

War and trauma are inextricably linked: This fact is so obvious that it can be easy to assume we fully understand its implications. Yet recognizing and comprehending trauma are stubbornly difficult tasks. There are good reasons, for instance, why veterans generally do not like to discuss their wartime experiences, especially not with those who have not shared them. And there are good reasons why war experience and trauma tend to resist narrative in general. Hemingway's writing addresses this challenge of representation in many ways, as critics and readers have recognized. Indeed, the meaning and effects of trauma amount to one of the more thoroughly considered and sophisticated elements of Hemingway's oeuvre. Therefore, trauma offers a valuable point of focus in the classroom, one that can help students see the complexity below the seemingly plain surface of much Hemingway writing.

Hemingway often focuses on war's impact at the level of the body, the human animal, demonstrating the entanglement of trauma and animality. Trauma forces us to recognize widely present but often suppressed elements of life, including personal weakness and vulnerability. In experiences of trauma, the human being is stripped down to bare life, exposed dramatically to mortality, and forced to recalibrate him- or herself. Such moments are often profoundly disorienting, and such disorientation is rarely temporary. Instead, it often permanently marks—physically and psychologically—those who undergo it. Exercised on the body, trauma thus permeates even our sense of what is "normal," of what is ostensibly outside of trauma. While many of these effects are harmful, enduring trauma can also be deeply instructive, producing profound knowledge and understanding, as in Hemingway's case. For students, at least to some extent, the same can be true. Carefully discussing war trauma not only enriches students' sense of Hemingway's work, it offers an entrée into discussing responses to trauma of many other kinds.

In writing about trauma, Hemingway consistently underscores our only partial control of our physical selves. While this fact applies to ordinary life—essential processes like breathing, digestion, and so on are basically beyond our conscious control—trauma exposes this strange reality of embodiment more dramatically. For instance, many injuries require assistance from others to heal, and lost limbs, psychic wounds, and the like reiterate the gap between the psychic and the physical self.[1] That gap leads, say, to phantom limb syndrome, or to events such as flashbacks, when a person physically inhabits benign circumstances while the psychic self replays intense traumatic experiences. These instances demonstrate how the common, everyday sense of a unified self obscures a more complex reality, a fragmented, even piecemeal selfhood possessed by everyone. Trauma simply brings that reality more clearly to the fore.

This chapter first explores cases of this disassembled selfhood in *A Farewell to Arms* and the short story "Get a Seeing-Eyed Dog," then relates such selfhood to Hemingway's thinking about animals and animality (the condition of being animal), especially in *For Whom the Bell Tolls*. In war, the conventional human/animal difference can erode, reinforcing the animal studies literature that shows the difference as inherently problematic.[2] These blurred human/animal boundaries point to the primary claim of this chapter: Partly because Hemingway had so much interest in and information about animals, he routinely used them to understand the meaning of injury or trauma, and more profoundly, the meaning of death. Animals, we will see, are essential to Hemingway's traumatic experience and vocabulary. Further, despite common fears that acknowledging human/animal kinship means sliding into immorality, I argue that Hemingway preserves a measure of moral human agency. Highlighting these ideas in the classroom can offer a compelling route into complex issues for students, who, once prompted, often readily grasp the metaphorics of animals. Further, students can come to recognize better how animals function not just as interpretive ciphers for humans, but as crucial flesh-and-blood companions.

Disability, Passivity, and War

Passivity and weakness have often been accented in considerations of twentieth-century wars. In his study *Soldiers Once and Still*, Alex Vernon notes, "One historical consensus about World War I is the unprecedented degree to which its soldiers were rendered passive by the new technology of machine guns, indirect fire artillery, and mustard gas" (74). Yet soldiers worked hard, then as now, to claim some measure of agency, some control over their wartime selves. In *A Farewell to Arms*, Hemingway's story of Lieutenant Frederic Henry's military service turns on his renewed assertion of a selfhood and agency outside of the military, which he deserts when he is threatened with an arbitrary assassination at the hands of fellow soldiers in the Italian army. The book nonetheless displays deep awareness that Henry's agency is always limited, often profoundly so. Consider the full shape of the plot: It begins with a brief spark of romance interrupted by a war that gets Henry hospitalized, where, in a much-reduced condition, his romance with Catherine genuinely blooms. Vernon underscores that Henry "falls in love with her in Book II only after his wounding, after finding himself in her care—after, that is, he finds himself in a passive position" (*Soldiers Once* 72). Yet Henry must return again to the fighting, and he finally deserts, as noted above, when it is clearly a situation of life and death. His desertion, then, at least does not begin as profoundly principled so much as immediately necessary. He is *forced* to retake control of his life.

Hemingway's much-quoted criticisms of war in *A Farwell to Arms* can seem to reinforce the power of an individual's perspective and agency: The great writer can stand outside of conflict and analyze it. But, read in context, these statements present insights that come to the character Henry in complex scenarios, which include a measure of passivity, reflection, and reaction, as distinct from action. Consider the following particularly famous passage:

> I was always embarrassed by the words sacred, glorious, and sacrifice and the expression in vain. We had heard them, sometimes standing in the rain almost out of earshot, so that only the shouted words came through, and had read them, on proclamations that were slapped up by billposters over other proclamations, now for a long time, and I had seen nothing sacred, and the things that were glorious had no glory and the sacrifices were like the stockyards at Chicago if nothing was done with the meat except to bury it. (*FTA* 184–85)

The soldiers' passivity is signaled, first, by the function of the passage in the immediate scene: The sentence preceding the quoted material reads, "I did not say anything," so Henry merely thinks the quoted words. They appear in the midst of a conversation with Gino in which the latter uncritically, unselfconsciously (indeed, arguably, intellectually passively) pronounces many of the terms Henry finds embarrassing. It is not easy to stand outside the ideology of war, but this text does not make Henry into a soapbox critic of such propaganda. Instead, the novel carves out Henry's space for *silent* reflection, embarrassment, an internalized response to the euphemistic clichés of war. In the conversation, partly because of his complex understanding of the patriotic Gino, Henry is wary of challenging that language directly. Further, the conversation occurs after Henry's injury, adding gravity to his privately considered thoughts and underscoring the soldiers' exposure to injury. Seen in this light, the passage shows how exerting a selfhood that matters can require stepping outside of sometimes programmatic roles, such as that of the soldier, into the more independent role of writer. It further indicates that all social roles (soldier, peace activist; student, teacher; and so on) involve some measure of passivity, some embrace of and surrender to norms that originate outside the self.

Second, consider the function of context *in* the passage: Its satire works by requiring that the reader recall the actual scenarios of war—"standing in the rain almost out of earshot"—and of wartime propaganda—"billposters over other proclamations." Both situations undermine the power of the speech act, exposing the flimsiness of the ostensibly potent declarations. The soldiers, given the trying circumstances of war, can hardly even hear these claims, and they are jaded from having been subjected to many others like them before on the much-used billboards. Hemingway's criticism undermines the pretentions of human language and human agency more broadly. That point is emphasized by the final comparison of soldiers to meat animals being slaughtered and then wasted. The soldiers' fate is worse than that of butchered food animals.

Such circumstances leave Henry no option but desertion. After evading execution, Henry, making his escape by hiding on a train, replays the recent events in his mind, reiterating his only-partial ownership of himself. "Lying on the floor of the flat-car," in a position that reiterates his vulnerable condition, he considers that his new knee "had been very satisfactory. Valentini had done a fine job. I had done half the retreat on foot and swum part of the Tagliamento with his knee. It was his knee all right. The other knee was mine. Doctors did things to you and then it was not your body any more. The head was mine, and the inside of the belly. It was very hungry in there. I could feel it turn over on itself. The head was mine, but not to use, not to think with, only to remember and not too much remember" (*FTA* 231). Even at the level of the body, Henry can claim only some control. His surgically repaired knee is, he thinks, the doctor's, and though Henry tries to reclaim his basic self in his mind and stomach, appetite and the activities of the stomach are largely beyond a person's control. Moreover, his very thoughts—indeed, more profoundly, his thought *processes*—are injured, damaged. He must resist the very process of remembering.

Henry's recognition that he does not own his whole body or even his mind is symptomatic or synecdochic of war in general. War estranges us from our bodies and from familiar places. As Fredric Jameson argues in "War and Representation," war is always liable to produce "an utter transmogrification of the familiar into the alien, the *heimlich* into the *unheimlich,* in which the home village—the known world, the real, and the everyday—is transformed into a place of unimaginable horror" (1538). That is, the homely (*heimlich*) becomes the unhomely; war creates homesickness even for those at home. These transformations attend not only to the horrors of the battles themselves, but to wars' results. When territory is "won," a strange new regime may make one's own home place foreign, even monstrous.

Hemingway reveals the damage to Henry's mental self not only through explicit statements, but formally and stylistically. Henry's mind constantly revisits past events in the book, demonstrating a point made by Cathy Caruth while introducing the book *Trauma:* The intensity and inscrutability of traumatic experiences show more general human limits, especially our inability to understand fundamental truths. Does anyone really understand death, for instance? Traumatic memories exceed a person's comprehension and control, as demonstrated by many Hemingway characters in many texts. In the passage about Henry's knee quoted above, Henry reveals awareness of these deep traumas in a backward way, by insisting he *does* own part of himself. Here is Hemingway's iceberg effect, in which the injuries that put self-ownership in doubt loom behind these simple sentences declaring self-ownership. At this moment, as in the larger plot of the book, Henry, per necessity, leaves the complexities of war and tries to return to the basics of life—eating, resting, enjoying quiet and loving companionship. This reduction of selfhood more nearly to the animal body helps to save Henry's sanity. Indeed, ironically, orienting himself this way helps to *rehumanize* him after the brutality of war. But we know that he cannot fully dispense with the past; even his knee is not his own, and his memories must be warded off.

Animals and Recovery

How does one go on after experiencing such selfhood-shattering events? It is exactly those difficulties that are the subject of Hemingway's posttraumatic story "Get a Seeing-Eyed Dog," in which a couple copes with a man's grave injuries, which have blinded him and left holes in his memory. The story details some of the couple's conversation, hinting at pieces of what the man, Philip, has forgotten because of the injury, but it focuses mostly on the difficulties the two face in their new lives, given Philip's condition. The woman in the story, who remains unnamed, attends to Philip carefully and lovingly, but he worries that her doing so will "destroy her life and ruin her." He considers that she was not built to be "good every day and dull good," to surrender so much of life's pleasure in the task of coping with his disability. Philip uses the erroneous phrase of the title to express these concerns, saying to her, "'I don't want you just to be a seeing-eyed dog.'" She corrects him, saying, "'it's seeing-eye not seeing-eyed,'" but the solecism aptly titles a story about human weakness and frailty, as Hemingway recognized in using it (*CSS* 490). The title underscores the story's larger argument about human weakness.[3]

The story evokes not only the man's particular disabilities of blindness and spotty memory, but human frailty more generally, including the difficulties of adjusting to a different form of life for both characters. This is an ordinary problem in questions of trauma, and the characters' difficulties amount to a kind of *cultural* disability. The characters attempt to work out new ways of dealing with daily life, as a person does following other forms of injury, life change, or cultural dislocation. For Philip, such challenges include his sensory experiences in the world. Near the end of the story, for instance, considering his loss of sight, Philip "tried not to feel her head and her lovely face the way a blind man feels," but he recognizes in the same sentence that "there was no other way that he could touch her face except that way" (*CSS* 490). This altered tactile sensing changes him and changes what her beauty *means*. Her attractive appearance has lost a major witness, a confirmation, because of her partner's blindness. Working to counter his disability in this moment, as I see it, Philip switches to speech, avoiding touch. He says, "'We'll go down now and have lunch in our old fine place by the fire and I'll tell you what a wonderful kitten you are and what lucky kittens we are.'" The words can still communicate his feelings to her in a familiar way, even if his gazing upon her cannot. To this suggestion, she allows, "'We really are'"—lucky kittens (*CSS* 491). Elsewhere in the story, Hemingway shows the man to rely on hearing, on scent, and on other senses in place of his lost vision. He seems, perhaps, to be adjusting well.

But the story ends with Philip's internal monologue, which tells another account, recognizing that he is "not doing too well at this." He doubly insists to himself that he "must get her away and get her away as soon as I can without hurting her" (*CSS* 491). From this perspective, the story's title takes additional resonance, functioning as a way of the man telling himself off, a kind of swearing to himself—as though the title has him saying to himself, *get yourself a seeing-eyed dog*. Yet, the woman insists that she will stay with him and help him. When he offers to sleep wrapped up with a pillow instead of her, she refuses. But it is clear to Philip that she must be sent away to enjoy herself. And so the title—"Get a Seeing-Eyed Dog"—is Philip telling himself to get a replacement for her, for her own good, and therefore, ultimately, for his own good in terms of the relationship. He must care for her in order to care for them both. As in *A Farewell to Arms*, Philip's insight appears in a silent, internal discourse in the story, a private thinking that runs contrary to his explicit statements.

This story's solution, in which an animal is intended to replace—meagerly—the pleasures of human love and companionship after a loss or trauma of some kind, appears in many Hemingway texts (see, for instance, "A Canary for One," "Cat in the Rain," and the passages about Boise the cat in *Islands in the Stream*).[4] In "Get a Seeing-Eyed Dog," trauma has intervened in the couple's life and alienated them from their familiar habits and modes of understanding, and even from their familiar values. For the man, caring means pushing his wife away, the opposite of what he or we would ordinarily expect. However, we should note that the expression of idealized companionship earlier in the story also relies on an animal register, on animal terminology, that of cats. As noted above, Philip's affirmative account of their relationship names them as "lucky kittens." This more positive use of animal terminology—especially with cats—runs throughout Hemingway's work as well.[5]

The complexities of the story and its title phrase, "Get a Seeing-Eyed Dog," mount when we recognize the importance of substitutions of various kinds. There is the concern about a pillow standing in for a lover; the idea of a dog replacing a human caregiver; and the classic form of human substitution, writing, which stands in for (or supplements) direct sensory experience. Philip fears he cannot physically write since he is blind. Thus, he develops plans to speak his stories into a "fine tape recorder," and then the woman will transcribe his speech (*CSS* 489), a further substitution. This approach will permit him to go on writing. It appears to be a success, and the woman acknowledges it as such. When he tells her of it, she exclaims, "'Oh, Philip—'" in admiration of his courage, which he modestly undercuts by cursing, "'Shit . . . The dark is just the dark'" (489). His disability is merely a practical problem. They will overcome it with this system of recording and transcribing.

But beneath the surface optimism lies a layer of deep skepticism, and it runs through the entire story. The dark is indeed dark. We have noted how Philip's brave exterior masks his serious private concerns about his wife and about himself. Similarly, we can infer some doubt about writing, more broadly as an undertaking. Writing about powerful and beautiful experiences can be a kind of pillow in place of an actual lover. Writing fills the place of direct experience, and resembles direct experience, but it cannot replace the real thing. Similarly, writing about trauma is a method of approaching it, understanding it better, but the actual traumatic events still commonly exceed controlled recollection and comprehension. Much recent war literature reiterates this point. Examples include Tim O'Brien's soldiers, in the title story of *The Things They Carried*, as they stutteringly repeat the phrase "Boom, down," trying to understand the sudden death of their comrade Ted Lavender; and Kurt Vonnegut's insistence on the difficulty of even writing his World War II novel *Slaughterhouse-Five*, a principle he built into the structure of the book, with its sudden and jerky movement through time and plot, as though the author himself cannot control the events. The list can be extended at some length.

One might understand such an account of writing as denigration, but it is more fitting to Hemingway's body of work to see it as realism, as recognition of human imperfection, mortality, and impermanence. We write, Hemingway continued to write, because every experience is unique and fleeting, and writing helps us to understand those experiences and thus more fully possess them. Writing also permits us to translate those experiences to others. Yet this work of getting the experiences down correctly requires the writer to acknowledge the gap between writing and reality. To put this point more broadly: We use substitutions like writing or animals because we need them to make it through, to make sense of events and to better communicate, as we are imperfect mortal beings. The obsessive regard for the act of writing thematized in much of Hemingway's work reveals this flimsiness in textuality; writing is an ability, but writing, especially nervous obsession with writing, also signals weakness and mortality. At the writer's back, he always hears "Time's wingèd chariot hurrying near," to cite the Andrew Marvell line Hemingway sometimes quoted.

### Living and Dying by the Horse

The powerful conclusion of *For Whom the Bell Tolls* relies on many characteristic Hemingway forms of understanding connecting war, trauma, animals, and animality. For one thing, the book's plot, especially its conclusion, assumes the fact of human dependence on horses in partnerships that stretch well back into human history and the history of war. Indeed, to talk about war at all has almost always meant talking about horses too.[6] It is therefore appropriate that Jordan and his band of antifascists make their escape at the close of the book on horseback. In that final scene, having thundered across the road on the stolen gray horse as the tank fires on his group, Jordan directs the horse up the slope to join the others. He says,

> "*Arre caballo!* Go on, horse!" and felt his big horse's chest surging with the steepening of the slope and saw the gray neck stretching and the gray ears ahead and he reached and patted the wet gray neck, and he looked back at the bridge and saw the bright flash from the heavy, squat, mud-colored tank there on the road and then he did not hear any whish but only a banging acrid smelling clang like a boiler being ripped apart and he was under the gray horse and the gray horse was kicking and he was trying to pull out from under the weight. (*FWBT* 460–61)

Jordan's escape lives and dies by the horse. The narrative testifies to this fact in part by making Jordan's final uninjured action a sympathetic patting of the animal in recognition of how hard the horse was running and how much Jordan depended upon him. When the shell hits, Jordan must be left behind because of his badly broken left leg and the group's extreme desperation.

Jordan is reduced then to a dying body, to his basic animal self. The horse is similarly exposed to death at this moment, which Jordan first realizes when "he heard the sound the horse was making" (*FWBT* 461). Agustín soon shoots the horse, presumably to end its misery, and offers the same to Jordan, asking, "'Do you want me to shoot thee, *Inglés?*'" (465–66). The horse and Jordan face the same plight, which Pablo's responses also reiterate. First Pablo sympathizes with Jordan facing his death, despite their troublesome relationship, asking Jordan of his leg, "'Does it hurt much?'" A moment later, befitting his deep affection for horses, Pablo is "looking at the gray horse on the slope with true regret on his face" (462). This presentation of the human being as a suffering mortal, a dying animal, in the face of war and trauma is one of the novel's central arguments, and Pablo looks upon the scene as a reader might, without surprise but with fellow-feeling for horse and human alike. Pablo's pity is further underscored when he does as Jordan asks and helps to extricate Maria from Jordan's *querencia*, his place of defense against death.

The likeness between humans and animals in death is a recurring motif in Hemingway's writing. He makes this point directly, with withering satire, in "A Natural History of the Dead," his piece of mock nature writing that upends Mungo Park's pious account of recovering from a grave situation in the African desert. Park, seeing a small flower, believes its creator must also have benign intentions for Park himself. Hemingway finds no such reassurance in the nature of war:

"One wonders what that persevering traveler, Mungo Park, would have seen on a battlefield in hot weather to restore his confidence." Although, Hemingway continues, there "were always poppies" and other pretty natural realities to see, there were also broken houses, holes blown into the earth from shelling, and many dead bodies. Hemingway observes of these last: "The first thing that you found about the dead was that, hit badly enough, they died like animals." The account then elaborates on the horrors of the dead and the dying, in stark contrast to Park's apparently naïve optimism (*CSS* 338).

There are many other similar examples in Hemingway of human/animal likeness in death: Francis Macomber is shot like an animal and dies alongside a buffalo; in *The Old Man and the Sea,* Santiago and the great marlin he catches suffer in parallel fashion, leading first to the fish's death and, implicitly, to Santiago's; and the hunted animals on Hemingway's African safaris become object lessons in death, a point developed further below. This leveling of humans and other animals is further reinforced by the final scene of *For Whom the Bell Tolls.* Jordan is lying on the ground. After Maria and the rest of the party have left, his suffering grows as he waits for their pursuers, working hard to remain conscious. He contemplates again and again whether he should "do that business that my father did" (*FWBT* 469)—that is, kill himself. He recognizes his impending death in any case, and he considers, for instance, that "if I pass out or anything like that I am no good at all and if they bring me to they will ask me a lot of questions and do things and all and that is no good" (469–70). In other words, if he passes out and is found, he is likely to be tortured and may risk revealing information that would hurt his comrades-at-arms. This scene turns around Jordan's insistence upon doing whatever he can to continue to help his cause while trying to cope with and mitigate his suffering. This moment also replays similar occasions in much Hemingway writing and life: "The Snows of Kilimanjaro," the proposed suicide ending to *The Garden of Eden,* and, of course, Hemingway's own demise. These moments near death reprise the values of life.

To survive, Jordan exhausts a number of trauma-coping mechanisms familiar from other Hemingway texts. He forces himself to imagine the rest of the group safely escaping: "Think about them being away, he said. Think about them going through the timber." But this distraction technique only works so long, and he considers, "*That's just as far as I can think about them.*" Jordan is also unable to help himself endure by recalling the distant past. He tells himself, "Think about Montana. *I can't.* Think about Madrid. *I can't.*" His ability to distract himself radically diminishes and the resources of mind and memory serve less and less well. Jordan's selfhood reduces to the thinnest shred of itself. It is only the thought that he can do something particular to help that keeps him going: "*And if you wait and hold them up even a little while or just get the officer that may make all the difference. One thing well done can make—*" (*FWBT* 470; emphases in original).

With this thought, Jordan convinces himself that hanging on is worthwhile, that it is not absurd. Willpower has the potential to matter, even though its importance is greatly reduced. As the pursuers arrive and Jordan waits for his moment to get off a good shot, Hemingway writes, "He was completely integrated now and he took a good long look at everything" (*FWBT* 471). At this point, the final step of the plot has been taken. Jordan's position in the much larger war effort is fixed and final, and in the end his importance is minimal. At first, this novel, like most narratives, lends individual lives meaning by staging its story at the personal level. It takes us inside singular characters, showing their thoughts and desires, their individual qualities, and so on. Yet this ending undercuts that system of meaning, backing out from individual lives like a camera reversing its tight focus, widening its view to show the larger landscape, the wider reality. These individuals appear among millions in a much, much larger effort. Thus, being "completely integrated" here means almost exactly the opposite of what Mungo Park felt when he thought himself on the edge of death, only to find hope in a flower. Jordan, instead, recognizes his *insignificance.*

His final contribution is to kill Lieutenant Berrendo, an event just beyond the close of the novel and the very thing he hoped would happen. But Jordan's luck presents one more ironic plot twist. Dying, he will have achieved another small act (small in the larger scheme of the war) that has the potential to be helpful. But staging this last act out of sight, after the text ends, reinforces Hemingway's larger point about the limitations of a singular person's importance in war. Jordan's last act is very much on par with the book's larger plot to blow a bridge, itself a small act with only the *potential* to be helpful, a potential that goes unfulfilled. Not only does the bridge blowing fail to achieve much, the larger effort against the fascists in Spain will fail.

Readers have recognized this futility or near-futility in the book's plot, as Michael K. Solow reports. Solow quotes Rovit and Brenner, who suggest of the book's close that Robert Jordan's minor triumph of courage is "'an absurdly meaningless event within the desperate flow of a losing war'" (Solow 104). This futility is signaled in a number of other ways, but one of clearest is the fact that Robert Jordan begins and ends the book in the same physical position: prostrate on his stomach on the ground, in the pine needles. This position indicates his serious involvement in the conflict at the level of the personal, the bodily, *and* it evokes his small, vulnerable mortality. Despite his intelligence, despite his serious attention to the complexities and ironies of war, despite his dislike of killing coupled with his sense of its necessity—despite, in short, all the elements that make Jordan a compelling character and this novel a compelling treatment of war, Jordan can be killed relatively easily, as we all can. All the sophistication and care in the world do not change that basic fact: the thin thread of mortal vulnerability.

Solow demonstrates that this view of war, so well realized and presented in *For Whom the Bell Tolls*, was hard won for Hemingway. For Solow, Hemingway's vigorous support of the Republican effort in the Spanish Civil War was at first uncharacteristically ideological and absolute. Solow suggests that Hemingway had bowed, to some extent, to pressure from critics on the left and had to work his way back into his more complex stance toward war by way of "his belief in and practice of aesthetic detachment" (112). Joining other critics, Solow views *For Whom the Bell Tolls* as successful in large part because of its sophisticated treatment of the nature of war, its insistent presentation of flaws among participants on both sides of the conflict, and, significantly, its perspective: Hemingway uses "omniscient narration for the first time in a major war novel." That is, Solow continues, "Hemingway's first-person presentations in his post–World War I novels, with their focus on individuality, have been displaced here by a collective voice" (112).

So *A Farewell to Arms* pulls the individual apart at the level of the body, while *For Whom the Bell Tolls* reduces the value of individual actions in modern conflict with a new complexity. But, crucially, the individual is still important to Hemingway. Much of his life philosophy, and the primary thrust of Robert Jordan's and Hemingway's own antifascism, hinges on valuing the individual's ability to make decisions for her- or himself, a kind of limited independence. Hemingway rejected fantasy-laden notions of the overwhelmingly powerful individual soldier, but he still believed honorable people sometimes must engage in war. Robert Jordan's character dramatizes this tension: he feels skepticism toward the war and his role in it, recognizing his relative insignificance, but he persistently recommits himself to his role in the war, right up to the end of his life.

### Africa, Animals, and Death

Hemingway's thinking about the individual's place in war was deepened by his persistent inquiry into matters of life and death *outside* of war, and even outside of humanity. His discoveries in those inquiries fed his understanding as he deployed it in novels like *For Whom the Bell Tolls*. James Plath, in his compelling essay "Barking at Death," argues that "Hemingway's first trip to Africa amplified a sense of his fragility and mortality in ways that not even the famous wounding in Italy had done" (301). Plath cites a number of reasons that Africa affected Hemingway so seriously: Hemingway's serious and painful case of amoebic dysentery, which led to his "being airlifted to Nairobi for eight days of hospital treatment"; several other dangerous events while hunting on the safari; and some moments of personal embarrassment (301). These experiences affected Hemingway's writing in minor ways, as well as in at least one major way, which Plath recognizes and names: "after Africa every main male character in every novel published during Hemingway's lifetime will die," including, of course, Robert Jordan (305). Hemingway's thinking about death was not isolated into silos; war trauma and other life traumas all contributed to his thinking about mortality in general.

Despite these difficulties, Hemingway enjoyed Africa immensely. Plath argues that a central reason why was because, especially on his second visit, "Africa helped him process his thoughts on such a difficult and complex subject" as death. Discussing Hemingway's writing about the second safari in *Under Kilimanjaro*, Plath notes, "Time and again an observation of an animal's death leads to a meditation on death, which in turn leads to an appreciation of life" (302). In sum, "both safaris then, gave him direct exposure to death, heightened by his feeling for life, and were followed by periods of fluent writing" (303).[7] The dramas of hunting, shooting, and watching animals die were clearly part of this whole process. Indeed, writing about the first safari in *Green Hills of Africa*, Hemingway justifies his harming and killing animals because, he says, "at least I knew what I was doing. I did nothing that had not been done to me. I had been shot and I had been crippled and gotten away. I expected, always, to be killed by one thing or another and I, truly, did not mind that any more" (148). While in his earlier years Hemingway understood our kinship with animals as rendering him and them equally killable, later in his life that kinship provoked in him less brutality and more sympathy; he came to a greater appreciation of, even deference for, the vulnerability we share with animals.[8]

Hemingway's insights into death accumulate sophistication and depth after each of his close passes with it. The major early pass, in Italy during World War I, profoundly marked his sensibility in ways that reverberated throughout his life and work. As critics have long recognized, he pursued many later experiences partly to make sense of this major early war trauma. But while Hemingway deeply sensed the power of trauma, and though he keenly understood the limits of the individual human, he was not absolutely passive in the face of these realities. He worked out a place in his life for meaningful activity. Death and trauma are two of the great themes of his work, as they are of human life in general, and because Hemingway studied them rigorously, with ferocious honesty, he rendered his difficult experiences in war and in life into great art and profound knowledge. Students reading his work can begin to grasp the depth of these ideas by addressing, at first, this simple question: How is death presented in this story?

## Notes

1. See Elizabeth Grosz, *Volatile Bodies: Toward a Corporeal Feminism* (Bloomington: Indiana UP, 1994), for a full account of the divide between the bodily and the psychic selves. Disability scholars like Rosemarie Garland Thomson (43 and passim) likewise show that "normal" people, those who are not ostensibly disabled, in fact experience many of the same limitations as those who are designated disabled.

2. See Wolfe (55 and passim) for one of many strong criticisms of the so-called human–animal difference. In short, these critiques remind us, first, that humans are animals, and, second, that there are many other animals who vary quite widely, so there is no single "human–animal" difference. Rather, there are *differences*. This distinction matters immensely in light of the history of designating a single, key human–animal difference (tellingly, that difference has been *variously* designated, as language ability, or tool use, or self-consciousness, among others).

3. Hemingway's title "Get a Seeing-Eyed Dog" evokes the practical solution of a canine companion for the blind. In the contemporary context, this animal solution has additional resonances: pairing dogs with veterans who have post-traumatic stress disorder is an increasingly common palliative approach.

4. For an example of Boise's depiction, see Hemingway, *IIS* 208.

5. For more on this issue, see Hediger 217–26.

6. According to David W. Anthony, humans began riding horses as early as 5000 BC, and this activity may have itself quickly led to new forms of dispute and fighting (222). But in Anthony's account, and also according to military historian John Keegan, the horse clearly assumed greater significance with the advent of chariot warfare, which lasted from 1700 to 800 BC (Anthony 222; Keegan 136). Following that, beginning around 800 BC, the earliest cavalries arose, archers mounted on horseback, and cavalries continued to profoundly affect the history of war, and history more broadly, for several thousand years. As Louis A. Dimarco writes, the "war horse and rider was a viable military weapons system for more than 3,000 years, far longer than any other military system" (ix). Horses remained valuable, even crucial, in conflicts through the World War II, including the Spanish Civil War.

7. Similarly, Vernon recognizes "the burst of writing that occurred upon his return from World War II" (*Soldiers Once* 73). Much of Hemingway's writing is directly motivated by trauma.

8. In "Animals," I address Hemingway's growing sympathy for animals late in life.

# The Poetics of Hemingway's *Death in the Afternoon*

Restaging the Experience of Total War

Christopher Barker

Introduction

When things become "particularly routine," one of the sitting associate justices of the Supreme Court of the United States retires to his basement to watch *Saving Private Ryan* (Liptak). As Mark Harris shows in *Five Came Back: A Story of Hollywood and the Second World War,* the iconic and deeply troubling scenes of U.S. troops landing on Omaha Beach are virtually shot-by-shot re-creations of actual film footage of that battle (476). Clarence Thomas's decision to review this re-creation of scenes of suffering and heroism speaks to art's potential, in the face of existential crises, to exert a moralizing force—or a *demoralizing* force: the ancient historian Herodotus noted that even the free-speaking ancient Athenians fined a poet, Phrynicus, for restaging the capture of one of their colonies.

The ambiguity of art as a way of exposing readers and viewers to death and dying speaks to a related set of very topical problems. Less than 1 percent of the United States' citizens learn about war firsthand, and only a third of the millennial generation has the opportunity to learn about war from immediate family members who have served in the military.[1] For veterans, the problem is inverted: the difficulty of dealing with the mundane nature of civil society after returning from war may result in a sense of dislocation, depression, and even suicide (Kemp).

A growing body of literature deals directly with the emotional survival of those who fought in the Great War. Such works sometimes assume that modern, total war is something new and unprecedented, but despite arguments to the contrary, in both scale and duration it is not. In the Roman battle of Cannae, fifty thousand Roman soldiers were killed in one day, an outcome equivalent to the worst single-day losses during World War I. A "battle of annihilation," argued German strategist Alfred Graf von Schlieffen (1833-1913), "can be carried out today according to the same plan devised by Hannibal in long forgotten times" (187-88). Total war is not a new phenomenon, and more importantly, for the average person, combatant or noncombatant, all war wherein there is a risk of death is a "total" war. For this reason, the need to rethink *all* wartime experience endures unchanged. As Adam Smith understood long ago, "Death, as we say, is the king of terrors; and the man who has conquered the fear of death, is not likely to lose his presence of mind at the approach of any other natural evil. In war, men become familiar with death, and are thereby necessarily cured of that superstitious horror with which it is viewed by the weak and inexperienced" (281).

Hemingway's writings can help us to understand this massively important human experience, and *Death in the Afternoon* has a central place in carrying out this task. However, even some sympathetic Hemingway scholars do not take the book seriously, while experts on the bullfight like John McCormick (xii, 240, 257) and amateur critics like A. L. Kennedy (passim) take Hemingway to task for romanticizing the bullfight. Others charge that Hemingway does not truly or authentically know the culture, language, and rituals that he lionizes (Herlihy-Mera 84–100). While the recent essays collected in Miriam Mandel's *A Companion to Hemingway's* Death in the Afternoon do much to dispel the loosest among these criticisms, there is a factual basis to criticism of the bullfight's cruelty; on first, and perhaps second, glance, it *is* a cruel display, in which as many as five horses can be killed in an afternoon—for mere sport, as Hemingway has a café waiter remark in *The Sun Also Rises* (201).[2] My aim in this essay is to reinstate *Death in the Afternoon* as a central text for retraining the eye to see and understand violent death, and to explain why Hemingway views the bullfight as an educative ritual. More broadly, I seek to show how self-understanding can be achieved by restaging our experiences so as to create critical distance and space for reflection.[3]

## Total War: Ernst Jünger

One way to introduce students to the phenomenon to be analyzed—violent death in "modern" war—is to immerse them in accounts of it.[4] Many autobiographies emphasize disillusion with war (e.g., Robert Graves's *Goodbye to All That*) or astonishment at the absurdities of war (e.g., George Orwell's *Homage to Catalonia*). Hemingway's war novels, which arguably draw substantially on his own experience, display a combination of astonishment, cynicism, and manliness regarding war. Few authors blatantly celebrate war. Still, it is the celebratory texts that are the best tests of Freud's observation that the Great War invited the "protest of the individual against the part he was expected to play in the army" (Freud). For the war enthusiast, the individual ought not protest the need to fight wars, because fighting completes him as an individual.

Ernst Jünger's autobiographical writings form the perfect introduction to trench warfare, presented without therapy. Unlike Hemingway, Jünger was a highly decorated officer who fought in the trenches in World War I, experiences for which he received the highest German medal for valor (the Pour le Mérite). He was also a rare proponent of total mobilization and of the use of modern technology in the waging of total war. The titular "storm of steel" of his best-known work is the unrelenting, unforgiving artillery barrage that claims the lives of "storm troops," old or young, skilled or unskilled (Jünger, *Storm of Steel* 61, 127, 168, 215, 222, 229, 280). Surprisingly, Jünger celebrates these storms both as the crucible of the human spirit and as the best educational route toward the development of full, manly maturity.

After students read a representative sample of Jünger's description of trench warfare, they should be challenged to answer this question: Is Jünger correct in arguing that human greatness and true nobility are best developed through immersion in total war? On the one hand, namely in his emphasis on seeing and on experiencing death up close and for the first time, Jünger shares with Hemingway a common educative purpose. On the other hand, Jünger argues that the immersion in total war is necessary and sufficient to develop the full human character, whereas Hemingway insists that a mediated or indirect experience of violent death is not only the best substitute for the experience of "action," but perhaps even superior to war experience. In Hemingway's view, the study of violent death is better performed at a certain distance from the action—that is, at a certain remove from harm.

Arguably, Jünger's celebration of total war conceals a key contradiction that helps us to understand Hemingway's fictional and nonfictional writings on war. Elucidation of this contradiction is found in his trench memoir, *Copse 125*, in which Jünger not only celebrates the world-sized storms of steel but also praises the aristocratic notion of honor and the "authenticity paradigm" (Wyschogrod 3–6), which is premised on the idea that the good life is capped by dying a good death. In *Copse 125*, Jünger's account of his life in the trenches of 1917, the career infantryman argues that the dogfight between fighter pilots, where two men meet face to face, knowing that only one will survive, is the true theater of greatness. "*Only* in the realm of air is the duel still possible today," Jünger writes, "and with it the chivalry that there below *had to die out* from the days of great armies, since it is always only the quality of the few." He rounds out the thought by arguing that "every time a flying-man falls as a burning brand to earth, a nobler issue is answered than that of being or not being" (*Copse 125* 91; emphases added).

In *Storm of Steel,* Jünger finds the same quality embodied in the storm troop commander, "the aristocrat of the trench" (Jünger, *Storm of Steel* 216), but his praise begs the question of whether an outright duel would not be a more efficacious way of testing a man's courage, or courage and skill combined.[5] As Richard Wolin summarizes the key contradiction, "The war of 1914–1918 had proved that in the modern age warfare was more dependent on the amassing of technological capacities rather than acts of individual heroism, and this realization left a deep imprint on all of Jünger's writing in the form of a profound *amor fati*" (119; emphasis in original). If this brief synopsis of Jünger's celebration of total war is accurate, it raises questions concerning the virtue of honor and its relation to the risk of violent death, which provoke his reader to address some of the most important moral and philosophical questions that we can ask. For Jünger, the answer lies in moving beyond celebrating individual greatness toward a "magical" symbiosis of free, noble individuals and materiel warfare (Barnouw 203, 210). But Jünger fails to persuade us when he argues that humans are simultaneously elevated in the crucible of combat and reduced to "a bit of nature, subjected to its inscrutable decrees and used as a thing of blood and sinew, tooth and claw" (*Storm of Steel* 56). Still, Jünger's memoirs usefully challenge students to face perhaps *the* central question raised by war: stripping aside ideology and mythology, how can one have an authentic death in war?

The Poetics of War Writing

Hemingway, like Jünger, learned about death while at war. After being wounded in World War I while serving as a volunteer ambulance driver, Hemingway bounced around Michigan, France, and Spain, becoming interested in the bullfight during his first trip to San Fermin in 1923. He ultimately published *The Sun Also Rises* in 1926, about a third of which concerns the fiesta in Pamplona, and *Death in the Afternoon* in 1932. Reflecting much later on his wartime shrapnel wound, in a letter to Thomas Welsh dated 19 June 1945, Hemingway writes that he "felt great fear [of death]" and "was really scared after wounded and very devout at the end" (SL 592). He confirms this impression in another letter, written to Ivan Kashkin on 23 March 1939: "In the war in Italy when I was a boy I had much fear" (480).[6] In his introduction to *Men at War*, a collection of war stories Hemingway edited in support of the Allied war effort in World War II, Hemingway reported that during World War I he lost the "great illusion of immortality" that is characteristic of youth (xiii–xiv). This insight that is repeated and underlined in his later fictional writings, in which manhood is achieved through conquering the fear of death rather than, say, through the loss of virginity.[7]

*Death in the Afternoon* is a book about this wartime experience of death, even though the war is mentioned only a dozen times. About this, at least, both Hemingway and Jünger agree: seeing involves training the eye to make sense of an experience by gathering facts under the umbrella of an interpretation of the world. For Hemingway, the new way of seeing the "real thing, the sequence of motion and fact which made the emotion" requires not just seeing a bullfight under the correct conditions (a sunny day, an "average" fight or a *novillada* [novice's bullfight]—an "undistinguished, honest performance"—and seats half-way up the amphitheater), but also a way of seeing death up close that allows moral reevaluation of the "meaning and end of the whole thing" (*DIA* 11, 18).[8]

The whole aim of *Death in the Afternoon* is to see the bullfight as an "integral whole" (278), in which both suffering and killing come to be accepted. Hemingway approaches the bullfight as a writer practicing how to observe and record "the actual things . . . that produced the emotion" (1). In the bullfight, he finds an encounter that isolates the phenomenon of violent death—"one of the simplest things of all and the most fundamental" (2). Most writers shut their eyes to this sort of suffering, but Hemingway uses the bullfight to reopen them, just as Judith Jarvis Thomson's variant of the trolley problem is used in ethics classes to get students to see the collision of moral intuitions—the desire to save the greatest number of persons and repugnance at causing harm. By starting with the experience of violence unclouded by one's own immersive participation in the action, and with one's sympathy partially displaced by watching a spectacle where animals, primarily, are the suffering victims, Hemingway begins the therapeutic process of dealing with suffering and the threat of one's own violent death by *seeing* death, which he calls "the unescapable reality, the one thing any man may be sure of" (256). In the reading offered here, Hemingway's method can be used to deal with any trauma that depends on reconsidering unexplained and misunderstood experience, although it is most effectively deployed in the case of the phenomenon we shun the most.

As Hemingway says at the beginning of *Death in the Afternoon*, after viewing the bullfight and reflecting on it, he changed his mind from thinking that the bullfight was "simple and barbarous and cruel" to conclude that it is actually "very moral" (2). How this occurs is the puzzle of the book.

First of all, Hemingway argues that the bullfight is not a sport or game, but a tragedy (22).[9] Mere games are about victory and defeat, and for the players, "the avoidance of death is replaced by the avoidance of defeat" (22). Games are fundamentally less serious than war or bullfighting,[10] and the bullfight is not on a complete par with war. Even Hemingway hesitates to directly compare battle with a bullfight because the latter is a mere "commercial spectacle" (154). Nevertheless, despite its commercial elements, as explored in Hemingway's works and in the secondary literature,[11] the bullfight, according to Hemingway, remains something greater than sport or spectacle: it is a tragedy.

Characterizing Hemingway's attempt to deal intelligently with death as a "poetics" of tragedy reflects the fact that, like Aristotle's *Poetics*, Hemingway's *Death in the Afternoon* is an account of how a specific art form (in this case, a particular sort of performed tragedy) elicits a unique emotional response. Hemingway is not the first artist to see the therapeutic appeal of tragedy: as Jonathan Shays argues, "the distinctive character of Athenian theater came from the requirements of a democratic polity *made up entirely of present or former soldiers* to provide communalization for combat veterans" (*Achilles in Vietnam* 229–30; emphasis in original).[12] The absence of this sort of sympathetic community is the theme of the Nick Adams stories, depicted through Nick's immersion in nonhuman nature and through the failures of his family, especially his father, to reinforce and to live up to Nick's conception of bravery.[13] Lacking a ready-made community, one must find it elsewhere, and Hemingway seems to have found it among the Spanish, who do not merely "live for life," as do the English and French (*DIA* 256).

The bullfight also meets the standard of tragedy that Aristotle abstracted from Greek tragedy. For Aristotle, the tragic drama is a highly structured performance with a beginning, a middle, and an end. Hemingway's bullfight is a drama performed in three acts (Kennedy 105–15), a drama that is so "well ordered and so strongly disciplined by ritual" that one can feel only the things that are at the core of the narrative (Hemingway, *DIA* 97ff).[14] Tragedy, according to Aristotle, is ethical in that it concerns characters who are good enough to elicit our fear and pity and who gain tragic wisdom about the fragility of the human condition through their errors. Dramatic tragedy, then, is the "imitation of an action that is serious and complete and has a [certain] magnitude" (Aristotle 1449b26–31). Comedy is distinguished from tragedy in that comedy concerns "inferior people" and "the certain sort of failure that is ridiculous and shameful" and "painless and not destructive" (1449a32). In light of this, Hemingway sees the honorable bullfighter as a figure of tragedy: the bullfighter can't run away or admit to fear without becoming instead a figure of ridicule (*DIA* 10). Only the frightened bullfighter is a figure of comedy. Hemingway also, controversially, describes the disembowelment of the horses as a comedy (6, 98); as inferior beings, the horses fit the comedic mold. Likewise, a poor bullfight, as when the bullfighter runs away or the injured horses run around the ring like "awkward birds," fits Aristotle's comedic criterion of a ridiculous and shameful failure. The aficionado, according to Hemingway, is "one who has this sense of the tragedy and ritual of the fight so that the minor aspects are not important except as they relate to the whole" (9). The bullfight, then, far from being "hysterical" or "blood-drunken" (Baker, *Life Story* 143; Young 97), is instead a tragic ritual that disciplines the person with a highly developed emotional response to suffering to focus on some aspects of the human drama unified under the umbrella of seeing death as the necessary end to life and violent death as a permanent possibility. Such a viewpoint requires acknowledgment of the cruelty and tragedy of all death, human and animal.

The Rules of the Ritual

Reconciling oneself to the fact of death requires concentrating on the purpose of the ritual. For Hemingway, the concrete aim of the bullfight is the ritual death of the bull. When this is accomplished, the spectator feels a sense of ecstasy—a "feeling of immortality" that "becomes yours" as the bullfighter brings death closer (*DIA* 206). It is, he contends, "as profound as any religious ecstasy" (213). As A. L. Kennedy writes in her own recent book on the bullfight, the bullfight captures both "Christian and pre-Christian urges to understand the termination of life and to celebrate survival"; it is not sport or art but "religious ritual" (81–82).

Hemingway's interpretation of the bullfight requires the relegation of the nonhuman participants of the bullfight to an instrumental status. He likens the bull to a canvas for a painter, a block of marble for a sculptor, or even dry powdered snow for a skier (*DIA* 15).[15] The bull that does not charge straight can, in Hemingway's interpretation, be "corrected" by skillfully placed banderillas. The light, lofty (*leventado*) bull is slowed (*parado*), first by the picadors, then by cape work, until he is finally exposed and heavy or leaden (*aplomado*), his head lowered and his energy sapped (147). The human participants in the bullfight are also subject to corrective pressures. Hemingway explains that spectators impose rules on matadors, by "punishing" them, for example. The spectators' role with respect to the matadors is to "impose the rules, keep up the standards, prevent abuses and pay for the fights" (164). For their part, writers and critics also attempt to impose the correct way of seeing upon the audience; they, in turn, can for different reasons fail to impose the right rules, leaving themselves open to the penalties of public criticism.[16]

In contrast to the orderly world of the bullfight, life as presented in Hemingway's novels has rules that are unfair or unintelligible, with punishments are arbitrary impositions rather than correctives. As Frederic Henry states in *A Farewell to Arms*, for example, "That was what you did. You died. You did not know what it was about. You never had time to learn. They threw you in and told you the rules and the first time they caught you off base they killed you" (279–80).[17] In *The Sun Also Rises*, the rules of the game are unintelligible: the fiesta in Pamplona is described as meaningless, nobody knows anything or anybody, and Jake tells the reader that he does not care about the meaning of life: he just wants to learn to "live in it" (152). In *Death in the Afternoon*, Hemingway charts one possible path toward understanding and reconciling oneself to the facts of life, by beginning to see the basic facts. In doing so, he finds that he can reconcile himself to the suffering of the horses—suffering to which he returns again and again in his writings, and which would be, without interpretation, indefensible.[18] Then he reconciles himself to the morality of the bullfight. Finally, at least with respect to the bullfight, he concludes that it is possible to know "what is good and what is bad" (*DIA* 98). Moral knowledge is possible, and moral action is possible, at least in theory. That is the lofty goal, or promise, of *Death in the Afternoon*. A short introduction to the type of person who deals intelligently with death secures Hemingway's point.

The composite term under which Hemingway discusses the virtue peculiar to the matador is *pundonor*. This is "honor, probity, courage, self-respect and pride in one word" (*DIA* 91). Honor dictates how closely the matador will work to the bull and whether he will use or avoid tricks (*trucos*) in doing so (178). Although honor can be lost in front of an ignorant or vicious audience, Hemingway argues that the spiritual quality of *pundonor* is retained not only when the actor is incorrectly evaluated but even when a matador's courage, self-respect, or honesty temporarily fails him. That spiritual quality is called *afición* (passion). Just as Jünger evaluates courage in competing and inconsistent frameworks of individual virtue and collective spirit, Hemingway, somewhat mystically and indulgently, describes it in *The Sun Also Rises* (136–37). That mysterious quality is presented with more clarity in *Death in the Afternoon*: passion (*afición*) is possessed by anyone who *understands*, through knowledge and science, how man dominates nature (*DIA* 21). A good matador who acts within the rules of the ritual will be frightened by the action but will bravely and temporarily ignore the consequence (death) that may follow from his working within the terrain of the bull. There is another sort of bravery, exhilarated bravery, where one permanently rejects thinking about the consequences of one's actions. Since this sort of bravery is unreflective, Hemingway criticizes it: it is "easier," he asserts, "to be stupid and naturally brave than to be exceedingly intelligent and still completely brave" (*DIA* 94).

In *Death in the Afternoon*, the essential difference between a good matador and a bad one—the subject of chapter 15 of *Death in the Afternoon*—lies in how he kills. Somewhat murkily, Hemingway describes the necessity of killing as a "rebellion against death" done with the "pagan virtue" of pride (233). Although in the context it is fairly clear that Hemingway intends "pagan virtue" to offer an alternative to Christian morality,[19] *how* killing can be understood as a "rebellion against death" is left unclear (233, 213). This is a problem in light of the thesis adopted in this paper, which is that the bullfight clarifies our finitude rather than denies it. I reconstruct Hemingway's solution as follows: If we all die sometime, but for the time being not yet, it is an easy leap to the commandment not to kill. Presumably, that leap is made because of a fear of death and an inability to see its necessity. But if the prohibition against killing were simply true, then Hemingway and all other combatants and quasi-combatants would sin—or get away with murder—when they engaged in or supported warfare.[20] It may be going too far into the realm of speculation to call the bullfight a schismatic, Spanish modification of Hemingway's own Catholicism, but his attempt to defend the "rebellion against death" in terms of the necessity of killing points to a problematic aspect of Christian morality's rejection of killing: what if your country asks you to kill, or what if this killing is a consensual mercy-killing, or what if your circumstances demand it? Hemingway seems to approach the morality of killing in the following way: by looking at a ritual as an ordered whole, we are liberated from individually shouldering all the responsibility for the crime of killing, an act which should be interpreted in terms of an openness to the necessity of death rather than to bloodthirst or cruelty.[21]

### The Natural History of Death

In the vignette at the exact center of *Death in the Afternoon*, "A Natural History of the Dead," Hemingway seeks to clarify his controversial interpretation of the point of the bullfight, and its relation to his own war experience. Here, Hemingway turns the power of observation and reflection directly on war deaths—vindicating the claim made above that *Death in the Afternoon* is primarily about wartime trauma.²² Earlier, we were confronted by a question prompted by the suffering of the horses: Can the brute fact of animal death be justified? In "Natural History," Hemingway invites the "naturalist" to observe the facts of human death in war. This story-within-a-story recounts deaths in war, imposed on men by other men, and compares these impositions to "natural deaths," such as death from Spanish influenza. Observing the order and beauty of nature, the humanist affirms that the Being who planted, watered, and perfected a little moss-flower cannot "look with unconcern upon the situation and suffering of creatures formed after His own image" (*DIA* 134). In this vignette, Hemingway invites us to consider who has the better part of the argument, the humanist or the naturalist. The conclusion he draws is that the naturalist is more enlightened about the real world: *all* human death is indecorous (139).²³

This thought is driven home in the last portion of "Natural History," where Hemingway stages an argument between an enlightened doctor and an army officer who wants to use morphine to kill a severely wounded man. Hemingway's officer argues for euthanasia and seems to have the better part of the exchange. Because we fail to understand the true nature of the human condition, our animal mortality, we often try to prolong life, seeing death as terrible and thinking that *anything* we can do to prolong life is justifiable. In another part of *Death in the Afternoon*, Hemingway says in his own voice that concern for the soul is mistaken when it leads to unnecessary suffering (220). For Hemingway, our human awareness of death sometimes causes us to deny death, or to cling on to life, even at the cost of inflicting great suffering. When we see life tightly structured by the rule of death, we may allow ourselves to forgive those who kill, and we may also learn to accept our own deaths as natural and unavoidable.

As philosophers remind us, human death is always "in some sense premature and violent" (Kojève 137). "A Natural History of the Dead" registers Hemingway's deep regret that "most men die like animals, not men" (*DIA* 83). Here, Hemingway is not the romantic naturalist, interpreting higher, human things like "family, church, and polity" in light of the spontaneous, natural things of our animal lives (Zuckert 184; Messent 123–42, 133). Instead, *Death in the Afternoon* insists on the higher value of human freedom. The danger of death to the *human* protagonist is, as Hemingway writes, "created at will" (*DIA* 16, 21). Likewise, death is "given" voluntarily as well, and it is the necessity of *voluntarily* accepting death that seems to transform the giving of death from a simple, indefensible cause of suffering into a "tragedy" (12). Humans are the only ones that understand their own deaths, and they must learn that life should not be prolonged against all reason. This is the concrete point to be learned from the "definite end" of the bullfight: to learn to accept death by seeing up close how death is "given, avoided, refused, and accepted" (256).[24] This is also, as Adam Smith wrote (quoted above), what we can learn from war.

Conclusion

Close readings of *Death in the Afternoon* and autobiographical memoirs of war such as *The Storm of Steel* help us to answer the question of whether it is possible to *choose* war, and whether it is possible for humans to be free even amid necessities such as suffering, war, and death. The tension between Hemingway's therapeutics and Jünger's wholehearted defense of poise (*haltung*) and courage amid suffering is elucidated in Hemingway's analysis of the character of the bullfighter, who voluntarily exposes himself to death and who exhibits *pundonor*, the composite virtue of the bullfighter.[25] Hemingway defends *pundonor* largely in terms of proper and even philosophical care of self. John McCormick, in contrast, emphasizes the exaggerated and excessive side of *pundonor* (45). Other authors emphasize and exaggerate the distorting side of Spanish honor. "Whenever I am perplexed about what a Spaniard might do under certain circumstances," James Michener writes, "it is instructive to ask, 'Under these circumstances what would a man do who subscribed to an acute or even a preposterous sense of honor?' And from endeavoring to answer this question I often find clues as to what the Spaniard will do" (Michener 61–62). For Hemingway, however, *pundonor* is essentially about one's relation to one's own inevitable death.

Whether or not you agree with Hemingway's elucidation of bravery and his argument that the Spanish take an "intelligent" rather than a preposterous interest in death, his conceptual analysis of the bullfight prepares us to see the "actual things" that activate the emotions of specific human beings in Hemingway's time. Hemingway's arguments may originate in a biographical accident (namely, Hemingway's service as an ambulance driver during World War I and his struggles to deal with the suicide of his father), and *Death in the Afternoon* may have originated as an exercise for the writer, who wanted to learn to report true things more accurately. But the encounter with violent death serves to teach readers of *Death in the Afternoon* about mortality beyond the battlefield—or the bullring.

In the reading presented above, the bullfight cannot become a grand metaphor for reality, explaining in full the economy or the sociology and politics of Hemingway's world, but it does present the observer with a way of learning how to see skeptically into suffering, something that Hemingway's journalism and his war experience failed to do. Its power as a guide to reflective seeing lies in its being about the most important things, like death, and in its presenting, at first glance, the same sense of unexplained suffering that Hemingway may have experienced in the war—the "why me?" thought. Its appropriateness as an analog for war and the human experience of mortality depends on our gut aversion to the suffering of the most obvious victims, the horses. *Death in the Afternoon* is first about animal suffering and then later, upon reflection, about human culture and accepting the fact that our deaths are always violent, disruptive potentialities that we loathe and fear but must nonetheless confront.

Hemingway's observation of violent death is careful enough that it allows us to see, in some sense, what is missing from his own narration of war in his war novels, and what is missing from Jünger's celebratory account of war: namely, a more complete accounting of the political and social ideas that motivate collective action. Wars are fought for a reason or reasons, and the phenomenon of war cannot be understood without reflecting on the political yearnings for justice and for the good community that animate war-making and war-makers. It is not only the case that the one experienced with war can see something about death, dying, and killing, although it was the purpose of this essay to support that point. It is also true that the one familiar with death can see true things about the meaning of war and about the search for a meaningful life that attracts us to risk life. (For a list of questions designed to start students exploring *Death in the Afternoon*, see Appendix D.)

## Notes

1. The percentage of the American population that has served in the military is less than 1 percent, and only one-third of respondents aged between eighteen and twenty-nine years have an immediate family member who has served. See "War and Sacrifice in the Post-9/11 Era: The Military-Civilian Gap," *Pew Research Social & Demographic Surveys*, 5 Oct. 2011, <http://www.pewsocialtrends.org/2011/10/05/war-and-sacrifice-in-the-post-911-era/>.

2. The statistic refers to the bullfight prior to the required use of the *peto* (the padded blanket that protected the horses' flank from goring) in 1928. I use it because Hemingway does not consider the *peto* a humane improvement, given the likelihood that the horses will suffer internal injuries from the impact (McCormick 35; Kennedy 108).

3. See Chris Barker, "Hemingway's *Death in the Afternoon* and the Fear of Death in War," *War, Literature, and the Arts: An International Journal of the Humanities* 26 (2014): 1–19, <http://wlajournal.com/wlaarchive/26/Barker.pdf>.

4. For the instructor, a particularly effective short summary of biographical statements about war, killing, and suffering is Donald Anderson's "Soldier-Artists: Preserving the

World," *War, Literature, and the Arts: An International Journal of the Humanities* (2013): 1–18.

5. Similar concerns have been explored in Joanna Bourke's *An Intimate History of Killing*. In Bourke's book, one pilot describes aerial combat as akin to the "lists of the Middle Ages, the only sphere in modern warfare where a man saw his adversary and faced him in mortal combat." This was man "alone," using his own skill, "single-handed, against the enemy" (47). Further testimonial evidence may also be found in the Somme section of John Keegan's *The Face of Battle: A Study of Agincourt, Waterloo, and the Somme*.

6. In the 1942 introduction to *Men at War*, an edited volume of Hemingway's choice of the greatest war stories ever written, Hemingway reprises his theme of care for our fear of suffering and death. The book, he writes to the young soldier or potential soldier, "will not tell you how to die" (xxii), but it can serve to "prepare for and supplement experience" and even to "serve as a corrective after experience" (xxvii). (All citations to *Men at War* are to the following edition: Ernest Hemingway, *Men at War* [New York: Bramhall House, 1982].) Reprising his own wounding at Fossalta, he writes that he regained his courage by telling himself: "Whatever I had to do men had always done. If they had done it then I could do it too" (xxii). He also repeats the lines from Shakespeare's Henriad that are "the best thing that is written in this book" (xxiii): "By my troth, I care not; a man can die but once: we / owe God a death: I'll ne'er bear a base mind / an't be my destiny, so; an't be not, so: no man is / too good to serve's prince; and let it go which way / it will, he that dies this year is quit for the next" (*Henry IV*, Part 2, III.ii.; Young 72–73).

7. Overcoming the fear of death makes Hemingway's Francis Macomber into a man.

8. All citations to *Death in the Afternoon* are to the Touchstone edition of 1960.

9. Contrast this attitude with, for example, that of the Pamplona café waiter in *The Sun Also Rises*, for whom the bullfight, rather than a spiritual event, is "all for sport. All for pleasure" (201).

10. To bear out this point, see Bernard Suits's masterful conceptual analysis of games: in utopia, we would not play games (or watch bullfights), even for the instrumental aim of self-knowledge (149–60).

11. See Adrian Shubert, *Death and Money in the Afternoon: A History of the Spanish Bullfight* (Oxford: Oxford UP, 1999).

12. An attempt to recapture the sense that drama can speak helpfully to soldiers has recently been made by the theater group Theater of War, which performs Greek tragedies for veterans.

13. Catherine Zuckert (1990) is particularly effective in explaining how Hemingway's war experience is restaged in the Nick Adams stories. In *Death in the Afternoon*, the contrast between bravery in the ring and suicide is explicit (Zuckert 11).

14. Hemingway's account carefully relates each of the three parts to the ultimate end of executing the bull, which is the "definite end" of the whole "action" (*DIA* 96–99, 454). A judicial metaphor—trial, sentencing, and execution—is also used by Hemingway to characterize the action (96). The trial portion contains the *suerte de varas* (act of the spears) in which the mounted picadors test and tire the bull: this is the time when the horses are injured. This is also the stage of the fight where, as Hemingway beautifully remarks, the bull is at his apogee, seemingly "winning" by clearing the ring of humans

by its end. This false victory sets up the tragic *peripateia* (reversal) and *anagnorisis* (recognition) of the next two acts, where the spectator recognizes that the bull's victory was fleeting and his defeat foreordained. The second act—the sentencing, in Hemingway's analogy—is the s*uerte de banderillas,* in which the *bandilleras* are placed. Finally, the bullfight ends with the *suerte de matar,* the execution of the bull: here, the bull is faced by "only one man who must, alone, dominate him" (98).

15. A *noble* is a bull that is "frank in its charges, frank, simple, and easily deceived" (Hemingway, *DIA* 426; see also the entry for "Franco" in the book's glossary). "All of bullfighting," Hemingway says, "is founded on the bravery of the bull, his simplicity and lack of experience" (*DIA* 145).

16. In *The Dangerous Summer,* an account of the 1959 bullfighting season, Hemingway offended his reading public through his insistence on the decadence of, imposing upon them what was seen to be a flawed, partial judgment of that matador.

17. All citations to *A Farewell to Arms* are to the following edition: Ernest Hemingway, *A Farewell to Arms* (New York: Scribner, 2012).

18. Hemingway revisits the same image of pack-horses dumped from the pier in Smyrna in "The Snows of Kilimanjaro," "On the Quai at Smyrna," and on two occasions in *Death in the Afternoon.*

19. He substantiates this by showing that in 1567 Pope Pius V banned the bullfight from all Christian nations except Spain on pain of excommunication, thus underlining the tension between mainstream Christianity and the bullfight (*DIA* 12).

20. In her book *An Intimate History of Killing,* Joanna Bourke notes how some combatants feel liberated by getting away with murder when they kill on the battlefield, insofar as they commit the most heinous act but are secure that they will not be persecuted for it (xix, 20). Bourke's reviewers, including Jean Bethke Elshtein, have taken her to task for defending or celebrating blood-lust. For further context, see Alan Confino, Paul Betts, and Dirk Schumann, *Between Mass Death and Individual Loss: The Place of the Dead in Twentieth-Century Germany* (2008); Michael Roper, *The Secret Battle: Emotional Survival in the Great War* (2009); and Gregory Thomas, *Treating the Trauma of the Great War: Soldiers, Civilians, and Psychiatry in France, 1914-1940* (2009). It is worth noting that liberation (getting away with murder) requires the *prior acceptance* of the commandment not to kill.

21. Alexandre Kojève expresses the thought that may be behind Hemingway's judgment concerning the morality of killing: it is "not the will to kill, but that of exposing oneself to the danger of death without any necessity, without being forced to it as an animal" that is humanizing and separates us from the given world (151–52). It is with respect to killing that a man has grace, which is an indescribable quality activated "in the presence of the danger of death" (51). Hemingway criticizes gypsy matador Rafael El Gallo, Joselito's brother, for a showy emphasis on riskless simulation of grace. "There is a whole school of bullfighting in which grace is developed until it is the one essential and the passing of the horn past the man's belly eliminated as far as possible" (*DIA* 212). Missing from this school of bullfighting are the "spiritual qualities" of the "simpler man," for whom killing and risking death are the core of the bullfight (232–33). El Gallo's stylizing results in "pure spectacle" rather than tragedy. As Hemingway wryly remarks, "There was no tragedy in it, but no tragedy could replace it" (213).

22. The centrality of "A Natural History of the Dead" is pointed out by Thurston (47–48).

23. Perhaps he writes in response to Wilfred Owen's poetic reflections on the decorum of patriotic death.

24. Some critics interpret Hemingway as obsessed with control. Nina Schwartz argues that Hemingway exerts his power over the reader by "producing a gap in the reader's knowledge, inscribing the reader as impotent slave to the master author" (52). Hemingway is said to have killed the father-figure but not the author-figure in his novels (Dragunoiu 868–92). Hemingway himself abets the aforementioned critical stance by stating his famous iceberg theory.

25. A good account of Jünger's *haltung* may be found in Dagmar Barnouw's *Weimar Intellectuals and the Threat of Modernity* (196, 211).

# "In Another Country" and *Across the River and into the Trees* as Trauma Literature

Sarah Wood Anderson

With veterans and soldiers so prominent in current American culture, students are drawn to readings of Hemingway that encourage awareness of the physical and mental wounds of his veterans. It is useful, therefore, to provide them with terminology, background, and interpretations of illness narratives so that they can direct their analyses. Recent critical work has identified the trauma of veterans in Hemingway's fiction, addressing structural choices—for instance, the lack of emotion as indicating trauma—and thematic choices—the threat trauma poses to masculinity, for example. Another useful aspect to observe is the conflict that Judith Herman identifies in *Trauma and Recovery* as "the central dialectic of psychological trauma": that is, "the conflict between the will to deny horrible events and the will to proclaim them aloud" (1).[1] It is worth recognizing, too, that trauma theorists have identified a contradiction in the method of therapy that urges victims to remember their moment of trauma. Cathy Caruth has written about the nature of trauma as unknowable, and consequently, untellable. Therapists have made clear that amnesia, in varying levels, is a common defense against trauma. There is something innate to trauma, therefore, about resisting the recovery of painful memories. Literary critics making use of trauma theory have explored the unspeakable nature of war and the codes of conduct that restrict veterans from recalling their experiences.[2]

Extending long-held discussions on Hemingway's representation of veterans, this particular lens of traumatic telling works well with many illness narratives, whether by Hemingway or other writers.[3] I suggest that Hemingway's *Across the River and into the Trees,* while presumably one of his least-taught novels, presents a valuable opportunity to understand the process of recounting trauma. The novel is uniquely suited for exploring the restrictions on traumatic confession as Cantwell both resists and overcomes them.

I often have students begin our discussion of Hemingway's writing by making a list of all the preconceived notions of Hemingway that they bring to their reading. I encourage them to put aside such notions as far as possible and examine the work through a particular lens, in this case mental trauma—more specifically, trauma related to masculinity. To aid in establishing that lens for *Across the River*, I often begin with another text, a short story such as "Big Two-Hearted River," "Soldier's Home," "Now I Lay Me," or "In Another Country," or, if time allows, the novel *A Farewell to Arms*, because much of the criticism concerning Hemingway's writing about trauma began with that novel.

Providing background on Hemingway's relationship with war trauma can be useful to students as a way of narrowing their focus. Working from the mainstream assumption that Hemingway's World War I experience—including his rejection by the United States Army, his enlistment as a Red Cross ambulance driver in Italy, and his wounding at Fossalta di Piave—influenced his portrayal of wounded characters, I suggest to my students that Hemingway's work emphasizes injuries partly in an attempt to reconcile the worthiness of a life spent fighting with the disabilities such a life often inflicts. Moreover, war injuries represent the injuries that civilians—at least Hemingway—collect throughout a normal life; the specialized case of the wounded soldier functions as an extreme example of the physical and mental traumas of human existence, something that Hemingway spent his career writing about.[4] The log of Hemingway texts in which characters struggle with painful memories is long and encompasses many of his major works, including *A Farewell to Arms, In Our Time, The Sun Also Rises, For Whom the Bell Tolls,* and *Islands in the Stream*. New critical approaches to the theory of the wound in Hemingway's life and fiction have updated a line of thought initiated by Edmund Wilson in the late 1940s and expanded by Philip Young in the 1960s. In general, they detail the relationship between combat or personal trauma and a defense of masculinity.

In *The Gun and the Pen: Hemingway, Fitzgerald, Faulkner and the Fiction of Mobilization,* Keith Gandal argues that Hemingway's participation in the Red Cross during World War I was intimately connected with his masculinity. His rejection by the United States Army undoubtedly wounded his pride and his sense of himself as a man.[5] Throughout Hemingway's oeuvre one can find allusions to serving in the ambulance service, as Hemingway did, as inferior to "true" military deployment. Hemingway was likewise embarrassed by the fact that he served in Italy rather than in the major theaters of the war. Together, these facts influenced his perceptions of how war validates or calls into question a man's masculinity.

Critics such as Diane Price Herndl,[6] Trevor Dodman,[7] and Alex Vernon[8] have developed useful ideas for examining certain texts, exploring, for example, how the patriarchal strictures of masculinity, medicine, and the military discourage Frederic Henry from telling his own story; or how, during the telling of trauma, the exact nature of a narrator's voice—with techniques of silence, resistance, and evasion—can reveal the extent of that trauma.

### "In Another Country"

Before a discussion of *Across the River and into the Trees*, I will provide a reading of "In Another Country," one of Hemingway's short stories from *Men Without Women*, because it introduces the key aspects of dissociation and emasculation. (As I mentioned earlier, there are other stories that would work equally well, such as "Big Two-Hearted River" and "Now I Lay Me.") Gary Brenner asserts that "'the thesis of *A Farewell to Arms* . . . is that no institution, belief system, value or commitment can arm one against life's utter irrationality'" (qtd. in Herndl 43–44). Wounded soldiers face just such irrationality when considering the mechanisms of war and the power structure of the military, within both of which they were injured. "In Another Country" is narrated by a wounded American soldier fighting in Italy and joined by Italian soldiers who are also victims of physical trauma. These wounded soldiers are instructed to attend a rehabilitation clinic daily, where they are strapped to new experimental machines that, in theory, heal their war wounds. For this story, I focus on the men as passive participants to their healing, their dissociation, and their emasculation.

The veterans, whose bodies were initially sacrificed to the machinery of war, are now ordered to subject them to the dehumanizing operations of dubious instruments by doctors who assure them too readily of full recoveries. The machines do all the work for the veterans, alternatively "lurch[ing]," "bounc[ing]," "thump[ing] up and down," and "flap[ping]" their respective body parts (*CSS* 206–7). The men have no faith that medical science can heal them; moving from the military machinery of war to the medical machinery of healing, they are drifting, detached, subject to grand schemes in which they are involved but have no control.

I also emphasize the soldiers' isolation, which is indicative of their mental trauma. The American soldier admits that his comrades pull away from him when they learn that his commendations were given primarily because he was an American instead of for acts of bravery, as theirs were. His camaraderie with this group of injured men dissolves, isolating him further. Such isolation compounds the psychological trauma he suffered as a result of his initial injury. He describes how he would "often lay in bed at night by myself, afraid to die and wondering how I would be when I went back to the front again" (*CSS* 208). Sleepless nights consumed with fears of death are certainly symptoms of post-traumatic stress disorder, an indication of the psychological wounding the American suffered in addition to his physical wounding.

The detachment that Hemingway describes in his soldiers has a clinical name: dissociation. According to Judith Herman, "dissociation appears to be the mechanism by which intense sensory and emotional experiences are disconnected from the social domain of language and memory, the internal mechanism by which terrorized people are silenced" (239). The soldier narrator of "In Another Country" describes action and not emotion. He tells what the soldiers do at the clinic, not how they feel about their injuries. He describes the major's crying but not how he felt to see it. Although the emotion behind action is left largely unspoken in much of Hemingway's writing, such silence in a story about war trauma points to dissociation.

Tied closely to issues of physical trauma are those of masculinity. Is an injured man, even more an injured soldier, still a man? Is he still useful and powerful?[9] Note where the American questions his bravery, and how his counterpart, the major, represents at once power in masculinity *and* emasculation. His sternness and his rank are undermined by an injury that has disfigured his hand, such that it is now "a little hand like a baby's" (*CSS* 44). More than being simply emasculated by his injury, the major is described as infantile. His hand is helpless, useless, and small. If, as Vernon says, Hemingway's description of pregnant soldiers feminizes them, then the major's infant hand marginalizes him to the most vulnerable position possible.

The description of his baby hand looms over his persona, even when the narrator learns that the major's wife has died and that the bitterness he feels stems from her death. He advises the American not to marry because he should not put himself in a position to lose things (*CSS* 209). But such is the condition of life. These soldiers have lost their complete bodies, their connection to those around them, their masculinity, their positions on the front lines. With such clear examples of dissociation, emotional repression, and emasculation, "In Another Country" prepares students to consider *Across the River* for the aspects of traumatic recovery it undertakes to display.

*Across the River and into the Trees*

Richard Cantwell in *Across the River and into the Trees* is a retired colonel in the United States Army who still suffers from combat injuries acquired in Italy during World War I. He returns to Venice, Italy, to hunt ducks, retrace his war experiences, and visit his new lover, the young and beautiful Renata. His injuries are still raw in some cases; for instance, he allows Renata to touch his wounded hand but warns her to be careful of the center because it is sensitive and can still crack open. He is only fifty years old, but he feels, acts, and is treated as if he is elderly. He is quite near death, having had his third heart attack just before the story opens, and the sense is that his war injuries have been too great for him to recover from. Like the American in "In Another Country," this soldier has endured both physical and mental trauma; however, the gaps between what the narrator reveals and what he keeps hidden are slighter than those of the American. The action of the novel centers on Colonel Cantwell's telling Renata about his war experiences. Such a premise allows for great detail concerning his opinions and attitudes about injury, his recollection of traumatic memories, and his healing from the wounds of war.

Students readily recognize Cantwell. He has many of the characteristics that we have come to expect in Hemingway's men: he is a masculine, thick-skinned, wounded, brooding fighter, who keeps friends intimately near and judges harshly those who do not suit his code of ethics and morality. Even though he loves deeply, he keeps himself private, remote. When he shares information, he does so sparingly. Having suffered greater physical damage than most, maybe all, of Hemingway's other male characters, he talks about his trauma, his injuries, and himself at great length, providing a unique opportunity to examine Hemingway's representation of physical and mental trauma and the process involved in remembering and recounting those experiences.

Renata encourages the colonel to tell her about the war, soon revealing that she hopes to rid him of his corrosive memories. He tells her several times, "'Nobody shares this trade with anybody,'" and later, when she says she wants him to recount his memories, he says, "'I don't need to purge'" (*ARIT* 126, 207). She is sweet and lovely, however, and his love allows her the freedom to urge him toward recovery, even though he still believes that she knows too little of war and brutality to comprehend his memories. "'Please talk,'" she says. "'I'm taking care of you'" (222). Her urging functions primarily to bring back Cantwell's repressed memories, forcing him to relive the battles and the injuries. Instead of moving him forward, however, the process takes him back into the battles themselves. The initial ineffectiveness of her plan aligns with her innocence and naïveté. Cantwell accommodates her ideas, even while he admits to himself that her strategy of drawing out his stories will not succeed in healing his wounds.

You might draw a comparison to the experimental machines of "In Another Country," for Renata's talk therapy is ill-suited for this indifferent subject, functioning only to emphasize the permanent effects of the soldier's injuries. Just as the lurching, jolting machine did not work properly with an injured body part attached, so too does Renata's psychological approach falter when it evokes foul language or memories that are too upsetting, too brutal for her to hear. Cantwell often omits the most violent details to spare her from learning too much of war's brutality. This resistance to telling the full story begins when he speaks to her portrait: he tells it that it is too young to hear the things he has to say. Then, when he is with her, she asks him (seven times in twenty pages) not to be so "bitter" or "rough." Most often it is his obscene language that makes her react; once, however, she says "'Please tell me about combat without being too bad'" (*ARIT* 224). Her requests for a gentler version of his story become a common refrain throughout the novel, revealing the chasm between the violence and crudeness of Cantwell's full memories and Renata's requests that he censor them as an ethical issue in itself. Encouraging the colonel to purge while negotiating the conditions under which he may do so complicates Renata's role as counselor and challenges the colonel's ability to comply.

You can ask your students to note the excuses that Cantwell employs for not telling Renata of his experiences, such as claiming that the details would "bore" her or that a soldier should respect the memories of those fallen by not telling their stories (*ARIT* 131). Note that this code of silence means that only fellow soldiers can know about war. "Real soldiers never tell any one what their own dead looked like, he told the portrait. And I'm through with this whole subject. And what about that company dead up the draw? What about them, professional soldier? They're dead, he said. And I can hang and rattle" (235). Cantwell defines a "real soldier" by what he does—that is, he is one who does not tell outsiders about fallen comrades. He holds to a code of silence and believes that the soldiers who wrote publicly of their impressions of war were "sensitive" and had "cracked" (129).[10] His methods of resisting the telling of his trauma, then, reveal much about his sense of masculinity.

Once Cantwell begins to speak of his trauma, his code of honor (upheld through silence) and Renata's innocence are not the only obstacles he must overcome. Students can also consider how Cantwell checks himself during his telling, thinking to himself while Renata sleeps in his arms: "Don't be bitter ... How can I remember if I am not bitter? Be as bitter as you want. And tell the girl, now silently, and that will not hurt her, ever, because she is sleeping so lovely" (*ARIT* 230). To be fully truthful in his telling, Cantwell must recount his stories either silently, while Renata sleeps, or aloud to her portrait in her absence. The figure of the portrait becomes an important compromise for Cantwell because he feels free to talk to the portrait in a way that he cannot to Renata.

Another example of the ill-fitting, jolting confession is when Cantwell begins to say things silently to Renata. "The Colonel told her all about it; but he did not utter it" (*ARIT* 227). This contradiction is significant because it emphasizes Cantwell's resistance to telling: it is a telling which does and yet does not take place. He tells Renata something, but he does not *say* anything. Equally, he tells her but she does not *hear* anything. This confession is both told and untold—and never received.

It is important to emphasize that *Across the River* functions not to tell Cantwell's traumatic memories, but to represent his process of reliving them. The narrator keeps the emotional details of Cantwell's confession out of the novel. It is important that readers understand how their experience of Cantwell's trauma differs from the one told to Renata. By leaving out information or presenting details out of context, the narrator protects the reader from the violence that so troubles Cantwell and upsets Renata. Readers find themselves locked in the silence that Renata desires.

From time to time, readers overhear information about troop movements or battles, but unless they have military training these scenes are largely meaningless. Hemingway himself addressed this style after negative reviews began to come in, "'Sure, they can say anything about nothing happening in 'Across the River,' but all that happens is the defense of the lower Piave, the breakthrough in Normandy, the taking of Paris and the destruction of the 22nd Inf. Reg. in Hürtgen Forest plus a man who loves a girl and dies'" (qtd. in Lisca 290). Hemingway asserts that these things happen in the novel even though they are not described. In terms of its omissions, much of his story is like Cantwell's confessions, which tell without speaking. The cryptic scenes of Cantwell's war trauma, as Hemingway crafts them, contain no emotion, few regrets, and no terror. They provide nothing that would traumatize. Readers consequently get an incomplete picture of the events, participating in the dissociation Cantwell experiences.

Try posing the following questions to your students: What does it mean that the novel functions to perpetuate the silence with which Cantwell wrestles? Is

Hemingway's intention to show the wounded soldier at fifty, rather than to show the full extent of what he has undergone? What does this incongruity, between the purpose of Cantwell's near-death talk therapy and the novel's silences about his trauma, mean in terms of trauma theory? Are we meant to see the injured soldier and watch as he struggles with confessing a past that refuses to be told accurately, to an audience who, for one reason or another, cannot receive it?

While other novels, such as *For Whom the Bell Tolls* and *A Farewell to Arms*, report battles that include protagonists' injuries and suffering, *Across the River* omits them. However, readers may be closer to Cantwell's thoughts than to those of most other Hemingway characters because of the nature of the story: the colonel's impending death allows him a reprieve on repressing his painful memories of the war and of past lovers, giving him, too, a freedom to express his love for Renata in a way that might not have been possible were he not soon to die. However, Hemingway leaves his readers with the sense that we do not get the full picture. Even during Cantwell's confession, we are bound by Hemingway's method of describing the action of a thing and not its emotion. Again, we may learn about troop movements and injuries, but not about the emotional ramifications of these events. Of course, if there were no emotional ties to these incidents, then there would be nothing to purge, nothing that Cantwell would need to reconcile. There is more to the story than we are privy to, and yet there is more overt discussion of trauma and the need to confess that trauma to someone else than we have come to expect in a Hemingway fiction. Why confess a story but leave out the emotion? How does Cantwell's telling of the story help him if he does not tell about his own feelings? What exactly is he purging?

Either Cantwell is holding back or Hemingway is. Or both. Perhaps Cantwell faces his inner emotional pain merely by telling Renata about the troop movements and invasions. Perhaps Hemingway wants to preserve Cantwell's masculinity by not showing his emotional purging. Whatever the reason for the omissions, all we have to work with are the action of the battles and the silence left by the gaps in emotional content. Our level of intimacy is thus seriously limited. We are close to Cantwell's pain, but not in it, near to the site of his trauma but kept from experiencing it. What we do learn is quite a lot about the debate to tell or not to tell and the fact that impending death is reason enough to let some rules about silence slide.

Cathy Caruth has written that "in extreme trauma one's sense of self is radically altered. And there is a traumatized self that is created. Of course, it's not a totally new self, it's what one brought into the trauma as affected significantly and painfully, confusedly, but in a very primal way, by that trauma.

And recovery from post-traumatic effects, or from survivor conflicts, cannot really occur until that traumatized self is reintegrated" (138). Cantwell, then, is negotiating between two selves—one, the soldier, whose masculinity is assured and one, a traumatized self, who is disabled, emasculated, and guilty. In her article "Traumatizing Feminism: Prevention Discourse and the Subject of Sexual Violence," Sara Murphy defines trauma as "the effects of an extraordinary event, an impact coming from outside the subject, which can only be integrated at the cost of the integrity of the subject itself" (73).[11] For Cantwell to reconcile his two selves, he must, in some ways, surrender his masculinity to Renata's love, give up his codes of silence, and speak.[12] Cantwell functions under strict codes in the telling of his trauma; one could argue that the codes, imposed by Renata and sometimes by himself, stem from grander schemes of the military or culture. The colonel tells about his experiences, but with much debate about who is free to speak of war (only those who are strong, injured, and not trying to write about it). I read Cantwell's outer resistance to speaking of his trauma as his inner struggle to retain the masculinity that his war wounds (both mental and physical) threaten.

### Madness in *Across the River*

In addition to Cantwell's resistance concerning his confession of trauma, his mental injuries contribute to students' understanding of the larger discussion of trauma in this novel and in Hemingway's other work. Hemingway indicates that there is something more to Cantwell's condition than physical injuries and a deeply rooted bitterness. Renata's refrain, telling Cantwell "'Don't be bitter'" and "'don't be so rough,'" suggests more than her desire for a gentler version of his confession; it is not like Hemingway to repeat details, so this frequency illustrates its importance. It is not just that Cantwell's language or his descriptions are too crude for Renata; it is that Cantwell's bitterness indicates that he has suffered a deeper injury, a mental one. To illustrate this, consider when the narration says, "Then he turned bad and he said . . ." (*ARIT* 224).[13] Being "bad" comes to mean more than a way of speaking; it illustrates the moments when the colonel falls into a mode of bitterness that can be seen as a manifestation of his madness.[14] Renata's refrains, then, signal his psychic instability, a condition from which she must calm him down. She is not only his confessor, she is also his therapist. Reminiscent of a patient on the psychotherapist's sofa, Cantwell often reclines on Renata's body as he talks, suggesting that Cantwell is engaged in the process of mental recovery.

Cantwell pointedly denies having mental problems. Aside from "combat dreams," which he says everyone has, he claims no ill effects from the war. There is evidence to the contrary, however. There are several instances in which his vulgarity reveals a greater psychic injury. You can direct students to his crude language as he recounts the invasion of Normandy, or his needless anger when a waiter asks him if he needs to sit down when his heart hurts (*ARIT* 204, 183). Each of these scenes reveals an outburst of anger instigated by feelings of insecurity, resulting in sudden the personality changes indicative of post-traumatic stress. The colonel's most overt display of madness, however, is not ambiguous because it carries with it a threatening image. At one point, Renata tells Cantwell that he must tell her more war stories. He reacts very strongly, as though she had commanded him to do something. "'*Have to?*' the Colonel said and the cruelty and resolution showed in his strange eyes as clearly as when the hooded muzzle of the gun of a tank swings toward you" (134; emphasis in original). That image of a gun barrel turning toward Renata lingers over the novel, bringing to light the cruel forces working in the colonel's mind. When his confession about the loss of his regiment surfaces, it reveals the guilt he feels over following dangerous and costly orders. Sorrow, even more than guilt, has made him unstable. When Renata becomes frightened and recants her "order," he recovers from the moment: "he smiled and his eyes were as kind as they ever were." His outburst was brief, but no less frightening for that, given the cruelty buried within. In that moment of madness, his perception of Renata's meaning was entirely divorced from reality. Renata describes these outbursts as "being bad," and the fact that she calms him each time implies that his behavior was irrational. Such a personality shift indicates mental trauma and provides a glimpse of the greater psychological wound he harbors.

By far the most significant threat to Cantwell's masculinity is coupled with a threat to his sexuality. Debra Moddelmog argues that "the obvious explanation for the recurrence of the wounded hero in Hemingway's work is that the wound marks a character's inner worth, especially his virility" (122). During their gondola ride, Renata asks again for the colonel to pleasure her by saying, "'Do you think we could once more if it would not hurt you?' 'Hurt me?' the Colonel said. 'When the hell was I ever hurt?' [Chapter end] 'Please don't be bad,' she said, pulling the blanket over them both. 'Please drink a glass of this with me. You know you've been hurt.' 'Exactly,' the Colonel said. 'Let's forget it'" (*ARIT* 147–48). The chapter ends mid-conversation, emphasizing the colonel's angry words about being injured with Renata's acknowledgment of his "being bad" at the start of the next. This scene illustrates several key points: the threat that disability poses to his sense of masculinity, Renata's ability to calm him after his outbursts, and his desire to "forget it." Vernon writes that "military and war experiences affect the soldier's sense of gender identity, which for the male veteran means his masculinity" ("War, Gender" 35). An *injured* veteran faces questions of wounded gender identity all the more.

By implying that the colonel might be too hurt to pleasure her again with his injured hand, Renata in effect emasculates him, questioning his virility and labeling him impotent. The colonel reacts by denying having ever been hurt, overcompensating in an attempt to confirm his wholeness and reject any disability. In discussing the sexual injury of Jake Barnes in *The Sun Also Rises*, Keith Gandal comments that "what Jake is missing . . . is not 'balls,' not guts; the spiritual stuff that matters in war. What Jake is missing is the stuff that matters most to a woman. . . . And what Jake has lost, *symbolically*, is the phallus as status" (147). The colonel never has to prove his sexual stamina because Renata is menstruating. His wounded hand, however, acting as an (already effective) sexual organ,[15] still must deflect questions of disability and effectiveness. "The wound ultimately increases rather than appeases the anxieties it was meant to deflect, moving the heterosexual masculine body into the realm of the female, the feminine, and the homosexual" (Moddelmog 121). Significant also to the colonel's emasculation is that, without penetration, Cantwell and Renata's lovemaking is nearer to lesbian lovemaking than it is to heterosexual intercourse. Peter Lisca discusses the star-crossed nature of their union, but what stands out is the threat to the colonel's masculinity and how it triggers his irrational outburst (292).[16]

Cantwell, like Jake Barnes in *The Sun Also Rises*, does not receive sexual pleasure, but he pleasures Renata with his *wounded* hand. Thus her suggestion of impotence strikes all the more deeply, emphasizing Cantwell's disability—suggesting a (more threatening) sexual disability—and igniting another outburst of anger. Despite her comment, the colonel does pleasure her, and therefore is given at least some of the sexual satisfaction Jake is not. Ultimately, however, the colonel's angry reply to Renata's suggestion of impotence repeats the harsh tone of his madness, implying that mentally he resembles the shell-shocked Nick Adams.

Miriam Marty Clark writes about three Nick Adams stories in which "illness remains unresolved . . . represented though never fully contained in narratives of original sin, Freudian symbology, and masculine heroism; addressed but never fully remedied by ordinary measures such as prayer, talk, or medical care" (170). Like Nick Adams in "Now I Lay Me," Cantwell for the most part functions normally with his trauma. Unlike Nick, however, who acknowledges the feeling of losing control of his mind—"I tried never to think about it, but it had started to go since, in the nights, just at the moment of going off to sleep, and I could only stop it by a very great effort" (*CSS* 276)—Cantwell does not acknowledge it. Cantwell's mental scars stand out as more prominent than those of other Hemingway protagonists, such as Nick Adams's in "Big Two-Hearted River," not only because of the frequent discussions about the need to purge but also as a result of their manifestations of anger and bitterness.

When Hemingway writes a mad man, this is what he looks like: imperceptibly insane, cruel, and rough when triggered. His brand of male insanity boarders on the sane. The colonel has only brief departures from control. Masked as sadness or bitterness, his mental instability is so slight as to be barely noticeable. The novel is suffused with his extraordinary masculinity; ultimately, his service record ensures that he is not feminized despite his (sexual) disability. Although the novel pivots around Renata's encouraging him to purge his bitter memories (and thus recover from his mental trauma), the focus tends toward his physical injuries, such as his scarred hand, weak heart, and impending death. Vernon has called "Big Two-Hearted River" the "most famous piece of fiction about war with no mention of the war in it" ("War, Gender" 34). I venture to describe *Across the River and into the Trees* as a fiction about psychic trauma with virtually no mention of madness.

Perhaps creating Cantwell is Hemingway's way of absolving himself for not doing more in the war; he joined the Red Cross ambulance corps after being rejected by the U.S. Army at eighteen because of poor eyesight. Vernon, Reynolds, and Gandal, among others, have discussed the feminized position of Red Cross workers and the impact that perception surely had on Hemingway's image of himself as a man. Teddy Roosevelt himself said that such work was for women and those unfit for service (Lisca 143; Vernon, "War, Gender" 38). "Hemingway could only be acutely sensitive to the implication of his Red Cross days, could only feel his male self-image undermined by his mode of war service" (Vernon, "War, Gender" 38). Thus undermined, he exaggerated his war experience and his personal heroics (39).

Gandal writes that Hemingway might have "consoled himself with the fact that his defective eye would probably have meant rejection by the American military from all branches of the service" (144), yet Jake Barnes's "humiliation" of being assigned to the Italian front (the "minor front") is "clearly derived from Hemingway's" (145). Given this, it is possible that Hemingway wrote Cantwell to compensate for his own lack of (proper) service. With nothing to shame him in terms of inadequacy or feminization, Cantwell carries the scars only of following orders and sending men to their deaths. *Across the River and into the Trees* is Hemingway's experiment in guilt from the other side—the guilt of a man suffering not from having done too little in the war, but from having done too much.

## Notes

1. Herman specifically identifies wounded soldiers who carry with them the memories of their combat experience and the burden of silence. "One of the many casualties of the war's devastation was the illusion of manly honor and glory in battle. Under conditions of unremitting exposure to the horrors of trench warfare, men began to break down in shocking numbers. Confined and rendered helpless, subjected to constant threat of annihilation, and forced to witness the mutilation and death of their comrades without any hope of reprieve, *many soldiers began to act like hysterical women*. They screamed and wept uncontrollably. They froze and could not move. They became mute and unresponsive" (20; emphasis added).

2. See Vickroy (207) and Herndl (38–54).

3. For instance, illness narratives of the modernist time period, such as H.D.'s *HERmione*, F. Scott Fitzgerald's *Tender is the Night*, and Zelda Fitzgerald's *Save Me the Waltz*, offer useful comparisons to those of Hemingway.

4. Hemingway suffered several serious injuries during his life, including a leg wound in World War I and others resulting from two plane crashes in Africa. According to Carlos Baker, "his injuries included a ruptured liver, spleen, and kidney, temporary loss of vision in the left eye, loss of hearing in the left ear, a crushed vertebra, a sprained right arm and shoulder, a sprained left leg, paralysis of the sphincter, and first degree burns on his face, arms and head from the plane fire" (*Life Story* 522).

5. Hemingway minimizes "Jake's humiliation by the army, in order to mask [Hemingway's] anger at the military" (Gandal 145).

6. From Herndl, consider two key ideas. First, consider how the patriarchal strictures of masculinity, medicine, and the military cumulatively encourage Frederic Henry to resist the telling of his own story for fear of accessing and then transmitting his painful emotions. "Plenty of critics have diagnosed Catherine Barkley as insane, unbalanced, or crazy," Herndl argues. "But critics almost always assume that Frederic Henry's malady is purely physical; he is the victim of shelling, in other words, but not shell shock. . . . I don't want to diagnose Frederic as insane, but I do want to cast some doubt on the precise nature of his malady, and raise the possibility that his illness is actually masculinity as it was presented to the World War I soldier" (39; emphasis added). Herndl locates this omission of his trauma in terms of Judith Butler's writing on the performance of gender, where the behavior of characters strengthens the norm of stereotypical gender roles. The second important idea in Herndl's article that informs our approach is her concept of "a narrative that in some ways resists its own telling" (44). In Frederic's case, she argues that "strategic silences" represent his resistance to revealing the full extent of his mental trauma or his emotional state (44).

7. Trevor Dodman's article "'Going All to Pieces': *A Farewell to Arms* as Trauma Narrative" supports the weight Herndl gives to the silences in the story by arguing that the narrator is fully involved in the telling of traumatic events. His attention to the exact nature of the narrator's voice during the telling of such trauma—with regard to techniques of silence, resistance, and evasion—informs my reading of trauma narratives, specifically, how the subtleties of narration can expose the nature of a character's deep trauma.

8. In his article "War, Gender, and Ernest Hemingway," Alex Vernon addresses the social constraints, loss of agency, and resulting emasculation that a soldier might feel during war. He interprets Hemingway's description, in *A Farewell to Arms*, of soldiers marching as though they were "six months gone with child" as "an expression of their experiencing the military and war as emasculating and thus feminizing insofar as the soldier's losing agency" (48). Vernon reads military service as a kind of entrapment, one that forces men into submission. "If pregnancy and childbirth for women signify and embody their social bonds, military service signifies a man's social bonds. Paradoxically, military service—and especially for American men headed to the Great War—serves as a liberation from domestic, economic, and social obligations, and a reassertion of manly autonomy, but also as the ultimate tie to society, one that demands the selfless sacrifice of the individual for society" (49). Henry is placed in an environment that, on the one hand assures him of his masculinity, while on the other, feminizes him by hindering him, ultimately contributing to the difficulty he finds in discussing his trauma. Like Vernon, Herndl sees military service as causing feelings of subservience and weakness. Herndl explains that Frederic is not able to find a voice to describe his suffering: "the stoicism that he embraces as an ideal (and that Hemingway employs as a style) keeps him from really being able to give voice to what he's thinking or feeling. He surrenders his own story to the intertwined stories of medicine (recovery from wounds) and masculinity (keeping quiet about his suffering). Frederic Henry tries to narrate a story that is culturally untellable" (46). The importance of *Across the River and into the Trees* is clear when you attend to this conflict between the desire to describe trauma and the complications involved in doing so because of the pressure from patriarchal systems of gender and sexuality.

9. Vernon reads Frederic Henry's position as a patient in *A Farewell to Arms* as one that inherently feminizes him: "He finds himself in a passive position, which in Hemingway's time was associated with the feminine and, in men, with the homosexual" ("War, Gender" 41). Vernon extends this idea to apply to all soldiers of World War I, arguing that the move of women to the work force, the changing roles of combat, and the mental hysteria of shell shock all contributed to their emasculation. "For male soldiers and front-line volunteers, like Hemingway, who passively suffered the new technology, the war paradoxically made men of them and unmanned them" (45).

10. When Cantwell does capitulate to Renata's demands for his confession, he tells his stories only to her, so while his audience is certainly inappropriate for the task, it is at least handpicked, not generalized, which perhaps absolves him of breaking this code.

11. "Because fragmentation creates a profoundly disturbing sense of self, victims go to great lengths to resist it. Consequently, the attempt to create or maintain a sense of agency and order and reject fragmentation is a common strategy of the narrators/ protagonists of trauma fiction" (Vickroy 24).

12. I am not locating this surrender in the larger discussion about modernist authors' mourning for the loss of masculinity, as Greg Forter has discussed. He describes their fixation on such a loss as making it "impossible to mourn or fully work through their losses—or to see in those losses an opportunity for reinventing masculinity in a less rigidly constrained, less psychically defensive, and less socially destructive fashion" (264).

13. Renata's comment, when she says, "I love . . . your strange eyes that frighten me when they become wicked," bears a mention here (*ARIT* 133).

14. What I read as madness, Lisca sees as the colonel's self-proclaimed "wild boar nature" (Lisca 294). He claims that the colonel, aware of his imminent death, is trying to be kind to those around him and to resist his more abrasive tendencies.

15. Lisca discusses the colonel's wounded hand as the hand of Christ (302).

16. Dana Fore writes that Barnes must "rid his consciousness of the idea that sexual mutilation can only trigger mental and physical 'degeneration' into homosexuality or invalidism" (81). Fore argues that Jake fails in reinventing his own sexuality and thus fails to save his relationship with Brett, but suggests that by the time Hemingway writes *Across the River and into the Trees,* he has perhaps developed his ideas of disability and sexuality, allowing the colonel to pleasure Renata (85).

# Part Four

# Ernest Hemingway Seminar

# Introduction

Alex Vernon

The three undergraduate student essays that follow were produced by seniors taking part in a Hemingway seminar at a small liberal arts college. Senior seminars in the Department of English at Hendrix College are capped at twelve students; this particular iteration, taught in the fall semester of 2012, enrolled nine. Students majoring in English are required to take one such seminar, which are often author-based. While we do not demand that students follow a strict course sequence for their major requirements, we do ask that they complete a certain number of courses at the different levels, and we regard these seminars as intensive preparation for the senior thesis they must complete in the spring semester of the final year. At this point in their careers, the students should be well practiced in the skills necessary to write a long essay of original literary interpretation.

For the first day of class, the students read a short biographical piece on Hemingway, Michael Reynolds's "Ernest Hemingway, 1891–1961: A Brief Biography," plus the early story that did not appear in *In Our Time*, "Up in Michigan." Besides the Reynolds essay, the semester's other contextual pieces are the segment on Martha Gellhorn in PBS's television series *Reporting America at War* and Hemingway and Joris Ivens's film *The Spanish Earth*. We view and discuss these prior to reading *For Whom the Bell Tolls* to introduce the students to the Spanish Civil War, a war few of them know anything about, the details and politics of which the novel relentlessly engages. Finally, Hendrix College's location and the generosity of the Hendrix-Murphy Foundation in Language and Literature afford me the opportunity to take the class on an overnight field trip to the Hemingway-Pfeiffer Home and Education Center in Piggott, Arkansas. I try to time this trip about a quarter of the way into the semester as another source for biographical context and as a community-building exercise (and also to take advantage of the fall weather). After a tour of the home, we hold class in the barn studio where Hemingway worked. We might carry on with the usual syllabus schedule; we might enjoy a presentation from the museum's director, Ruth Hawkins, on her book *Unbelievable Happiness and Final Sorrow*; we might do something more creative. After dinner, back at the bed and breakfast, we'll crowd around a television and watch a Hemingway-related film.

We begin our studies with *The Garden of Eden*, and then return to the beginning of Hemingway's career and read chronologically through most of his major novels and select short fiction:

1. *The Garden of Eden*
2. *In Our Time*
3. *The Sun Also Rises*
4. *A Farewell to Arms*
5. "The Short Happy Life of Frances Macomber" and "Snows of Kilimanjaro"
6. *For Whom the Bell Tolls*

Usually half of the students have studied a Hemingway text with me before: *A Farewell to Arms* in the lower-level American War Literature course; *In Our Time* in the modernism course; or *The Garden of Eden* in the postmodernism course. About a quarter of the remaining students have read a little Hemingway in high school or on their own. The course does not bear "war" in its title or deliberately focus on it, but war clearly is an aspect of every Hemingway book on the syllabus and it becomes a regular part of our conversations.

Beginning with *The Garden of Eden* shakes up the students' expectations and conventional understanding of the Hemingway ur-text. When we move on to other texts, students more readily initiate stimulating lines of inquiry. They are trained to be on the alert not only for complex expressions of gender and sexuality, but also for race and imperialism, authorship and craft, family and individuation, innocence and experience, selfhood and war, nostalgia and betrayal, memory and imagination, art and mortality. This unfinished novel by a mature writer studying a version of himself at an earlier stage of his career, a version of himself who likewise finds himself looking backward, has students looking for patterns and developments. The book's own play with the blurring of the nonfictional into the fiction introduces a discussion about Hemingway and biographical interpretation; at some point I read from Hemingway's entry in Mary's safari diary.

The class meets twice a week for seventy-five minutes. I have no agenda for any text or class meeting—I find that prompting great conversation requires very little from me other than using my own curiosity and expertise to occasionally oil the wheels. I do have a few tried-and-true moves, such as providing the excised ending of "Big-Two Hearted River" ("On Writing") on the last day we discuss *In Our Time* and brainstorming as many symbolic reasons as we can for Catherine's and the baby's deaths at the end of *A Farewell to Arms*. Generally, however, though I sometimes quickly introduce a potential reading, I prefer to foster the students' creative, critical, and collaborative interpretative processes. I want to embolden them to pursue their interests and to achieve originality accordingly.

We conclude each of the five books with two critical articles selected by a student pair or trio, who then lead class discussion that day. The two articles could analyze the same issue but from different approaches; they could cover different subjects altogether; or they could employ different scholarly styles. I ensure that, in addition to reflecting on the content of the essays, we spend some time discussing them as essays. *How do they work?* Thus, by the time the students begin to draft their own essays, they have a library of ten models. Invariably, the students find articles about a text relevant to a text later in the course. Conversation about the two Africa stories, for example, frequently draws on articles about *The Garden of Eden,* and a student's own final essay for the course will as often as not refer to or discuss an article *not* primarily concerned with the text on which the student has focused his examination.

The only other course assignment I require from the students before they turn to drafting their final essays is a "book report" on a scholarly work of their choosing, with my guidance and approval. The book might or might not focus on Hemingway; I encourage English majors to select a book that just might prove useful to their senior thesis as well as their Hemingway studies. I also suggest that they consider texts from different disciplines. For a student planning on a psychoanalytic approach to a different text for her thesis, I would recommend Carl Eby's *Hemingway's Fetishism: Psychoanalysis and the Mirror of Manhood.* A student in this particular class had a thesis interest in issues of race, sexuality, and incest in Faulkner, so I suggested she read and report on Walter Benn Michaels's *Our America: Nativism, Modernism, and Pluralism.* A student in an earlier class, fascinated by the male rivalry in *The Sun Also Rises* and excited by his Introduction to Literary Theory course, where he had encountered Eve Kosofsky Sedgwick's *Between Men: English Literature and Male Homosocial Desire*, chose René Girard's *Violence and the Sacred*. I directed a student curious about *A Farewell to Arms* and *For Whom the Bell Tolls* as tragic novels to Terry Eagleton's *Sweet Violence: The Idea of the Tragic*. One year Noël Sturgeon's *Ecofeminist Natures: Race, Gender, Feminist Theory, and Political Action* helped a student write a brilliant essay on "Up in Michigan" by giving her the basics of a school of thought she had not previously studied.

This requirement is intended to stimulate the critical imagination, to provide context beyond the text-specific articles they will find in electronic bibliographies as they research their own projects, to enable them to connect projects across courses, and, most fundamentally, to create low-stakes curricular space for intellectual curiosity. These books do not always prove pertinent to the immediate coursework, but the assignment gives students credit for exploratory reading, underlining its intrinsic value. I give them a reading day, and they come to class with a front-and-back handout for their classmates to supplement a five- to ten-minute briefing about their book.

The senior thesis, on a topic of the student's choice with faculty approval, runs twenty to thirty pages; I require my senior seminar final essays to run sixteen to twenty pages. In accordance with department guidelines for the senior thesis, I rarely permit a student to tackle more than one text—although an essay certainly can, and often does, employ other texts in its analysis, through passing reference, by framing a particular interpretative moment, or in appending a note that suggests ways of expanding the interpretation beyond the studied text.

The schedule allots a full week without class meetings for generating the first drafts, and then three to four days workshopping no more than three essays a day. A student is required to provide written feedback on the other drafts considered on his or her day. All drafts are due to me electronically forty-eight hours before the first workshop. Students with later workshop dates are welcome to distribute revised versions to all of us up to twenty-four hours before their assigned day. If the math dictates an uneven number of drafts each day, the first workshop will see a lighter load, because this day tends to invite questions about my expectations and indeed about structural and stylistic *possibilities*. As few English courses to this point have required essays of this length, the idea of a sectional organization comes as a welcome surprise. During the first workshop we usually talk about introductions (*More than one paragraph! Entice and be specific but don't spoil your conclusion!*), conclusions (*Truly conclude—don't waste anyone's time summarizing!*), and the skillful use of notes, plus I field the usual questions about stylistic preferences from students I haven't taught before. The last workshop day is the second choice for a light day in terms of draft numbers, giving me time to provide students with tricks and tips on enhancing their prose for the upcoming final couple of drafts.

I check my own comments until the end of discussion on a particular draft, and I do not write my own one-page feedback until after the workshop. The students' insights and questions are an essential part of my process. Their counsel complements and challenges my own; their articulations routinely give me better language for expressing my advice and concerns. Waiting until after the workshop to deliver my own feedback also allows me to write briefly and quickly, as I can reference workshop comments and target my elaborations. I don't have to make a point of referencing peer comments in my own letter because I simply can't help doing so. The workshops are scheduled for the last meetings of the semester, and the final essays are due at the start of the college's set final exam period for the course. Students thus have a week or more to revise and refine their essays before submission.

The following student essays were the three best from the fall 2012 class of nine. Whatever contributions the course structure made toward their brilliance, I really need to credit the other students in the class, my department and college colleagues, and the writers themselves.

I wouldn't call Hendrix an exclusive liberal arts college. Its acceptance rate is fairly high. Still, Hendrix is widely recognized as the top undergraduate institution in Arkansas, for several years now having received annual national recognition as an up-and-coming school and a best-value school. Roughly half of our students come from out of state. The English major draws some amazing students. I sometimes feel dispensable: our good students will excel regardless of the particular body at the head of the class.

While its professors have freedom in course design, the English Department has established a scaffold by course level to standardize expectations. How a particular course develops skills in close reading and substantive integration of secondary sources, for example, remains up to the professor. My departmental colleagues are known both for their rigor and their care. They demand a great deal from students and from themselves. By the time the students show up for the first day of a seminar, they have enjoyed a thorough preparation. They do most of the course's discussion work.

The three student writers of these essays were high achievers. Josephine Reece double-majored in philosophy and English. Her thesis on H.D.'s volume *Sea Garden* won the department's Best Thesis award. Zack Hausle majored in philosophy and minored in English. Anna Broadwell-Gulde double-majored in English and in environmental communication (a self-designed course of study). All three graduated with distinction and other honors. Both Josephine and Anna won Fulbright teaching opportunities for the year after graduation, Josephine in Korea and Anna in Brazil.

One can discern these students' backgrounds and interests in their Hemingway essays. The philosophy students brought their talents for literary theory to the table, with Josephine applying Elaine Scarry's *The Body in Pain: The Making and Unmaking of the World* to *The Sun Also Rises,* and Zack applying Michel Foucault's ideas about biopower to *A Farewell to Arms.* Anna, the communications student, taught herself Walter Ong's *Orality and Literacy* in order to fashion an original approach to the different kinds of storytelling in *For Whom the Bell Tolls.*

The results speak for themselves.

# Perceptions of Pain in *The Sun Also Rises*

Josephine Reece

Only two-thirds of Hemingway's bullfighting novel, *The Sun Also Rises*, takes place in Spain and only part of that in Pamplona as Jake, Brett, and their entourage act out their absurd love affairs to the music of the fiesta. The characters move not so much between locations as between drinks, their dialogue and concerns often mundanely and depressingly realistic. Expatriates, they exemplify the lost generation, idly spinning their wheels, with no purpose or motive as they drink their way across Europe. However, the novel is more than a depiction of overgrown teenagers who cannot get over their angst. Rather, it expresses beneath the surface a deep anxiety over pain and its expression, a preoccupation mimicked in the bullfighting ritual. The final bullfights bring these disparate characters to an aesthetic climax, reducing their circular story, for a moment, to a standstill in the bullfight's violent movement. Romero's bullfighting becomes an aesthetic act in which perceptions of pain are transferred to aesthetic effect. In this way the bullfight mimics Jake's own transference of pain through his narration of the novel.

Bullfighting in *The Sun Also Rises* is evaluated based on its ability to transcend the physical realm by becoming aesthetic. The bullfighting Jake calls "good" is equated with classical art, but he describes "bad" bullfighting in physical terms. Good bullfighting is always described as "straight," "pure," "natural," "smooth," all words that call to mind the classical beauty of Roman columns and statues (*SAR* 171, 223). As their relation to the classical suggests, these words describe good bullfighting in terms of a sculptural object, rather than pinning the sense of beauty onto a single movement or action. The bullfight is beautiful in the relation between the movements of the matador and those of the bull in this dance to the death. Bad bullfighting, in contrast, is described as "twisted" and full of "contortions" that leave behind "an unpleasant feeling" (171). These descriptions, though still visual, also evoke bodily feelings of disgust and discomfort. Guilt and embarrassment are types of social pain often described in physical terms. Someone experiencing fear or nervousness might say "my insides are twisted in knots" or "writhing." In her book *The Body in Pain*, Elaine Scarry states that "the vocabulary for pain contains only a small handful of adjectives" and so people often describe pain "as if" some agent (the cause of pain) or "bodily damage" were present (15). For example, someone feeling pain in the arm might say, "It feels like rats are gnawing on my arm," seeking to make the invisible pain tangible to others. In this way, Jake's use of the word *contortions* in describing bad bullfighting not only refers to the body of the bullfighter but also attempts to articulate physical pain.

Such articulation here is interesting, since it suggests not exactly communication, but the creation of the communicable. To *articulate* is to put the disparate parts of one's internal feelings together into a framework that will be understandable to others. Scarry claims that pain is unique in being particularly resistant to articulation. Observers of a person in pain will find that pain doubtful, yet for the person in pain, the pain is undeniable and certain (4). If someone wants to convey happiness, he tends to describe the object of their happiness. There are many words with which to do so—*wonderful, lovely, awesome, pleasurable*—and each one conveys to the listener that the object described is giving the speaker pleasure. But when a person wants to describe her pain, there is no object to which she can refer. There is no "it" to be the subject of adjectives. A person may say, "That song was wonderful!" if a song gives her pleasure, but if she has a pain in her arm it would not make sense to say, "My arm is horrible." She might say "My arm feels horrible," but even then the feeling of pain is not revealed. While listeners can experience the song that induces wonder, they cannot experience the arm that induces a "horrible feeling." Thus the listeners must remain in doubt.

If the speaker creates an object for his pain, however, his articulation becomes more successful. So in the example in which he says, "It feels like rats are gnawing on my arm," the feeling of pain is communicated because the listener now has an object to which to attach the pain, the sight or imagining of which can give the listener a sympathetic sense of pain. In *The Sun Also Rises,* Jake refers to bad bullfighting in terms that mirror this sort of pain articulation. In this case, the bullfight itself becomes the object through which pain is relayed to the audience. However, the context is distinctly different. Usually, the person experiencing the pain articulates it in a hypothetical object, but in this case the object (the bullfight) is real and visible while the pain attached to it and the one experiencing the pain remain undefined.

Scarry contends that "intense pain is also language-destroying," so control of pain is a control of language as well (35). Scarry explains the relationship between pain, power, and articulation through the example of torture. Torture creates an illusion of power for the torturers by destroying the victim's world (with pain) and reinforcing their own world (with articulation). In this way, language and an individual's pain are implemented by the agent of torture to convert "the vision of suffering into the wholly illusory but, to the torturers and the regime they represent, wholly convincing spectacle of power" (27). The first part of this claim is that pain is world-diminishing for the person to whom it belongs, while "intense pain is world-destroying" (29). The agent objectifies this world- and language-destroying aspect of pain and then denies it through the interrogation (29). In this way, the denial of pain "becomes a second form of negation and rejection" for the person in pain; her existence, which has been reduced to the undeniable fact of the pain, is negated, alienating her totally from her surroundings (56).

Instances of pain litter *The Sun Also Rises:* implied images of Jake's war wound, Romero's bruises, Belmonte's pain, Cohn's broken nose, the count's scars, Vincente Gironés's killing by the bull, Brett's longing, the wounding and deaths of the horses and bulls in the bullfights, and the goring of the steers. The preeminence of pain in the novel and the corresponding attention it gives to narration—what should be told, what makes good writing—make Scarry's theory of torture as the unmaking of the world a useful lens in analyzing the novel. Within the narrative there are two different presentations of pain—those associated with the bullfight and those occurring in the lives of the characters. These two kinds of pain are defined by spectatorship: the pain of the bullfight is meant to be viewed, whereas the pain of the characters is viewed only tangentially. These two kinds of pain are then brought together in the main bullfighting scenes of Belmonte and Romero, both of whom represent good bullfighting in the novel.

That the bad bullfighting is associated with the body in pain is an aspect of Jake's narration as much as it is a part of the bullfight. In his descriptions, Jake is creating a moral framework for the aesthetic portrayal of pain because he is using the bullfight as an object to help him understand and come to terms with his own pain. Jake claims that the bad matadors simulate an "appearance of danger . . . while the bull-fighter was really safe" (*SAR* 172). What makes bullfighting bad is when the danger is "faked" (171). In the essay "The Uses of Authenticity," Timo Müller claims that Hemingway creates for himself a pose of authenticity by portraying authenticity in his novels, a posture which "finds its most complex expression in bullfighting" (31). For Müller, Jake Barnes's association with bullfighting and especially Montoya's cult of *aficion* link Jake with the Spanish countryside and authenticity, a term that here denotes a "healthier social and natural environment" (31–32). Authenticity then grants "social capital" to the person who postures herself effectively (31). However, Müller focuses solely on the cult aspects of *aficion* and does not comment on what appears to be Jake's own creation of authenticity through his narration. In defining bad bullfighting as "faked," Jake makes a direct appeal to authenticity as a value. In this case, however, what defines faked is the absence of danger, so what is authentic (as opposite to faked) is the presence of danger. Jake juxtaposes the "appearance" of the bad bullfighting style with an implied reality. In describing and defining these differences, Jake aligns himself with the authentic, dangerous reality. However, the amount of truth underlying that presentation is debatable. What is revealed, though, is that danger is the source of bullfighting's aesthetic value, the danger of impending pain. When the bad bullfighters fake the danger, their effect is less aesthetically good because their bodies are no longer at risk of pain.

Good aesthetics, then, require an acceptance, a transformation of possible pain into an aesthetic object. What makes bullfighting good is the consciousness of pain presented in the correct way. Bullfighting becomes real when the bullfighter is truly in danger. The danger makes the fact that they remain whole and unhurt appear to the audience beautiful, because it is surprising, and because its truth may be undercut at any moment. Jake states that "Romero's bull-fighting gave real emotion, because he kept the absolute purity of line in his movements and always quietly and calmly let the horns pass him close each time" (171). In this description, Jake defines good bullfighting as that which arouses "real emotion," and such emotion stems from the extent to which the bullfighter submits himself to the idea of pain. The passing of the horns—the image of future pain—is transformed into an aesthetic object in which the absence of pain appears effortless and is enacted for "purity of line" rather than avoidance of pain. In this way, when the bullfighter is dedicated to the action as opposed to the result, the act of bullfighting becomes aesthetic. In order to achieve this, he must set aside the possibility of pain evoked by the horns, allowing his danger to become the basis for a new creation: the bullfight.

The aesthetic bullfight would not be possible without these two things: the bullfighter's relinquishment of his future pain, and the consciousness of that pain in the spectators. Brett and Jake see that what was "beautiful done close to the bull was ridiculous if it was done a little ways off," because they perceive that the beauty comes from the prolongation of danger, the matador's sustained exposure to injury (*SAR* 171). When the bullfighter is exposed to danger, the audience can participate in all his fear and tension as the probability of pain is again and again controverted. Thus it can be seen that the relationship between the audience and the bullfight centers around pain, but in a way that does not fit completely into Scarry's schema. Scarry notes that the pain experienced in torture results in a strange feeling of "isolation and exposure" for the victim (53). The victim is isolated by her pain, but this pain is meanwhile being objectified for the regime's use, so it is also exposed in that way, recognized but ignored. The victim has "all the solitude of absolute privacy with none of its safety, all the self-exposure of the utterly public with none of its possibility for camaraderie or shared experience" (Scarry 53).

The bullfight likewise involves isolation and exposure, but in the bullfight their functions are controlled, creative, and aesthetic. The difference is again in the mode of spectatorship: in the bullfight, the bullfighter has exposed *himself*, and while his exposure does not allow for camaraderie, neither does it invite ridicule. Rather, the bullfighter objectifies himself, gives himself up to the audience's gaze, and in doing so becomes a giant, becomes a god. The bullfighter's relationship to the crowd is the opposite of the relationship of victim to torturer because in the bullfighter's *choice* to objectify himself he is raised up, rather than cast down. His spectacle is not a spectacle of power as it becomes for a torturing regime, but a spectacle of creativity, an aesthetic assertion of selfhood.

As for isolation, which in torture occurs through the physical pain of the victim, in the bullfight it manifests as the bullfighter's physical isolation in the ring, which brings with it the possibility of pain. In torture, the victim is in constant pain, so that the pain at each moment reduces her world to nothing, isolating her from all else (Scarry 35). In the bullfight, the possible pain acts in the opposite manner, so that as the bullfighter avoids pain at each moment (pain that is present in the fear of the bull's horns) he is brought closer to the audience members, who are able to experience the thrill of fear and to triumph over pain from the safety of their seats. Brett's comment, "These bull-fights are hell on one . . . I'm limp as a rag," illustrates the way in which the crowd participates in the fight, taking on the sustained fear which the bullfighter gives up, so that in the end Brett is exhausted (*SAR* 173). The matador's body becomes a site of worship for the crowd as he objectifies himself, allowing the crowd to experience the prevention of pain, which is the creation of the aesthetic object, over and over again. In this way, the bullfight becomes a continual act of renewal, in which every move the matador makes is an aesthetic triumph over the possibility of pain.

The crowd members have already become unified with each other through participation in the fiesta, and it is in the pantomime of the bullfight that they are again able to assert themselves as individuals in the face of death. The fiesta that surrounds the bullfighting is a unity which can be described as "boiling over," as the many people involved are subsumed into the entity of the fiesta itself (215). The bullfight, however, exhibits the social distinctions which are erased during the fiesta: there are the "sword-handlers and bull-ring servants," the matadors and the picadors (215). Each person in the bullfight is defined by his specific job, which becomes his identity for the bullfight just as, during the normal state of affairs, the people enjoying the fiesta are defined by their occupations. The bullfighter's resistance to isolation allows the crowd to experience the individual, the bullfighter, asserting himself against the leveling power of society and death. However, the assertion is not an assertion for himself but an assertion for everyone, and thus the aesthetic climax of the bullfight is when the bullfighter becomes one with the bull. In this moment, all distinctions are torn apart in what is ostensibly the most distinct of experiences, killing versus being killed. This is the moment the crowd loves, for they go to "the corrida to be given a tragic sensation," to feel internally the bullfighter's aesthetic assertion (218).

Romero and Belmonte are both described as "all alone" in a crowd of people (*SAR* 216). "Neither," Jake states, "seemed to have anything in common with the others" (216). In this way, Romero and Belmonte represent twin demigods, the objects of the crowd's aesthetic appreciation.[1] Thus it is no accident that in the novel they who subvert pain in the bullring have their own personal pain painstakingly described by Jake. Seen in relation to one another, Belmonte and Romero present two opposite modes of experiencing the pain that they bring with them into the bullring. Belmonte's pain is repetitive and all-consuming. It shows itself in his face, which grew "yellower ... as his pain increased," and in his jaw, which "came further out in contempt" as the crowd jeered him (218). The physical pain from his sickness and the mental pain from the crowd's derision are expressed together in his face, and the one feeds on the other. In this way, Belmonte's pain is partially created by the crowd, which cannot understand his pain and so increases it. This pain, which Belmonte did not choose to confront (as he chooses to enter the bullring), is nonetheless evident during his performance in the ring, denying the crowd the triumph over pain that it expects. It is not that the crowd truly ignores Belmonte's pain but that it acknowledges it while despising it, a response that increases Belmonte's suffering. Belmonte in turn attempts to express his pain, to strike back at the crowd through the deeply ironic clenching of his jaw, so that the more the crowd derides his skills the more he stands on principle of technique (218). The indifference that he projects to the crowd contrasts with the "correct" indifference that Romero displays, projected toward the bull (221).

The rhythm of the Belmonte section suggests the way in which Belmonte and the crowd negatively feed off one another so that the public "felt defrauded," as Belmonte stuck out his jaw "in contempt . . . and finally the crowd were actively against him and he was utterly contemptuous and indifferent" (*SAR* 218). Belmonte's terrible, wolf-like smile is directed to the crowd as an answer to their insults, and as a mockery of his own pain (218). Everything Belmonte does is in reference to the pain, which he clutches tight, like his jaw. The pain has come to determine the color of his face, his ease of movement, his choice of bulls, and his very concept of himself (218-20). The throbbing of his pain is emphasized throughout this section through the repetition in the long sentence:

> Sometimes he turned to smile that toothed, long-jawed, lipless smile when he was called something particularly insulting, *and always the pain* that any movement produced grew stronger *and* stronger, until finally his yellow face was parchment color, *and* after his second bull was dead *and* the throwing of bread *and* cushions was over, after he had saluted the President with the same wolf-jawed smile *and* contemptuous eyes, *and* handed his sword over the barrera to be wiped, *and* put back in its case, he passed through into the callejon *and* leaned on the barrera below us, his head on his arms, not seeing, not hearing anything, *only going through his pain.* (*SAR* 218-19; emphasis added)

Every action in the sentence is framed with the words "always the pain . . . only . . . his pain," so that at each moment the pain is present and pushing against the reader's consciousness as it pushes against Belmonte, pushing out his jaw. In this way the pain infects every moment for Belmonte, eventually consuming everything, even perception, and he is stuck in the motion, "going through his pain." Jake's description reinforces Belmonte's pain as internal, close, personal, as it affects Belmonte physically and mentally. Jake implies that Belmonte fails in his bullfight because he allows his pain to come between himself and the audience, between himself and his art. In a way this is so, since Belmonte "picked the bulls out for their safety," because he was afraid of his pain and the danger of the bulls (*SAR* 219). However, Jake, in his description, offers another possible explanation for Belmonte's failure, which comes from the existence of two different Belmontes: the Belmonte who Jake sees in the ring and the Belmonte of legend, who exists in the minds of the audience. The Belmonte who Jake sees is the Belmonte who is suffering. Yet Jake implies that the rest of the crowd is so blinded by the legend of Belmonte that the real Belmonte becomes a ghost in comparison to his legend: "Fifteen years ago they said if you wanted to see Belmonte you should go quickly, while he was still alive. Since then he has killed more than a thousand bulls. When he retired the legend grew up about how his bull-fighting had been, and when he came out of retirement the public were disappointed because no real man could work as close to the bulls as Belmonte was supposed to have done, not, of course, even Belmonte" (218). In this way, Jake sets himself apart from the rest of the crowd in his connection to and understanding of pain. This example, though unmentioned by Müller, fits into his framework of authenticity. Müller believes that *The Sun Also Rises* reveals authenticity as a construct, the performance of which is a "strategy for success in the literary field" (34). In this case, Jake is using his narration (a literary skill) to posture himself as a more authentic experiencer of pain than the rest of the crowd. Only he is able to view and understand the pain behind Belmonte's actions and, in so understanding, separate Belmonte the man from Belmonte the legend. In this way also, Jake brings himself closer to Belmonte as a privileged observer.

In using pain experience as a measure of authenticity, Jake not only sets himself up as more authentic than those around him but also places pain once again at the center of his aesthetics, where authenticity is good and whether something is good or bad depends on the manner in which pain is avoided. By expressing his pain visibly, Belmonte denies the members of the crowd the sensation of tragedy they desire and prevents himself from becoming the sculptural object of the tragedy. Both his legend and his personal pain get in the way of the audience's gaze so that it cannot see Belmonte's "greatness" (*SAR* 220). Jake is explicit that the greatness is still in Belmont at least some of the time, but that makes no difference to his aesthetic success. In this way, the aesthetic success of a bullfight is a construct, just like authenticity, constructed among the bullfighter, the bull, and the audience. Belmonte does not fail in the same way as a "decadent" bullfighter using a "false aesthetic," a bullfighter who fails because the he only pretends to give himself up to the danger of the bull (219). Belmonte still works in the "terrain of the bull," but he does so in full knowledge of the pain, which only serves to intensify it (217). Unable to let his pain go and unable to resist bullfighting, Belmonte puts himself in a terrible borderland, where his pain is not only present but confronts him at every moment. Just as, in the truly aesthetic bullfight, the audience is confronted at every moment with the bullfighter's delicate survival, Belmonte is confronted at every moment with his pain and the fear of pain. If Romero becomes immortal as art, Belmonte's immortality has been stolen by his legend.

Belmonte's actual bullfighting is hardly described. In the narrative, as in Belmonte's life, the experience of pain takes over and it, rather than Belmonte's actions, provides the content of Jake's description. Romero's scene, in contrast, focuses so much on the actions of his bullfight that his personal pain is almost forgotten, and the text enacts the bullfight's ability to "wip[e] that out a little cleaner" (*SAR* 223). Romero is entering the fight after having been beaten by Cohn the previous night, a beating that left "his face . . . smashed and his body hurt" (223). Yet despite his personal pain, Romero achieves the aesthetic objectification that Belmonte failed to achieve. Jake states that Romero relinquishes his pain, implying that since it does not touch "his spirit," Romero is able to release himself to the movement (223).

In the work with the first bull, Romero's "hurt face had been very noticeable . . . all the concentration of the awkwardly delicate work with the bull . . . brought it out" (*SAR* 223). Romero's pain is more visible with the first bull because the pain cannot be transferred to the spectators, not through any fault in Romero, but because the bull is faulty. The crowd knew "nothing very fine could happen with a bull that could not see the lures," just as no dance can be truly beautiful if one of the dancers has learned only half the steps (221). Romero cannot give himself up to the choreography because his partner cannot keep the beat, and so because the movement between Romero and the bull is imperfect, Romero's relation to the crowd is also tainted. The crowd wants Romero to conquer a perfect enemy, a bull worthy of his godlike state. Without a worthy opponent, the anticipation of pain, the feeling of tragedy that the crowd yearns for, is unattainable.

The crowd's dissatisfaction with the first fight is then contrasted with their absolute approval of the second fight, which they "did not want . . . ever to be finished" (*SAR* 221, 223). Here Romero's exposure to the bull is so perfect and his triumph at each moment so seemingly effortless that the longer he remains in the ring the more godlike he becomes. Jake describes the feeling of viewing the bullfight, saying that "each pass as it reached the summit gave you a sudden ache inside" (223). In this way, the pain that Romero carried into the ring has been "wiped away" by his transformation into the aesthetic object. He, unlike Belmonte, has no legend, no prior aesthetic image to compete with, and so is more objectifiable. It is through his objectification that the crowd can participate in the nearness of pain through the "sudden ache inside" (223). The transfer of pain from the bullfighter to the spectators thus makes possible the aesthetic and in a sense constitutes it.

The relation of the bullfighter, bull, and crowd to pain is complicated by the fact that Romero and the bull are described several times in unity. Jake calls them "one sharply etched mass," says that "he and the bull were one," and adds, "without taking a step forward he became one with the bull" (*SAR* 221, 222, 224). Romero achieves aesthetic oneness with the bull as together they represent one etching, one mobile sculpture. As mentioned earlier, this unity is unique, since it represents the aesthetic climax of the bullfight, but it is also a moment that ought to be disparate. On the very basic level of experienced pain, the experience of killing is entirely distinct from the experience of dying. However, the experience is described as a unity, a oneness of being that goes beyond physical proximity. This moment is presented in the text as the culmination of the bullfight as aesthetic act and, as such, also represents the final transference of pain. It is the bullfighter who all along is exposed to pain, but it is the spectators for whom the imagination of pain is performed. What is beautiful in the bullfight is the bullfighter's avoidance of pain, his seeming immortality, but in order for the crowd to be aesthetically satisfied it must have tragedy; it is the bullfighter who ought to die in order to fulfill his role as aesthetic object.[2] The bull could not be the object from the start because he is too far from the crowd for them to identify with him. The bullfighter is the crowd's object, its pain surrogate. At this last moment, however, the bull takes the bullfighter's place. As they merge to become one, the bull's death stands in for the bullfighter's imagined death.

The relation between Jake's narration and the two bullfighters is evidenced in the choices Hemingway made in revising the main bullfighting scene. As noted before, the scene takes place following Robert Cohn's beating of Romero and the death of Vincente Gironés[3] and is meant to wipe "all that out" (Svoboda 61). However, Jake too was knocked out by Cohn the same night he attacked Romero (61). As Frederic Svoboda claims, the bullfighting scene "works structurally as an antidote to the sordid happenings of the preceding chapters" (61). Given that, as Romero wipes out his pain, the writing offers the reader relief and release from the tension of the novel. In revision, Hemingway changed the scene to focus more completely on Romero and to reduce Jake's narration, which originally comprised a "running commentary on his reactions to Romero's actions" (61). While in this revised version, Svoboda still sees Jake's role as that of "narrator and expert commentator on the bullfight," he does not expand on what it means for Jake to narrate this scene, coming as it does after a night in which Jake has been strangely twinned with the man who is going to fight perfectly in the bullring (62). Both Jake and Romero have been beaten by Robert Cohn, who takes that action out of jealousy over their involvement with Brett. Now, in the bullfighting scene, Romero "wipes away" his pain. But how does Jake deal with his pain?

Just as Romero brings his personal pain into the aesthetic arena of the bullfight, Jake brings his own personal pain into the aesthetic arena of the novel. The whole narrative is haunted by the specter of Jake's war wound. Throughout the novel he never describes or reveals the nature of his wound, although his hints make it clear that he is impotent (SAR 39). Ira Elliott, in his discussion of masculinity in The Sun Also Rises, states that Jake "is bound by a 'masculine' signification and desire which is 'untrue,'" and that his body physically "cannot do what his appearance suggests he can" (Elliott 84). In this way, Jake's pain has been transformed: originally deriving from a physical wound, it now derives from a wound of absence—that his societal signification as a male (which he also accepts) is not matched by a performative ability. Jake's statement that he tries to "play it along and just not make trouble for people" illustrates his discomfort with the issue (SAR 39). He sees the wound as a cause of trouble, not just for himself, but for others. His own pain, the inability to fulfill what desires he may still have, can become a source of pain for others, like Brett, causing a ripple of pain to travel outward through the whole group. Since the pain of his inability, like physical pain, is invisible to the outside world, he is isolated by it and finds it difficult to express. "I . . . felt like crying," he says. " . . . I felt like hell"—but only in relation to Brett (42). In this way she provides an object for his pain to become visible, to become expressible. However, even she is hidden, since none of his friends know he is in love with her. Jake's reticence causes him more pain later, when Robert Cohn continually confides his love troubles with Brett to Jake, not knowing that each word is a source of suffering for Jake himself.

Jake and Romero are also twins in their control of their aesthetic creation. For Romero, the aesthetic object is himself. Pointedly, in his narration of the last bullfighting scene, Jake implies that aesthetic creation has the power to erase pain. For Jake, then, it is through his narration (his voice, articulation) that he attempts to blot out his own pain. However, this structure is a performance on Jake's part; the idea that acting aesthetically, creating, can eradicate personal pain is set up within the narration by Jake himself. That the pain is "wiped out" for Romero is entirely subjective and based on Jake's own wish to "wipe out" his own pain. In this way, Jake's narration of the bullfighting scenes is also an enactment of his desire for healing. Yet in the way he describes the bullfight, Jake also creates a Müller-like structure of authenticity that not only provides the possibility of healing pain through art but also implies that Jake himself is an authentic example of such an act. Müller claims that Jake Barnes is presented in the text as a man of "literary merit," which grants him authenticity and social capital (33). According to Müller, literary aesthetics, like bullfighting, are concerned with "getting it right"—that is, with creating a more authentic, more original art object (33-34). Jake is an authentic writer because he "takes the material at hand—his friends and his travels—and makes a good book of it"; thus Müller believes that the text is meant as Jake's novel and that Jake's success as a writer is meant to define Hemingway's own pose as a writer (34, 40). For the purposes of this essay, what it is important to hold onto is Müller's estimation of both writing and bullfighting as examples of performative posturing, and his assertion that Jake Barnes is an authentic literary character (34). Jake's narration can be seen as setting up the criteria for its own success. Jake uses the bullfights to craft a narrative in which pain can be alleviated through the aesthetic act. At the same time he applies this logic to the narrative as a whole, using the criteria he set up within the bullfights to bring the narrative to a similarly therapeutic conclusion. The most important part of the bullfight, the act it depends on for aesthetic success, is the correct mode of dealing with pain, which is to allow the pain to be transferred to others. The bullfighter's pain is transferred first to the audience, but then to the bull. For Jake likewise, aesthetic success depends on transference of pain, and he achieves this through his doubles, Pedro Romero and Robert Cohn. Romero and Jake become doubles, as described before, because of their relations with Brett, their suffering at the hands of Cohn, and their control of aesthetic action. Robert Cohn and Jake are twinned as writers and because they are both in love with Brett. Robert Cohn is repeatedly called a steer in the early Pamplona scenes, but it is Jake Barnes who is like a steer in fact because of his impotence. The accusation illustrates Jake's own inability to signify externally his internal (hidden) condition, an inability that prompts anger when others signify in the "wrong way" (Elliott 84). Jake's anger and frustration with Cohn are in fact facets of anger toward himself. That Cohn and the homosexuals in Paris are all described by Jake as "superior" indicates that Jake is frustrated with Cohn because he has the performative ability of a man but is not performing—that is, can be mistaken for a steer (84). Jake's estimation of Cohn fluctuates based on his own state of pain, so that he can claim, at dinner in Pamplona, "We all felt good and we felt healthy, and I felt quite friendly to Cohn" (*SAR* 155), when, three pages earlier, he had admitted, "I liked to see [Mike] hurt Cohn. I wished he wouldn't do it though, because afterward it made me disgusted at myself" (152). Here Jake's feeling of health is associated with a friendly feeling toward Cohn, but when Mike is cruel to Cohn, Jake enjoys his pain. However, Cohn's pain is coupled with Jake's disgust as well. When Jake humanizes Cohn, his disgust finds its true object—Jake himself—but when Jake sees Cohn as the aesthetic object, he is able to displace his own pain onto Cohn, who becomes his surrogate.

Jake effects a displacement of pain through his narrative, crafting his theory of authenticity into the bullfight and then mirroring that example in the surrounding narrative, almost as if the bullfight were the Greek chorus to his tragedy—slightly removed and explaining the pattern the action will follow. At the end of Book 2, after the bullfight, Jake and Bill go to the café, where Jake "watched Belmonte," the man who holds his pain close (*SAR* 225). Jake, who also holds his pain close (admitting it to no one, least of all himself), sees in Belmonte his own synthesis of pain, the failed aesthetic, and so his pain is multiplied. He says twice during the meal "to hell with Cohn," and then, asked how he feels, replies "like hell" (226). Here Jake's anger at himself is muddled together with his anger at Cohn. The continued use of "hell" places them together, despite the fact that it is all simply Jake's feeling of suffering, which he projects onto Cohn. Jake proceeds to get very drunk to forget his pain, and when he wakes up again the world is "very clear and bright and inclined to blur at the edges" (228). Structurally, this passage marks a transition, since it is the end of Book 2, and the alteration of the world's appearance seems to imply some form of transformation. What the transformation entails, though, can only become clear through a comparison with Book 3.

The ending of Jake's narrative, Book 3, is only twenty pages long, and in those twenty pages Robert Cohn is mentioned only twice—once by Jake in his internal narrative in a brief aside about his hotel room and once by Brett (236, 246). That Cohn disappears so thoroughly in the ending is strange for a character whose history marks the beginning of the story. Brett's comment that Romero has "wiped out that damned Cohn" is true for the narrative quite literally, as Jake never mentions Robert Cohn again (*SAR* 246). Cohn is absent because Jake is completing, in this final book, his aesthetic project. By erasing Cohn from the story, expunging his presence except as history which can be wiped out, Jake mimics the bullfighter's killing of the bull, the final transference of pain. In the bullfight, the imagined pain, which was always the bullfighter's, is perceived to be present first in the crowd and then in the bull, whose death (a succumbing to pain) the crowd witnesses. Jake, in his narrative, has done the same thing with Cohn. The final book is Jake's act of killing, where Cohn is finally removed from existence in the narrative. The pain, which has always been Jake's and which compels him to write the narrative, is transferred through the narrative, through the reader's interpretation, onto Cohn. The reader acts as witness to Jake's act of transference and to the final removal of Cohn altogether, an act in which Jake frees himself from his own pain, if not forever, then for these few moments contained at the end of novel. In this end, we can read Romero's comment to be Jake's also, when Brett asks, "You kill your friends?" and Romero replies, "Always" (190).

## Notes

1. Although I am using *demigod* in a different sense, it was Timo Müller's essay, "The Uses of Authenticity: Hemingway and the Literary Field," that first gave me the idea that Romero might represent a deity in the text.

2. In describing the relation between the bull and the bullfighter, I am borrowing some structure from René Girard's discussion of sacrifice and surrogate victims in his book *Violence and the Sacred*. He states: "Sacrificial substitution implies a degree of misunderstanding. Its vitality as an institution depends on its ability to conceal the displacement upon which the rite is based. It must never lose sight entirely, however, of the original object, or cease to be aware of the act of transference from that object to the surrogate victim; without that awareness no substitution can take place and the sacrifice loses all efficacy" (5). Where Girard's discussion concerns displacement of violence in societies through sacrificial ritual, my essay is concerned with the displacement of pain through aesthetic ritual.

3. Gironés's death and funeral present a moment of pain in the text which is not channeled aesthetically or displaced but finds its way out of the bullring and into the streets of Pamplona. In this scene, the reality of pain and death is reasserted in the narrative in the figures of Gironés's "wife and two children" (*SAR* 202).

# A Farewell to the Armed Hospital

Military-Medical Discourse in Frederic Henry's Italy

Zack Hausle

*A Farewell to Arms* pulls no punches in its first chapter. With its opening salvo, Hemingway drops the reader straight into the universe Frederic Henry and Catherine Barkley occupy, one of staggering natural beauty regulated by war and death. In two pages, the book sets up major themes of naturalization, place, war, and throws us into the Italian front of World War I. At the surface of the text, Hemingway is preparing us for a great war story, the ominous movement of troops preparing for inevitable bloodshed over the course of the next three-hundred-odd pages. This interpretation, however, proves to be deceptively simple. The chapter closes with two brief lines on the impact of cholera on the troops: "At the start of the winter came the permanent rain and with the rain came the cholera. But it was checked and in the end only seven thousand died of it in the army" (*FTA* 4). Formally, these sentences are stated so simply that they seem an afterthought. The content they contain, however, helps to provide structure for most of the book. The vast medical apparatus of the military here "checked" the grave threat of cholera; the prosperity of the military operation is conditional upon a ubiquitous structure of health and medicalization that holds the sick world at bay. This theme of health and medicalization, particularly as it relates to the military, is a central concern of the text.

Upon further examination, buried in the description of the soldiers moving through the Italian countryside is a description of them marching as though "six months gone with child" (*FTA* 4). This is at least superficially bizarre. Given the context of medicalization, however, this image enters a web of comprehensive relations brought about by the war. In being likened to women "gone with child," the soldiers are both carrying the catalytic elements of death—the swelling of the apparent pregnancy is actually rounds of ammunition—and embodying the potential for reproduction. Putting aside the obvious irony of this description, the image of soldiers bearing ammunition as producers of life recognizes the enmeshed nature of the preservation and production of bodies and the instruments of death. What this chapter presents us with is a system of war, health, medicalization, and sexuality that comes to define the course of the text.

It is in this vein that the idea of biopower, popularized by Michel Foucault in a series of texts during the 1970s and 1980s, emerges as a useful lens of analysis for understanding *A Farewell to Arms*. Most generally, biopower is the field of analysis that addresses the politics of the body, and how specific mechanisms and techniques of power ascribe roles and functions toward the furthering of specific goals. I would, however, like to attach a caveat to this notion. The notion of biopower as a holistic, comprehensive phenomenon is difficult to draw from Foucault's writings; by the very nature of his work, Foucault aimed to resist what he termed scientific discourses. These are totalizing fields of knowledge that admit for little creativity or criticism, which he presumes most fields of authoritative knowing to be. As such, it would be difficult to provide a quotation that fully captures biopower as a gestalt. With this in mind, I will deploy some of the aspects of what Foucault believes to be biopower. I hope that the quotations I use here help to illuminate the specific direction of my analysis. Biopower is not best understood as a comprehensive tool of analysis, but rather as an inquiry into the specific techniques and instantiations of how power occurs: "[It is less] a 'theory' of power and moving toward an 'analytics' of power; that is a toward a definition of the specific domain formed by relations of power, and toward a determination of the instruments that will make possible its analysis" (Foucault, *History of Sexuality* 94). Foucault emphasizes the diffuse, network-based character of the typical manifestation of biopower: "This [the system of politics of the body] is an extremely complex system of relations ... subtle in its distribution, its mechanisms, reciprocal controls, and adjustments. It's a highly intricate mosaic" (Foucault, *Power/Knowledge* 62).

Perhaps the central concern of this politics of the body is what it is a strategy toward; the teleology of biopower in general is toward the maintenance of a healthy and useful population: "This is the emergence of the health and physical well-being of the population in general as one of the essential objectives of political power ... Different power apparatuses are called upon to take charge of bodies ... to help and if necessary to constrain them to ensure their own good health. The imperative of health—at once the duty of each and the objective of all" (Foucault, *Power* 90). This is the rationalization for all the techniques of health, hospitalization, role-assignment, and place designation—all the facets of being are kept in check by a comprehensive regime of control designed to keep the population healthy and useful.

Hemingway's literature can serve as a tool to interrogate the constituent phenomena of biopower. Foucault puts heavy emphasis on the concept of a subject constituted as a dual subject; persons are importantly considered both subjectivities and targets of medicalization, sexualization, and all the other processes that end up constituting a coherent person in the context of institutions. To this end, Foucault deploys old journals from French prisoners and the ledgers of nineteenth-century reformeries—an evidence set with obvious limitations. Insofar as literature provides the sort of specific emotional and personal context that can't be gleaned from prison statements or psychiatric records, it adds another dimension to understanding the particular technical effects of biopower.

Before I begin in earnest, I'd like to make a few important methodological notes. Acknowledging that in dealing with biopower we are not dealing with some science in its totality but instead a "mosaic" of diverse strategies, my approach in this paper is to address four different areas of inquiry that help to illuminate the sort of regime that may ultimately constitute the modern politics of the body. These four areas of inquiry—the institution of the hospital, the role of place in controlling bodies and livelihoods, the roles ascribed by the war and health apparatuses, and the curious matter of Catherine Barkley's pregnancy—all directly reflect areas of concern that ultimately constitute a broader regime of control brought about by the conditions of the war. As such, there will occasionally be overlaps in inquiry. I think this speaks mainly to the structure of tactics that constitute biopower, however, and ultimately reflects the pervasiveness of its effects. That Foucault never approached literature itself makes this line of inquiry somewhat more difficult, but to ameliorate that concern, I engage with the work of a number of scholars on the constituent techniques and issues that help to constitute an analysis of biopower. Hopefully, this interdisciplinary engagement will serve as an advantage as well.

Hospitalization and the Medical Regime

In *A Farewell to Arms*, the institutions of health—particularly the hospital—are nearly ubiquitous. Frederic Henry is an ambulance driver, Catherine Barkley is a V.A.D. nurse, much of the narrative action takes place in hospitals, and the extensions of military health into the battlefield are often explicit in local treatment and field hospitals. Frederic Henry even goes so far as to say that his "room at the hospital had been our own home" for him and Catherine (*FTA* 153). This is compounded by three other instances in which he talks of going "home to the hospital" (117, 118, 134). Foucault is particularly interested in the implications of the hospital, describing it as "an essential element in medical technology" with a role of "elaborat[ing] a complex system of functions in which the hospital comes to have a specialized role relative to the family . . . to the extensive and continuous network of medical personnel, and to the administrative control of the population" (Foucault, *Power* 103).

In *A Farewell to Arms*, we see the articulation of a world structured by medicine, and by the hospital in particular. In applying Foucault's description of the typical hospital regime to the novel, however, we must acknowledge an interesting additional wrinkle: we are primarily interested in the institution of the military hospital, both as a set of regulating ideas and as a literal place. This particular instantiation of the hospital has specific implications for a consideration of the text, as Diana Herndl argues. While Foucault states that the purpose of biopower is ultimately to maintain a healthy, well-regulated population, Herndl notes a perverse echo of this with regard to military hospitals; such hospitals are structured under the assumption that "the point of military medicine is to heal men to the extent that they can go and face death again" (49).

This interpretation of the function of the military hospital ties neatly into an analysis of biopower. Herndl posits that "the discourses of medicine and masculinity in this novel join forces to colonize male subjectivity, to remake men as fighting machines" (4). Herndl notes two instances in which success as a soldier as judged in the hospital context is directly determined by a man's willingness to put himself in the line of fire: first, when Rinaldi questions whether Henry was injured while doing something "heroic," and second, when the officer marks that Henry was injured in the line of duty so as to avoid being accused of shirking duty. Although the hospital is at least nominally meant to heal, in fact, the only legitimate reason for being in the hospital—which, in most cases functions as the only sanctuary from war for a soldier—is because of grave injury in the line of fire.[1] This particular role of the heroic, body-sacrificing soldier gains greater importance when contextualized by the grave consequences that accompany Henry's eventual desertion. It is obvious in the case of the text that the role of the hospital is not strictly to heal or to control a population but to prepare a population for readiness in combat.

## The Hospital and Medical Expertise

"But what's the idea of a hospital without a doctor?" (*FTA* 87).

Henry here seems to be channeling Foucault's understanding of the signification of the hospital. As the agent of the hospital, a place in which it is necessary to "articulate medical knowledge without therapeutic efficiency," the doctor becomes the "great adviser and expert . . . in the art of observing, correcting, and improving the social body and maintaining in it a permanent state of health" (Foucault, *Power* 100). In this case, the hospital is truly useless without a doctor, without the avatar capable of imparting medical knowledge. Henry seems to agree with this, questioning the purpose of a hospital staffed only by nurses, who constitute peripheral agents of the hospital. Not only does Henry question the purpose of a hospital without a doctor, though; in relation to Valentini, he revises this claim to ask what the idea of a hospital is without a decorated doctor. The first we hear of Valentini is that "he was a major, his face was tanned and he laughed all the time," and Frederic Henry notes his exit with the statement that "there was a star in a box on his sleeve because he was a major" (*FTA* 99–100).

Frederic Henry's judgment of the doctor treating him on the basis of rank—and particularly, the value of his opinion as a relative function to his rank—is telling of the function power serves in developing intellectual authority. Initially, before discussing the doctor's rank, Henry assures the first captain that he values his opinion. Yet despite the assurances of the house doctor that the first captain "is an excellent surgeon" and that he would "rather have his judgment than any surgeon I know," Henry is skeptical. His skepticism stems from his belief that if "he [the first captain] was any good he would be made a major" (*FTA* 98). Despite assurances from someone familiar with the first captain's medical proficiency, Henry's assessment of medical capability is bound up with his assumptions regarding military capability. The doctor Henry asks for as a replacement, Valentini, is a major from the Ospedale Maggiore, a prestigious medical institution in Italy. This doctor, however, does not seem to have the same practical medical expertise as the first captain, and quickly exclaims that he will have "ten drinks" when offered one by Henry (99). Throughout this entire section, Henry's repeated musings on the doctor's status as a major obscure his recognition of Valentini's seeming deficiencies in knowledge. The text critically exposes Henry's enmeshing of military authority and medical expertise in his choice of doctor. The decision-making process was not contingent on the opinions of those apparently qualified to make judgments on medical expertise—the house doctor in this case—but instead on Henry's conflation of the institutions of the military and health. The result of his choice is that he is able to return to the action of the war much sooner—an ability directly related to the differential diagnosis of the higher-ranked medical officer. This is, after all, why he initially sought a second opinion—his desire to be capable of fighting the war again. The first doctor, the captain, despite his medical experience, did not give Henry a response pursuant to the aims of the military hospital, which Valentini promptly does.

Valentini's dialogue is also worthy of examination on this tack. His offer to "do all your maternity work free" and his comment that Catherine "will make you a fine boy," have several implications (*FTA* 99). The first phase of inquiry is Valentini asking Henry how he did that "rotten thing," but it quickly shifts to the subject of reproduction. Valentini, who comes into the story and wins Henry's approbation as a result of his rank, immediately offers to provide reproductive services, implicating these in the military regime. Interpreting this through Herndl's lens of the military hospital as functioning to repair men only to the extent that they can die in war, we can also view the child with regard to this function: the child, the son of a figure already implicated by the war, is brought into the world by the avatar of the military-health discourse in what seems to be a harmless, pro bono gesture. However, the child is part of the population being produced as war-fodder, fated to die as a result of its place in the discourse of military health. This contention is supported by Valentini's referring to their unborn son as a "fine boy." Not only does Valentini refer to Henry as a fine boy in his injured state, but Henry, later in the text, refers to one of his fellow patients, who is severely wounded, as a "fine boy who had tried to un-screw the fuse-cap from a combination shrapnel and high explosive shell for a souvenir" (108). Although "fine boy" is the sort of description that Henry employs for people throughout the text, this specific phrasing is restricted to Henry—particularly in the context of injury—and the critically injured boy in the hospital.

Place, Territory and the Body

Geographic space and territorial concerns play an important role in Hemingway's work. According to Foucault, geographic concerns, and particularly the way institutions manifest themselves in geographic space, can play a critical role in the machinations of the politics of the body (Foucault, *Power/Knowledge* 77). More than being exercised on a population, biopower is exercised on a population in a certain territory with certain geographic and topological implications. Within the world of *A Farewell to Arms,* the geographic locus of biopower is Italy as a whole. The state's apparatus of military medicalization is apparent, with the focus on the hospital being the core of this territorial dominance. What makes the biopolitics of territory most critical in this narrative, however, is the way in which Frederic Henry and Catherine Barkley attempt to use territory to create place of resistance to the techniques of biopower—to the hospital. I will discuss this toward the end of the section.

Frederic Henry noted the way the real effects of the war implicated real places:

> There were many words that you could not stand to hear and finally only the names of places had dignity. Certain numbers were the same way and certain dates and these with the names of the places were all you could say and have them mean anything. Abstract words such as glory, honor, courage, or hallow were obscene beside the concrete names of villages, the numbers of roads, the names of rivers, the numbers of regiments and the dates. (*FTA* 185)

Beneath the guise of gratuitous decoration and glorification, you have the "concrete names" that determine the actual content of the war. There is a certain cynicism that accompanies this statement by Henry. Despite all the dressing and obfuscation, Henry is able to demystify the techniques of power and determine their real targets: the places and people directly affected by the military ideology that controls their population. Perhaps the most salient example of an attempt to glorify and obfuscate the reality of place concerns Italy, as both nation and location in geographic space, and comes during an interchange between an Italian army officer and the battle police during the Italian retreat from Caporetto.

> "It is you and such as you that have let the barbarians onto the sacred soil of the fatherland."
> "I beg your pardon," said the lieutenant-colonel.
> "It is because of treachery such as yours that we have lost the fruits of victory."
> "Have you ever been in a retreat?" the lieutenant-colonel asked.
> "Italy should never retreat." (*FTA* 223)

Not only should Italian soldiers never retreat, "Italy" should never retreat. Through the metonymic use of *Italy* for the Italian army, the battle police lay bare the implications of the territorial strategies of military-health. The nation and geographic place have claim to the people of the Italian army—such a strong claim that death is the only appropriate retribution for a retreat. The retreat, constituting an attempt to escape the territorial obligation held by the Italian army for each of its soldiers to risk death, is unquestionably[2] a punishable violation of military laws, regardless of whether it was appropriately mandated or not. This is because of the geographic implications of military power.

There could be an even greater signification held by the tactics of geography, however. Gene Washington's analysis of the significance of the "good place" and "dead angle" in Hemingway's play *The Fifth Column* interprets certain places in the work of Hemingway to hold specific meanings. The good place, or *querencia*, is a consistent theme in Hemingway's works. "It may be argued that every major Hemingway narrative contains a good place ... a good place that features a close human relationship ... and/or a good place that features a relationship with a special location" (Washington 132). Washington characterizes the *dead angle*, a term borrowed from military parlance that signifies protection from fire for some geographic reason for another, as a specific sort of good place in Hemingway's work. The tactical nature of biopower makes this sort of good place particularly interesting when analyzing the politics of the body—use of the dead angle is a tactically oriented defensive response to an aggressive strategy. Analysis of the dead angle provides insight into the geographical strategies deployed by the Italian government through the refuge Henry and Barkley seek.

The most apparent example in *A Farewell to Arms* of a dead angle as a good place is the town in Switzerland to which Henry and Barkley escape following the retreat from Caporetto. This is also the crux of their resistance to the military-medical regime of the hospital: by escaping to Switzerland, a "good place" isolated from the reach of the hospital institution, Henry and Barkley attempt to escape the damaging and proscriptive impacts of biopower. Immediately following Henry's escape from the battle police, it becomes obvious that his only refuge is to escape the geographic influence of the military entirely. The simple exchange between the barman and Henry—"'I don't want to be arrested.' 'Then go to Switzerland'"—is a tersely stated reflection of the territorial extension of biopower (*FTA* 283). For his desertion of the military—for his abdication of his body as a resource for the Italian military-medical system—he must escape the territory they control in order to avoid death.

Switzerland, then, is a good place—and, in its use as refuge from the effects of the military in Italy, a dead angle—"a country where nothing makes any difference" (*FTA* 303). Switzerland, at least for a time, serves as both a demilitarized and a demedicalized place. In fleeing, Henry forces Barkley into abdicating her duties as a nurse; as a direct result of his own act of resisting overwhelming military force, Henry and Barkley flee from Italy and away from the influence of the war. The armed neutrality of Switzerland functions as an alternative to the militarization that dominates the rest of Europe—it provides an apparent escape from the framework of institutions and expectations that constitute wartime existence. In sharp contrast with Italy's battle police, with their interrogations and executions, Switzerland's guards are unquestioning and benign. In dialogue, Frederic Henry contrasts the Italian regime with the Swiss:

> "No," I said. "What's the procedure in going to Switzerland?"
> "For you? The Italians wouldn't let you out of the country."
> "Yes. I know that. But the Swiss. What will they do?"
> "They intern you."
> "I know. But what's the mechanics of it?"
> "Nothing. It's very simple. You can go anywhere." (*FTA* 241)

The technical approach of the Swiss police differs substantially from that of the Italian military, with a much less invasive process of control of his geographic location—and this difference in place and control is borne out in their experience in the text. Even in Barkley and Henry's encounter with the police in Locarno, their discussions are less related to control and possession than to petty squabbles and bureaucratic inconveniences. The most contentious discussion the two officers have concerns which city in Switzerland is the best for "winter sport" (280–81). This passage is a far cry from Henry's confrontation with the battle police during the retreat from Capporetto, which set him onto this path of translation in the first place.

In Hemingway's writing, however, the safety provided by the good place is not lasting. Washington argues that the collapse of the good place—the end of the protection of the dead angle—is a tragic inevitability in Hemingway's work (129). Certainly in *A Farewell to Arms* the act of translation proves to be limited. When Henry and the pregnant Barkley move to Lausanne because "that's where the hospital is," reminders of the war return (*FTA* 307–10). Henry, reading the newspapers in his hotel, is reminded of the German offensive taking place at that moment. Their good place has also been necessarily ruptured by the coming child. The dead angle has collapsed as a result of the child, forcing Barkley and Henry out of their Swiss idyll and back into the world of hospitals and war. Once they have reengaged in this context, the looming deaths seem inevitable. There is no more dead angle; they have returned to the direct line of fire.

### Role-ascription, Military Health, and Sexuality

It is likely that the great romance between Frederic Henry and Catherine Barkley never would have come about outside of wartime.[3] The meeting of an American volunteer and a British military nurse came about not by true coincidence but as the caused result of a unifying military institution. Their common space, which operates as a precondition for the relationship between the two, is entirely conditioned by the expectations of the institutions of the military and health in the text. *A Farewell to Arms* engages differently with the discursive ascription of roles, although the roles fulfilled and negotiated by Barkley and Henry are very different from the roles fulfilled by gendered masculine expectation. Still, these roles possess much of the same gendered function, as is indicated by Barkley's characterization of her placement as a V.A.D. nurse: "The Italians didn't want women so near the front. So we're all on special behavior. We don't go out" (*FTA* 25).

There are two elements of significance in this description: first, that the roles of women in the military-health institution are circumscribed by a set of norms inherent to the discourse, and second, that social activity—and sexual activity, as indicated by Barkley's qualification that "we're not cloistered" (*FTA* 26)—is restricted by the parameters of "special behavior." Later, Barkley remarks that if her superiors were to find out that she and Henry were intending to marry, she would be sent away. Although she is not formally cloistered, the standards of the Italian army substantially restrict the range of her formal options regarding sexuality and even marriage.

> I wanted us to be married really because I worried about having a child if I thought about it, but we pretended to ourselves we were married and did not worry much and I suppose I enjoyed not being married, really. I know one night we talked about it and Catherine said, "But, darling, they'd send me away."
> "Maybe they wouldn't."
> "They would. They'd send me home and then we would be apart until after the war." (*FTA* 115)

The mores of the military medical institution thus very neatly regulate not only Barkley's specific role as a V.A.D. nurse but also the conditions of her body through control of her sexual existence. She is not helpless, however. The proscriptions laid down by the hospital and the war play a formative role in the sexuality that does occur but seem intended to limit it rather than eliminate it;

sexual options are narrowed and channeled into what seems an accepted but unacknowledged sort of resistance. Barkley's and Henry's awareness of the roles they are required to play as a result of the circumstances of war signifies this, as they consciously adopt certain rules and perspectives in their approach to sexuality. Their conversations early on indicate this active flouting of regulations, including the rule they make regarding Henry's dalliances with prostitutes.

Sex with prostitutes is an integral part of the military experience, and it may help to explain Barkley's experience of feeling like a "whore" when decontextualized from the hospital. After all, women are presented with two sorts of functional roles: either their role as members of the V.A.D., in which they are at least nominally prescribed a sort of "special behavior," or the role of prostitute—a dreaded external specter. Rinaldi describes the prostitutes as having become "old war comrades" who are no longer "girls"—the war has so implicated them that they are more fellow veterans, subjects of the military regime, than untouched "girls" (*FTA* 65).

Catherine Barkley expresses her concern over the differentiation of these roles in her questioning of Henry over his previous sexual history.

> "How many have you—how do you say it?—stayed with?"
> "None."
> "You're lying to me."
> "Yes."
> "It's all right. Keep right on lying to me. That's what I want you to do. Were they pretty?"
> "I never stayed with any one." . . .
> "When a man stays with a girl when does she say how much it costs?"
> "I don't know."
> "Of course not." (*FTA* 104–5)

Although Barkley is clearly aware that Henry has had sex with prostitutes, she would rather claim ignorance so as to be able to claim faithful adherence to the narrative of genuine romance. And it is explicitly role-playing, with both of them acknowledging that they are mutually accepting Frederic's lies. This role-playing is not one-sided; initially, the entire relationship is contingent on Frederic pretending to be her fiancé in the first romantic encounter. Henry, after all, acknowledges that this is a game: "This was a game, like bridge, in which you said things instead of playing cards" (*FTA* 30). Just like bridge, the dialogue here is contained by a set of guidelines and rules that allow for certain actions but proscribe others. This game exposes the norms and expectations that come into play in the formulation of interaction between the genders, but reproduces them nonetheless.

Yet another example of this role-playing comes even earlier in the text, when Henry first tries to kiss Catherine: "I leaned forward in the dark to kiss her and there was a sharp stinging flash. She had slapped my face hard. Her hand had hit my nose and eyes, and tears came in my eyes from the reflex.... 'I'm dreadfully sorry,' she said. 'I just couldn't stand the nurse's-evening-off aspect of it'" (*FTA* 26). Barkley here directly confronts the role that she is expected to play. She acknowledges both the usual sexual proscription that accompanies her role as nurse and the tacit expectation of sexual libertinism that accompanies the allowed lapse of that role (the "nurse's evening off" she refers to). She shows a momentary hesitance about fully embracing the narrow avenue of seemingly "taboo" sexuality—which seems to be the primary context of male fantasies brought about by the wartime situation. Foucault holds that this sort of game-playing with taboos is a natural part of the proscriptive discourse, one it must have in order to function in the manner it does. He asserts that taboos do not "set boundaries for sexuality, [but instead] ... extend the various forms of sexuality." Further, they "produce and determine the sexual mosaic ... [they] all form the correlate of the exact procedures of power" (Foucault, *History of Sexuality* 46–47). This is to say, the taboo and the proscription in the end perform a positive function; there is a positive account of sexual behavior that emerges from the terms of proscription. Barkley and Henry's experience clearly bears this out. Ultimately, they must be made to have sex—otherwise, the population does not replenish itself as it needs to do in the military discourse. It's worth recognizing, however, that it must occur in a very specific way.

The Pregnancy

In all these questions of the control of bodies and population, the issue of Catherine Barkley's pregnancy is a central concern. Foucault tracks a "medical—but also political project for organizing a state management of marriages, births, and life expectancies; sex and its fertility had to be administered" (Foucault, *History of Sexuality* 118). In *The Birth of the Clinic*, he characterizes a turn from sex as a private issue to sex as an issue of mechanical reproduction; this specific sort of reproduction and administration in the context of military health seems to be suggestive of the reproduction of the child being directly implicated in the logic of the military hospital established earlier. This is to say that all the strains of biopower eventually culminate in Catherine Barkley's pregnancy and the ultimate death of her and the child. Aimee Pozorski alleges that the entire war may in fact hold some culpability for the death of the child, as "this phrase also solidifies the tenable connection between the deaths of soldiers in war, and the deaths of the soldiers' babies. The phrase 'war baby' alone suggests that these babies, born under the sign of war, are already slated for death; they are already dead, a significant subtext of literatures of genocide" (80). Alex Vernon holds that in order to escape the "social ties" created by the war, both Catherine Barkley and the child must die; this constitutes Frederic Henry's final escape from the impact of the war ("War, Gender" 49). I would argue that both of these accounts have truth: the conditions of the war are such that the "social ties" binding Frederic Henry are manufactured; they are the result of an intersection of the techniques of the military and health. As such, the child is necessarily implicated in the war in a fatalistic way.

It seems to be tacitly accepted from the outset that Barkley and Henry's child is already implicated in the discourse of military medicalization. Perhaps the most revelatory passage in this context occurs when Barkley and Henry discuss the future military position of their unborn child. Although the discussion is brief, it almost immediately follows the initial revelation that Barkley is pregnant. The discussion is one of the speculative games frequently played by the two regarding their future following the war. The only question is whether the child will be "a lieutenant commander" or a "general" (*FTA* 141). Barkley resolves this by joking that if the war is "a hundred-year war," their child will have the chance to do both. This short passage not only implies the prospect of ongoing war, but also suggests the way in which the very possibility of reproduction in war is entangled with the conditions of the war itself.

The pregnancy culminates in an oft-cited passage in which Frederic Henry describes the inevitably of the death of his just stillborn son:

> Maybe he was choked all the time. Poor little kid. I wished the hell I'd been choked like that. No I didn't. Still there would not be all this dying to go through. Now Catherine would die. That was what you did. You died. You did not know what it was about. You never had time to learn. They threw you in and told you the rules and the first time they caught you off base they killed you. Or they killed you gratuitously like Aymo. Or gave you the syphilis like Rinaldo. But they killed you in the end. You could count on that. Stay around and they would kill you. (*FTA* 327)

This is the moment at which the narrative strands of biopower culminate in the text. Henry's harried, almost hysteric sentences, alternate between desperate statements to his stillborn son and second-person statements about the cruelty of war. Interestingly enough, he ascribes intentionality to a "they" responsible for the death of both the rhetorical "you" and Catherine. This intentionality is suggestive of the possible tactical nature of the techniques of the politics of the body throughout the text—the system of medicalization and military death has been strategically imposed by the ambiguous "they," possibly the obscure agents of power and war who have created this milieu. Pozorski argues that Henry sees the death of the child as an intentional act, describing it as murder: "By establishing an analogy between a choking, murderous stillbirth and death at the front, Hemingway here translates the stillbirth as murder in two senses, with the infant's death ultimately appearing as 'gratuitous' as Aymo's death" (82). Now that the regime has become clear, the death of the child is somewhat merciful. The process of medicalization is revealed to be a process of dying, which the child has avoided entirely by dying at the outset—never living, in fact. Although at this point Catherine has not yet died, Henry understands that it is only a matter of time. The realities of war and their impact on the body have become obvious to him. Ultimately, the careful management of life, behavior, and loyalties, serves only to validate Herndl's claim that the entire enterprise of control and management is to restore men enough to confront death once more—which Henry has now recognized as an inevitable reality of the life he has engaged in with Catherine and his stillborn child.

## A Final Farewell to Arms

The analytics of biopower help to expose a regime of control hidden just beneath the surface in Hemingway's text. A war story at first blush and an epic love story at the second, *A Farewell to Arms* is in many ways the narrative of military medicine and its diffuse but ubiquitous impacts on those entangled in the war. These four different areas of inquiry—the impact of the military hospital, the role of territory in the politics of the body, the way in which in the military-health complex shapes the attitudes of individuals toward sexual activity, and the seemingly inevitable tragedy of Catherine's pregnancy—create a coherent picture of the variety of techniques and expectations deployed by the Italian army and the medical apparatus of that army to control and maintain a fleet of willing and able bodies to fight the war. The mosaic overlap of techniques described by Foucault should be apparent as well. None of these strategies is truly discrete, and Frederic Henry at times seems to be acutely aware of these linkages. Nonetheless, together, there is something like the massive apparatus of war, health, and reproduction suggested by Foucault, given a real human element through the lens of Frederic Henry's and Catherine Barkley's experience.

This narrative, then, ends with the end of this discursive reality as well. I believe that Frederic Henry's final farewell to arms, rather than coming as a result of the death of Catherine and their child, comes in the last sentence of the text. The book ends with a simple, declarative sentence that seems more reflective of the beginning of the text than of Henry's hysteria a moment earlier: "After a while I went out and left the hospital and walked back to the hotel in the rain" (*FTA* 332). After Henry tells the doctors to leave and finally rids himself of the world of medicalization, the text ends. In his experience in the Swiss idyll, the clock was merely running down to the time he would have to return to the hospital—to the place that ascribed certain roles, possibilities, and obligations. Not only has he broken his social ties with the death of his war-generated family, he has broken his discursive and institutional ones. Placing *A Farewell to Arms* as a memoir of sorts written well after the chronological close of the novel's action, this narrative choice seems to reflect a Frederic Henry conscious of and reflective upon the role that military and medical institutions played in this period of his life—a substantively constitutive one.

### Notes

1. This is also pretty significantly tied up with masculinity, but the relation between bodily selflessness in war and masculinity is too broad to treat effectively within this essay. Vernon, Moddelmog, and Herndl all treat the issue in varying manners, and do it much better than I could here.

2. Both literally and figuratively. Frederic Henry states that "they did not answer. They did not have to answer. They were battle police" (*FTA* 112). That inquiry runs one way.

3. In this section, I neglect the homosocial and homosexual undercurrents that play a fairly large role in a number of contemporary interpretations of the text. I do not mean to completely ignore a large section of the contemporary literature on *A Farewell to Arms* and war, but I believe that the specific sorts of impositions coming from above did not necessarily prescribe the homosexual tension in the text, in the same way that certain prohibited sexual behaviors were almost encouraged. The only case in which I demonstrate a resistance is in the case of the geographic escape, but only because I believe the contrast highlights even more starkly the territorial imperative of the battle police.

# Pilar's Turn Inward

Storytelling in Hemingway's *For Whom the Bell Tolls*

Anna Broadwell-Gulde

The dichotomy between interiors and exteriors is complicated by oral communication, a mode of relaying information that at once highlights the external, embodied speaker and preserves the interiority of the information relayed through its momentary aural presence, unable to be objectified by the gaze or destroyed by the touch. In his seminal work *Orality and Literacy,* Walter Ong emphasizes the difference between speech and other forms of communication and perception. "Sight isolates, sound incorporates," Ong claims, illustrating the way in which sound "pours into the hearer," different from the way that sight positions the observer outside what is observed (Ong 71). Though a written text, Hemingway's *For Whom the Bell Tolls* highlights the importance of storytelling through the character of Pilar.[1] Unable to read, Pilar nevertheless has a keen aural perception that contrasts with Robert Jordan's attachment to the written text, evident in his desire always to record through writing.

The distinction between oral and literate cultures is understood as a difference in both the employment of language and the understanding of the self. Ong suggests that literate people visualize language, relegating it to a thing-like realm of objects, representations, and labels, whereas oral people rather understand language through speech. Unable to visualize words, oral people do not view language as representation but rather perceive language, through oral communication, as part of their embodied experience, inseparable from the world around them. Historically, as writing allowed for a higher level of abstract thought, people have become more self-reflexive, their thoughts suggesting a higher degree of self-awareness.[2] Through her storytelling, Pilar demonstrates her embeddedness in oral culture, both in her employment of bodily language and in her situational thinking, which Ong suggests is characteristic of oral cultures.

Pilar's position as storyteller, however, is complicated by her shifting perspective as she tells her stories. At times, Pilar speaks through direct address, a perspective that creates an intimate storytelling environment inside the cave of the Republican band. At other moments, however, Pilar adopts a narratorial voice that filters her language, creating a disjunction between the text and Pilar's storytelling. Still other moments reveal Pilar's thoughts rather than her speech through a limited omniscient perspective. The three main stories that Pilar orates suggest a progression or movement from the exterior to the interior self, both in the content of the stories themselves and in the structure and method of storytelling employed.

The first tale, the Valencia story, recalls Pilar's experiences there with her lover Finito some time earlier. Almost Edenic in nature, this story focuses on the external interactions between two people at the beginning of a relationship. Just as the content of the story suggests a focus on the tangible, physical, and external body, so, too, does the storytelling mirror the subject matter of the tale. Maria and Robert, in the beginning of their own relationship, ask Pilar simple questions, which she answers with her tale, a storytelling structure that displays the importance of the external self to oral culture and highlights the interaction between storyteller and listener. Pilar's second story, the war story, illustrates a shift inward. In this story, Pilar speaks "as though she were speaking to a classroom; almost as though she were lecturing" (*FWBT* 98), a detail that acknowledges the separation between Robert Jordan and herself (as a difference between oral and literate culture) and suggests Pilar's shift to an interior self through her possession of knowledge that elevates and separates her from the listener. The story also displays division between speech and writing through a narratorial presence that sometimes belies Pilar's direct address. The final tale, the Finito story, illustrates an ultimate turn inward, away from the external quality of oral communication, and it is through this interior monologue that *For Whom the Bell Tolls* suggests the isolation of the self from others in preparation for death, foreshadowing Robert Jordan's necessary isolation from the other band members at the time of his death.

### Valencia as Eden: The Exteriority of Storytelling

Pilar's deep voice prefigures her appearance as she enters the novel, shouting a cascade of expletives at the man with whom Robert Jordan speaks. Such an entrance not only highlights the importance of the spoken word but also confirms the portrait that Rafael had painted of Pilar earlier. Through Rafael, Pilar is painted as a strong, authoritative woman who emasculates the men in the band by commanding them to shoot, taking their guns from them, and telling them to carry Maria to safety. Our initial understanding of Pilar is through her leadership in the war.

Pilar's aural entrance into the story, then, and her tale of time spent in Valencia with her lover Finito, allow her to establish herself as cocreator of the text: Pilar recalls her own Eden in Valencia and mirrors Milton as the authorial and creative presence who retells of a prelapsarian world before it was corrupted by political entanglement and the ravages of war. Indeed, Pilar declares that she did "all things" in Valencia (*FWBT* 84), echoing S.B.'s poem "In Paradisum Amissam,"[3] which first appears as a commendatory poem in the second edition of Milton's *Paradise Lost*: "You who read Paradise Lost, sublime poem of mighty Milton, what do you read but the story of all things?" (qtd. in Lieb 71). Even the progression, from lying by the water, to eating together, to making love, seems to recall Adam and Eve's initial encounter in Eden and is, similarly, without temporal concern or awareness of mortality:

> We made love in the room with the strip wood blinds hanging over the balcony and a breeze through the opening of the top of the door which turned on hinges. We made love there, the room dark in the day time from the hanging blinds, and from the streets there was the scent of the flower market and the smell of burned powder from the firecrackers of the *traca* that ran through the streets exploding each noon during the Feria . . . We made love and then sent for another pitcher of beer with the drops of its coldness on the glass. (*FWBT* 85)

The repetition of "we made love" and the sensorial descriptions (visual, olfactory, tactile) contribute to the imagination of this idyllic place that seems to exist out of time, just as Milton's Eden did before the fall. Routines are established, but there is no hurry, no end in mind. Here, in a locus amoenus unharmed by war, Pilar and Finito make love, secluded from outside intrusions.

Pilar and Finito become part of this idealized place as Pilar paints a picture of their days spent eating, making love, and sleeping, giving no indication of communication between the two lovers other than relaying Finito's desire to continue to sleep, even when beer is brought to drink. A place is idealized, bodily needs are satisfied, and sensations are satiated, but, as actions subsume reflection, the interior self is never revealed.

Positioned directly after Maria and Robert's initial lovemaking scene, this story of an Edenic past echoes Maria's own desire for a new beginning—her hope that making love with Robert can reclaim her virginity and her innocence. Though she is clearly already physically and psychologically affected by the war, Maria is re-created to embody Eve's innocence in her alignment with the natural world—the world of Valencia before it was corrupted. Tainted by the intrusion of the airplanes, which rumble overhead, signifying the imminent threat of the Nationalists and the present corruption of Valencia's Edenic past by the Republican government, Pilar's first story ends in an external and aural threat from above. The smell of the burned powder from the firecracker explosions, which innocently contrasts with Rafael's recollection of the train explosion earlier in the novel, now seems ironic in the face of new, even more powerful, explosive, and *corrupting* technologies.

### A Turn Inward: Withholding Information and the Beginning of the Fall

The oral (aural) quality of Pilar's second story, the war story, is highlighted not only by the method of storytelling and the content of the story but also through the withholding of information, a distinction that sets up a dichotomy between Pilar's listeners within the text and the reader of the text. In this story, in which Pilar speaks "as though she were speaking to a classroom; almost as though she were lecturing" (*FWBT* 98), knowledge of the town where the siege took place is restrained from the text. The aural quality of Pilar's storytelling is definitively lost in this textual moment, where the previous intimacy afforded through direct address is lost.

Such a withholding of knowledge can be understood by examining the progression of Pilar's stories from a recuperation of the Edenic to an acknowledgement of the post-Lapsarian present. The "fall," then, is not the attainment of a forbidden knowledge but rather the recognition, through Pilar's shifting perspectives (not through herself directly) of the distancing and separating effect of knowledge on human interactions. Detailing the Republican siege of a Nationalist town, Pilar's second story provides important background information for understanding the band's dynamics.[4] Pablo's reticence and disillusionment with the band is contextualized through this story, which demonstrates his stoicism, his cruel indifference, and the calculating manner in which he kills the fascists. In the progression of the novel, this story is crucial to realizing the previously unknown histories of the novel's main characters. Significantly, Jordan worries whether Maria "should not listen" to this story

(*FWBT* 99), perhaps fearing that the recounting of a history beyond the present moment could shatter Maria's Edenic recreation of herself.

Pilar, as storyteller, retreats from the engaging question–answer structure of her first story, demonstrating her self-conscious removal from her listeners, a shift inward that seems to reflect the distancing effect of knowledge itself. The deliberation about whether or not even to tell the story widens the distance between the speaker and her listeners and raises the level of anxiety and anticipation surrounding the story's telling:

> "Tell it," said Robert Jordan. "And if it is not for her, that she should not listen."
>
> "I can hear it," Maria said. She put her hand on Robert Jordan's. "There is nothing that I cannot hear."
>
> "It isn't whether you can hear it," Pilar said. "It is whether I should tell it to thee and make thee bad dreams."
>
> "I will not get bad dreams from a story,"[5] Maria told her. "You think after all that has happened with us I should get bad dreams from a story?" (*FWBT* 99)

Maria and Jordan cannot remain within an imaginary Eden, and just as this story reifies the idyllic Republic by detailing the atrocities Republican band members committed, so, too, does it bring about the fall for its listeners. Maria's insistence on it as a mere *story* that cannot affect her emphasizes her innocence before she and Robert Jordan are tainted by the aestheticized interior of the fallen reality of Pilar's tale.

The hand-holding imagery that pervades *Paradise Lost* also characterizes Robert and Maria's affection, highlighting the importance of physical, bodily contact in the compression of time. Robert Jordan's hand, tainted by Pilar's palm-reading, which seems to foreshadow his fate, is the same hand that demonstrates his affection for Maria, perhaps reinforcing the idea of free will within a finite existence, echoing the end of *Paradise Lost* in both the acknowledgment of limited time and the insistence on the importance of human relationships in the time remaining. Pilar may be withholding information from the reader, but Robert and Maria *hold* this story in their hands, in their shared proximity as listeners: "Robert Jordan stretched himself out, his shoulders against the ground and his head against a clump of the heather. He reached and found Maria's hand and held it in his, rubbing their two hands against the heather until she opened her hand and laid it flat on top of his as they listened" (*FWBT* 99). In pausing their movement and listening to Pilar's story, Robert and Maria demonstrate a frame audience that highlights the oral quality of *For Whom the Bell Tolls*.

Walter Ong suggests that throughout literary history, residual elements of oral culture can be located in texts.[6]

The use of aesthetic language to describe wartime atrocities allows listeners to visualize—to make somewhat concrete—what would otherwise be a complete abstraction to those who are not familiar with the events being told. By withholding the precise location of where the siege took place—"'It was this town,' and she named a town" (*FWBT* 98)—and in using abstract language to require imagination on the listener/reader's part, Hemingway demonstrates Pilar's movement from a concrete, physical exterior to a more abstract interior. Even in her use of abstract, aesthetic language, however, Pilar details the importance of the physical body by requiring listeners to imagine her stories in terms of a delineation of beauty and ugliness. Jordan does not realize that Pilar's discussion of beauty prepares him (and us) for her aestheticization of war in recounting the Republican siege of a Nationalist town; by establishing herself as "ugly" but having "felt beautiful" her whole life (97–98), Pilar problematizes using such an aesthetic as a value judgment, thus foreshadowing the application of such language to wartime atrocities.

Speaking with Maria, Pilar first essentializes and then argues for the contingency of beauty/ugliness, demonstrating her own wavering, ambiguous position. Avowing her ugliness, Pilar claims, "*Vamos*, I'm not ugly. I was born ugly. All my life I have been ugly" (97). Then, in a quick reversal, she claims:

> Yet one has a feeling within one that blinds a man while he loves you. You, with that feeling, blind him, and blind yourself. Then, one day, for no reason, he sees you ugly as you really are and he is not blind any more and then you see yourself as ugly as he sees you and you lose your man and your feeling ... After a while, when you are as ugly as I am, as ugly as women can be, then, as I say, after a while the feeling, the idiotic feeling that you are beautiful, grows slowly in one again. It grows like a cabbage. And then, when the feeling is grown, another man sees you and thinks you are beautiful and it is all to do over. (*FWBT* 98)

Feelings momentarily belie visual perception, even becoming generative ("like a cabbage"), demonstrating their alliance with the natural world. Visual perception, in contrast, is linked with the irrationality of the human mind—"one, day, *for no reason,* he sees you ugly as you really are"(emphasis added)—perhaps suggesting the contingent, subjective nature of visual perception. Unlike aural perception, which surrounds and subsumes the listener, visual perceptions dissects and isolates what is in view.

By establishing the contingency of beauty and ugliness, Pilar then frames her story of the Republican siege of the Nationalists in terms of this language, in order to demonstrate the situational (rather than ideological or essential) nature of actions and events.

> "Does what I say not hold interest for you, *Inglés?*"
> "You speak very well. But there are other things that interest me more than talk of beauty or lack of beauty." (*FWBT* 99)

Jordan's initial critique, then, is undermined by Pilar's story, in which her aesthetic language, in its ability to capture the nature of the siege, engages his attention, memory, and impulse to write. Jordan claims that he is not interested in hearing "talk of beauty," an affront to Pilar but also a demonstration of his own investment in the cause—carrying out his work/duty in a pragmatic and practical sense but not pausing (or trying not to) to consider his subjective perception of his actions. Jordan confirms this position in his statement that he would "form judgments . . . afterwards" (*FWBT* 136)—visually aesthetic judgments are usually made immediately—after he writes down/objectifies/solidifies the narrative itself.

Pilar brings the unfamiliarity of the war into the familiar and *bodily* world of visual perception by aestheticizing the tools used for killing and the method of killing. Linking the *guardias civiles* to herself—"they were all tall men with the faces of *guardias civiles*, which is the same model of face as mine is" (*FWBT* 100)—Pilar compares the *civiles*' appearance to herself. She then uses visual imagery to describe the enemy's speech, further highlighting the aesthetic and synesthetic nature of her storytelling: "I have never heard such a tone of voice. It was grayer than a morning without sunrise" (*FWBT* 101). Pilar describes the pistol Pablo used to shoot the *civiles* as an "ugly thing" and then describes the entire massacre as "a thing of great ugliness," changing the adjective *ugly* to a noun, *ugliness*, to suggest a concreteness in abstraction (*FWBT* 101, 118). Pilar needs to abstract the massacre in order to distance herself from it. Observing most of the action during the siege, Pilar reflects this position through her use of visual language, moving herself from observer to artistic figure. Pilar is able to externalize the interiority of the war experience by using visual and aesthetic language to capture a remarkably personal experience of war.

Unlike the Edenic Valencia story, where the temporal distinction between night and day was inverted, demonstrating the lack of awareness of a future or past time (the cyclical nature of the story reflecting the conflation of space and nonlinear time), this story rather frames the killing in a day. Sectioning off the atrocity as an event in time, Pilar's war story creates a level of dramatic unity that reflects the novel's three-day structure. Pilar begins her story at the beginning of a day, "early in the morning when the *civiles* surrendered" (FWBT 99), and ends her story with the shining moon and the image of Don Guillermo's wife crying on the balcony. Pilar states that there was "no sound but the splashing of the water in the fountain," yet she could "hear a woman crying" (129), suggesting that Don Guillermo's wife's tears merge with the water, providing a natural cleansing of the "great ugliness." Approaching the abstract through the illusory image of Don Guillermo's wife on the balcony, the story is nevertheless grounded in the aural sounds of splashing water and crying.

The external self presented in the Valencia story is complicated in this war story, where killing satiates the desire for having sex. The "fall" is two-tiered in that it is reflected both through the shift in perspective (commenting on the distancing effect of knowledge) and in the content of the story itself. The Edenic Valencia story, where bodily needs were met without thought, mirroring Maria's hope to erase the past through her present relationship with Robert Jordan, "falls" when Pilar demonstrates a subversion of bodily and sexual needs: Pilar speaks of having a "belly-full" after the killing (*FWBT* 119), and Pablo no longer desires sex after killing the fascists. Pilar feels "hollow" inside after the killing, a word that Robert Jordan uses to describe his feeling while having sex with Maria (127, 378), complicating the distinction between the effects of killing, eating, and having sex. By using bodily language to describe her feeling after the killing, Pilar brings the reader closer to the embodied experience of the aftermath of the massacre. Such language supports Pilar's position as a representative of oral culture, demonstrating that nothing can ever truly be removed from the body. The guilt and shame that Pilar felt are described as a "belly-full"—a physical and concrete description that anchors the listener in the present moment.

### Preparing for Death: Finito's Story and the Abandonment of Orality

In her final story, the description of Finito's attenuating body and encroaching death and the separation between speaker and listener demonstrate a shift in Pilar as storyteller. Pilar stands before the cooking fire when she recalls her relationship with Finito, his fear of bulls, the weakening of his physical body in his sickness, and his inability to eat. In her embeddedness in oral culture, Pilar demonstrates a kind of situational thinking that Ong notes is prominent in most oral cultures and that contrasts with the analytic and abstract thinking of literate culture.[7] "Oral cultures," states Ong, "tend to use concepts in situational, operational frames of reference that are minimally abstract in the sense that they remain close to the living human lifeworld" (49). This characteristic is reflected in Pilar's recollections of Finito's inability to eat as she cooks and of her caring for him—the extreme attention to his physical body that demonstrates her passion for him—as she leans over the fire. It makes sense, then, that it is while Pilar stares into a cooking fire, a medium of consumption and heat, that she is reminded of her final days with her lover, days in which his own inability to eat—to consume—is foregrounded and Pilar's passion/love for Finito is figured in terms of caring for his enfeebled physical body.

Mortality is highlighted in this story, even more so than in the war story in which the actual killing was abstracted. As Pilar recalls Finito's final days, she remembers holding his hand, just as hand-holding has become important for Maria and Robert Jordan: "he would go to sleep and she would lie there, holding his hand in her two hands and listening to him breathe" (*FWBT* 189).

While Pilar's earlier story about the Republican siege of the Nationalist town demonstrates the success of oral communication—so much so that Robert Jordan wants to "write down her story because it was better than Quevedo" (*FWBT* 134)—her recollection of Finito rather emphasizes the failure of language and communication. Pilar's thoughts reside in her mind—unarticulated—her shaking head (the disgust for her audience's lack of understanding) mirrors Finito's own repeated negation—"No! No! No!" (188)—which is a denial and refusal that we, as readers, do not fully understand. Finito's repeated "No!" is finally accompanied by the coughing up of real blood: speech conflates with a physical and bodily reaction, demonstrating the physical, rather than representative or abstract, nature of language itself. In his work *The Spell of the Sensuous*, David Abram, reflecting on Merleau-Ponty's *Phenomenology of Perception*, argues for the carnal, the fleshlike, quality of language, claiming that "the gestural genesis of language, the way that communicative meaning is first incarnate in the gestures by which the body spontaneously expresses feelings and responds to changes in its affective environment, is spontaneous and immediate and not an arbitrary sign" (74).

Thus, in this regard, language is primarily a bodily experience before it becomes abstract or representative. Previously, Finito had been coughing up blood into a napkin, maintaining proper discretion and giving "an appearance of great gayety and enjoyment" (*FWBT* 187). Finally, however, the body belies propriety when Finito speaks out: "'No!' very loudly and a big blob of blood came out and he didn't even put up the napkin and it slid down his chin and he was still looking at the bull and he said, 'All season, yes. To make money, yes. To eat, yes. But I can't eat. Hear me? My stomach's bad. But now with the season finished! No! No! No!'" (188). Such a negation is, somewhat ironically, also an affirmation of self. In his refusal to agree with the custom of displaying the bull's head, Finito claims a place for matadors outside the usual ceremonial, historical, and cultural aspect of bullfighting, affirming instead personal and practical reasons for being a matador—to make money to be able to feed himself—asserting the importance of the bodily over the symbolic. Just as Finito is not understood by the others at the banquet, so, too, is Pilar misunderstood, her listeners quick to make simple assumptions as to why Finito should not have been a matador—his "short stature" and being "tubercular" (184). Pilar shakes her head, refusing verbal articulation, which proved inadequate, a turn inward prompted by the misinterpretation of her story.

This turn inward, however, is not a turn inward in the self-reflective, self-conscious manner that Ong suggests is shaped by literate cultures (print allowing such self-reflexivity and affording higher levels of abstract thought). Rather, Pilar's thoughts remain on Finito's physical body, maintaining the physical, bodily connection of unspoken language, further reflecting Pilar as an emblem of oral culture and storytelling. Her final thoughts turn to Finito's physical body, delicately conveying through language the same tactile movements of her hands over his body: "rubbing the legs, chafing the taut muscles of the calves, kneading them, loosening them, and then tapping them lightly with her folded hands, loosening the cramped muscles" (*FWBT* 189).

Pilar's thoughts in these moments are revealed through interior monologue. To the band members, she appears merely to be fulfilling her role as cook, but through the text Pilar reveals an internal self that demonstrates conflict with her external environment. Her storytelling conveys an understanding of relationships within the novel and this turn inward suggests a relinquishing of narrative power in order to allow the rest of the story to unfold: "What a people they are . . . What a people are the Spaniards . . . And I hear it and say nothing. I have no rage for that and having made an explanation I am silent" (*FWBT* 189). This statement resonates on the level of the novel, as Pilar's relinquishing of narrative control ultimately mirrors Robert Jordan's relinquishing of control over his own fate.

Such a silence also recalls previous narrative silences in which Pilar refuses to tell a story. Describing the Republican siege of the Nationalist town as "the worst day of [her] life until one other day," Pilar reveals that the "worst day" was when the fascists "took the town" (*FWBT* 129), but she never actually tells this story, though she promises to tell it to Robert Jordan. This refusal to articulate is, to some extent, even more horrifying than Pilar's description of the Republican siege, for it acknowledges the inexpressibility of the situation, highlighting the failure of oral communication accurately to describe experience. Kate McLoughlin understands the articulation of the inexpressibility of war as a demonstration of communication-by-implication: "Absence conjures up presence: a reader informed that a battle is too shocking to be described is likely to envision horrors exceeding anything that straightforward description could invoke" (18). The result is a "curious disempowerment that confesses smallness and ineptitude" (18). Pilar's mastery of storytelling is a two-fold example of McLoughlin's description of the strategies for adequately describing war: first, by describing the Republican siege as a "thing of great ugliness," Pilar denatures the realist image through aesthetic terms. Second, in her refusal to tell the story of the "worst day," Pilar establishes a narrative silence that is magnified by the imaginative freedom afforded her listeners.[8]

Resounding Voices

In the progression of stories, Pilar moves from an authorial/Miltonic (approaching godlike) presence in her telling of the prelapsarian Spanish world to a human lover whose focus on the mortal body places her among those exiled from the garden. In his epic war novel, Hemingway creates a storyteller who etches herself into her narratives, demonstrating the importance of place for identity in oral culture. But it is not just Pilar who moves toward an interior self through the progression of her storytelling—Robert Jordan learns by listening. Through Pilar's stories, Jordan learns that "there's no one thing that's true. It's all true. The way the planes are beautiful whether they are ours or theirs" (*FWBT* 467). Even in his use of "beautiful," aesthetic language that he previously devalued, Robert Jordan suggests his acceptance of a subjective value judgment that blurs the lines of "theirs" and "ours." Equally important, Jordan illustrates the limits of language and abstraction in his statement "It's all true," perhaps indicating that he cannot adequately express his felt experiences through the construct of language. In the final scene of the novel, tactile images subsume Jordan's interior thoughts as he becomes "completely integrated" (471).

It is not this final scene, which suggests Jordan's union with the Spanish earth and culture, that reveals how Robert has changed through developing his sensitivity to orality, however. Jordan is dying, and the shift from an interior monologue to the third person limited omniscient perspective suggests a narratorial presence that draws us out of Jordan's stream-of-consciousness. Rather, it is important to turn to Jordan's final conversation with Maria to examine how his sense of self has changed as a result of their relationship—a relationship cultivated through Pilar's storytelling and guidance.

Many critics have argued that Robert Jordan's farewell to Maria either implies her possible pregnancy or suggests that Jordan has metaphorically become part of Maria, since she represents the Spanish earth. Though Robert Jordan is continually characterized as deaf throughout the text, he does seem to have changed by the end. Through listening to Pilar's stories, he has moved from the pleasure-seeking Edenic beginning with Maria to recognizing the limitations as an academic/intellectual—realizing the failure of this kind of knowledge during wartime—to finally accepting his own death.

In his journey, Robert Jordan has moved to a greater acceptance of the importance of bodily presence, as evident through his relationship with Maria (he was previously told by Golz that there was no need to find a girl during war). Jordan has learned from Pilar's storytelling, and his final goodbye with Maria suggests not that he is part of her so much as that he may be willing to let a part of himself go (a movement outward toward an understanding of self as constituted in oral cultures):

> "Thou wilt go now, rabbit. But I go with thee. As long as there is one of us, there is both of us. Do you understand?"
> "Nay, I stay with thee."
> "Nay, rabbit. What I do now I do alone. I could not do it well with thee. If thou goest then I go, too. Do you not see how it is? Whichever one there is, is both."
> "I will stay with thee." (*FWBT* 463)

The union pictured at the end of *For Whom the Bell Tolls* is not unlike Adam and Eve's union in Milton's *Paradise Lost* as they leave Eden:

> With thee to go,
> Is to stay here; without thee here to stay,
> Is to go hence unwilling; thou to me
> Art all things under Heav'n
>
> They hand in hand with wand'ring steps and slow,
> Through Eden took their solitary way. (lines 615–18, 648–49)

In both of these endings, there exists a simultaneous togetherness and separateness. Adam and Eve leave Paradise "hand in hand" but take "their solitary way," suggesting the singularity within the pair. Similarly, Robert Jordan claims that he is now part of Maria, yet he knows that he must die alone. In both of these endings, the simultaneous presence of going and staying conflates movement and stasis, suggesting that to go is also to stay together but to stay also represents a going on or continuing with passing time. Robert Jordan declares he must "go" (leave himself/die) while Maria begs to "stay" with him, recalling the final lines of *Paradise Lost* in which "slow" and "way" rhyme with "go" and "stay." Sound cannot be contained in the realm of objects; it emanates from the interior self, but, through articulation, speech leaves the self. The interiority of sound exposes the exterior self to a listening other, "staying" long enough to be understood but always "going" with the passing of time. Indeed, the literal and figurative going and staying at the end of *For Whom the Bell Tolls* recalls the quality of oral communication even in the written text's effort to represent, preserve, and objectify it.

## Notes

1. David Cole views the function of storytelling in *For Whom the Bell Tolls* as educational for Robert Jordan, a way to initiate him into the Spanish culture. He claims that storytelling is interwoven in the novel for the purpose of anticipating the action to come (22–30). I would argue that storytelling has a more essential purpose in the novel in that it functions to heighten the distinction between oral and literate cultures (by demonstrating differences in sensory perception, thought processes, and self-identity between Pilar and Robert Jordan).

2. David Abram explains the self-reflexivity gained by literate cultures by examining how reading and writing function to remove us from perceiving the world around us: "The letters of the alphabet, each referring to a particular sound or sound-gesture of the human mouth, begin to function as mirrors reflecting us back upon ourselves. They establish a new reflexivity between the human organism and its own signs, short-circuiting the sensory reciprocity between that organism and the land" (187). I would argue that Robert Jordan, in his desire to write down Pilar's story and in his visual objectification of Maria (seeing her tell her story to his students in Montana), illustrates his devaluing of the importance of place in oral communication. Writing both "displaces the participation between the human senses and the earthly terrain" and "disengages [stories] from the diverse places from which they came" (185). Writing thus gave way to a "notion of a pure and featureless space" (185), abstracting the stories from their earthly and bodily connections.

3. For the purpose of this argument, I will be considering Hemingway's invocation of *Paradise Lost* to comment on the progressive interiority experienced through Pilar's

storytelling and its relationship to the separating and isolating nature of knowledge. It is important to note, however, Wolfgang Rudat's invocation of Milton to comment on gender roles in Hemingway. In his article "The Other War in *For Whom the Bell Tolls*: Maria and Miltonic Gender Role Battles," Rudat claims that Maria rebels against the subjection of women to men by taking charge of her sexual experience with Robert, "leading the way" in the heather and telling him "I want to kiss, too . . . Yes, yes. Everything as you" (*FWBT* 166) (reminiscent of Catherine Bourne's "I can do anything and anything and anything" [*GOE* 15]). In Jordan's "androcentric" treatment of Maria during their initial interaction (Rudat 15), he reflects the fascists' rape of Maria. Thus, Maria takes revenge on her rape through taking control of her lovemaking with Robert. Rudat claims the "ground-moving" that they experience parallels the earth's moving in response to Adam and Eve's fall (Rudat 16). Thus Maria, initiated into the knowledge of the "ground moving" idea, as presented by Pilar (viewed here as the "tree of knowledge" but who I contend echoes Milton's own voice), also functions in a slightly satanic way in that she brings about this experience for the uninitiated Robert. Ultimately, however, she brings Robert away from his self-indulgent ideas of sexual pleasure (he refuses onanism) and toward recognition of the importance of the continuance of both genders ("I would like to bear thy son and thy daughter" [367], Maria says). Rudat claims that in this way Maria defies the stereotype of the submissive Eve and argues that it is through parallel scenes of comparison and contrast with *Paradise Lost* that Hemingway differentiates Maria's character (8–24).

4. Like the background story in *Paradise Lost* of Satan's disillusionment with the archangels, Pilar's story details Pablo's killing of Nationalists and subsequent disillusionment with the Republicans.

5. Eve's temptation to eat the fruit is first presented to her through a dream/vision in which she *hears* the snake speaking to her.

6. Ong points out that the fictionalization of readers, from Chaucer's *Canterbury Tales*, in which fictional people tell stories to one another, to the direct address to a "dear reader" in Jane Austen's novels, suggests a progression from framing a narrative through oral communication to acknowledging the presence of the literate reader (101–2).

7. Interviews with illiterate peasants demonstrate this situational thinking: In a study by A. R. Luria cited by Ong, oral and literate people were asked to identify the outlier in a group of objects (hammer, saw, log, and hatchet). While the literate persons categorized—and abstracted—the objects to think of the three "tools" and the log as the outlier, the oral persons rather used situational thinking to determine, for example, that the hatchet should be thrown away since it could not cut up wood as well as the saw (50–52).

8. Furthermore, Robert Jordan's impulse to write down Pilar's story seems to follow McLoughlin's explanation of the duty felt by those involved in war to write about their experiences, either to give a voice to those who died or to explain why the deaths occurred. Jordan's position, however, is complicated by the fact that he does not envision writing about his own experiences but rather wishes that he could write down Pilar's story. Such an artistic impulse follows Hemingway's own belief that fiction can convey truths more accurately than can recorded experience.

# Appendix A

Character List, with Pertinent Scenes

*The following is a list of the characters available to testify, as well as some initial thoughts about what passages, issues, or scenes might be relevant. Of course, this is not meant to be exhaustive. Please feel free to focus on other incidents or ideas you find in the novel.*

**Agustín**: likely to be a strong witness for the prosecution.

Agustín is a brave and committed soldier, and also one who retains a strong moral perspective. While he is always willing to die, it isn't at all clear what he would think of the mission if he knew that it was pointless. Midway through the novel (*FWBT* 277), Jordan tells him that Segovia can be taken and the war can be won. There is no evidence Agustín ever abandons his conviction that he is fighting a battle that is a military necessity, rather than an ideological one.

In other words, Agustín would be unlikely to willingly risk his life on a mission with no military value. That is clear in the scene in which he weighs Jordan's and Pablo's importance as equal (95). He is not willing to simply dive into the mission without concern for escape. While willing to fight, he is not one to foolishly waste lives.

Another scene to look at is Agustín's disgust at Pablo's treachery. In this he shows his own moral code, by which he places the lives of the men (even though they are outsiders) above both the mission and Pablo's favoring of his own men (*FWBT* 455). What if he knew that Jordan had stood by silently, in full knowledge of Pablo's plans? Hasn't he given Pablo permission to kill those men? Confronted with this fact, Agustín may well treat Jordan with much less respect.

**Anselmo**: most likely to be a key witness for the defense.

Anselmo stays at his post in the snowstorm past all reason, which would seem to indicate that he shares Jordan's stubborn adherence to orders. He wishes to perform his duty well and sees this almost as an end in itself, regardless of the validity or efficacy of the orders he has been given. However, Anselmo's devotion to duty is not pure. He at least considers leaving and criticizes the overly rigid set of orders that keeps him in the snow (*FWBT* 191–92). There is therefore a possibility that Anselmo, too, would have little patience for Jordan's intention to follow his orders beyond any rational end. This is particularly so because the orders will cause so many deaths—on both sides.

On the other hand, despite his belief in the republic, Anselmo's need to test his own courage to face battle without running also motivates his participation in the mission. He, too, is capable of bravado.

**Berrendo**: a telling witness against Jordan.

In a key scene, Berrendo agrees to charge El Sordo's position even though he believes doing so is a foolish waste of effort. However, Berrendo makes two key distinctions that Jordan does not. First, although he agrees to charge, he does so under protest. Second, he is deeply reluctant to order anyone else to go. When asked by the captain to condemn the sniper's confession of fear, Berrendo makes it clear that he regards the man's reaction as dignified and accords his humanity a weight that a military command does not cancel (*FWBT* 318–19).

Further, since Berrendo doesn't seem to have the means to follow Pablo's band anyway, he may see Jordan's desire to kill him as less than heroic, as just another barbaric act that war demands—as he sees his own decision to cut off of El Sordo's head.

**Golz and Duval**: both staunch witnesses for the defense. (The person who is playing Golz should also be ready to play Duval, since these two characters are so closely aligned.)

In the opening scene, Golz makes exactly the same decision that Jordan makes at the end—to go ahead with a costly attack even with the near surety that it will fail. "Has any attack ever been as it should?" he asks (*FWBT* 5). But Golz is determined to go forward with this for roughly the same reason Jordan does later: he views the gesture as important, regardless of the result.

Similarly, Duval, Golz's chief of staff, declines to call off the airplanes at the end, even though he knows that the surprise is blown and the offensive doomed (429–30).

**Robert Jordan**: the defendant.

The defense team might cite any of the passages in which Jordan sees his mission in the broadest possible strokes, in particular, his vision of the bridge as necessary for the good of mankind (*FWBT* 43), or the passage near the end where he weighs his life and finds the mission worth it (469).

The prosecution team might cite as powerful testimony any of the numerous passages in which Jordan questions his own motives. Most telling is the passage cited in the indictment, where Jordan sees himself as becoming his own enemy (162). Also effective are passages where Jordan admits how he really feels about those around him, particularly his admission, in the conclusion, that he is probably lying to Maria (466), and his inability to remember Eladio's name (455).

**Maria**: a willing witness for the defense, but a possible witness for the prosecution.

Although Maria, as Hemingway portrays her, would try her utmost not to hurt Jordan through her testimony, she could be confronted on cross-examination with some of the internal thoughts that Jordan does not share with her. This is particularly true of the end of the novel when Jordan sends her away—and denies her the death that she wants—by filling her ears with arguments of her obligation to live on (*FWBT* 462–64).

Why isn't she allowed to stay? Jordan admits later he doesn't entirely believe what he has told her. Shouldn't he have respected her wish to die in the manner that she finds suitable?

**Pablo**: a principle witness for the prosecution, but with some evidence useful for the defense.

Pablo regards Jordan's actions—particularly his willingness to sacrifice individuals for the mission—as supremely foolish. This is exactly what Pablo decides not to do. And at the end of the novel, Jordan decides that the well-lived moment, above all, provides meaning to life. Pablo would have no sympathy for this ideal.

It's also important that Pablo sees Jordan as complicit in his own murders. Since Pablo regards Jordan is fully cognizant of what Pablo does to get enough horses for everyone (*FWBT* 392, 403–4), he (rightly?) regards Jordan as capable of acting quite cynically when his interests are at stake.

**Pilar**: a witness probably most useful for the defense, but with testimony that could benefit the prosecution.

Pilar's loyalty to the Republic is absolute, and although she recognizes the futility of the attack once Pablo leaves, she, like Jordan, remains committed to it. This makes her a powerful witness for the defense. On the other hand, Pilar values life and sensation in a way that Jordan does not. She calls him a "cold boy" exactly because she regards his dedication to his duty as a kind of mutilation of the soul (*FWBT* 91).

One scene to consider is the interlude where Pilar talks about the death of the bullfighter Finito's death (182–90). For Finito, at the end of the day, the practical reality of being gradually killed was no match for the inner necessity to persist in the ring. Even though the blows are killing him, he continues fighting. But although Pilar acknowledges the beauty of this, she is also aware of the waste and tragedy.

# Appendix B

Trial Day Schedule of Events (For a 75-minute class period)

Course of the Exercise

1. Last minute prep (5 minutes)
2. First trial (25 minutes): follow A-F below
3. Intermission (please fill out the verdict sheet for the first trial now) (5 minutes)
4. Second trial (25 minutes): follow A-F below
5. Fill out verdict forms and academy awards sheets (10 minutes)
6. The jury renders verdicts in both trials/closing discussion (5 minutes)

The Trial Process

A. Prosecution opening statement (1 minute)
B. Defense opening statement (1 minute)
C. The prosecution makes its case (8-11 minutes):
   First prosecution witness (2 minutes)
   Defense cross examination (1 minute)
   Second prosecution witness (2 minutes)
   Defense cross examination (1 minute)
   Prosecutor's closing statement (2 minutes)
   [If time allows]
   Third prosecution witness (2 minutes)
   Defense cross examination (1 minute)
   The prosecution rests
D. The defense makes its case (6-9 minutes)
   First defense witness (2 minutes)
   Prosecution cross examination (1 minute)
   Second defense witness (2 minutes)
   Prosecution cross examination (1 minute)
   [If time allows]

Third defense witness Witness (2 minutes)
　　Prosecution cross examination (1 minute)
　　The defense rests
E. Prosecution closing statement (2 minutes)
F. Defense closing statement (2 minutes)

# Appendix C

Valid Objections in the Trial Process

Objection 1: Misreading of the Text

This objection may be made when a character asserts something that is directly contradicted by the text.

This is most clear in factual matters. If Pablo denies murdering the men from the other band, for example, the opposing counsel has grounds for an objection. Note that this objection prevents characters from lying, even when lying might be true to their personalities.

Note also that the characters cannot deny having the thoughts and ideas that are recorded in the novel, even if no one overheard them. Jordan, for example, cannot deny that he was willing to proceed with the mission despite his conviction that everyone would be killed (*FWBT* 371). No one heard Jordan say this other than the sleeping Maria, but since it is in the text, Jordan cannot deny that it happened.

Objection 2: Out of Character Behavior

This objection may be made if a character radically departs from his or her personality in a way that seems to directly contradict the novel. Agustín, for example, cannot treat Pablo with respect and reverence. We know that he hates him.

Objection 3: Wild Speculation

This objection can be made when the actor introduces events, facts, or opinions that have little or no basis in the text. For example, Maria cannot claim to be pregnant. It is true that she and Jordan had sex, and it is true that she *might* be pregnant. But there is no basis in the novel for claiming that she actually is.

Note: there is some room for interpretation in testifying. Pilar may, for example, discuss what she sees in Jordan's hand. Although in the book she is never explicit about what it is, we are given plenty of evidence that what she has foreseen is Jordan's death.

# Appendix D

Teachers' Questions for *Death in the Afternoon*

1. Hemingway argues that the aficionado becomes indifferent to the horses' suffering. This judgment constitute the real threshold premise of the text: to see the bullfight as a tragic ritual is to accept the necessity of death, not for sport or honor, but as an antecedent fact of life that makes sense of what suffering, honor, sport, and other practices mean. Is the suffering of the horses unforgivable? Is Hemingway's apology persuasive? Why or why not?

2. It is the death of the bull that is the definite aim of the bullfight. The death of a bullfighter, when it occurs, is an accident of the ritual rather than its goal. One bullfighter reportedly commented of Hemingway's book: "We do not go into the plaza to die. . . . Why does this Hemingway not call his book *Life in the Afternoon?*" (McCormick 236). The bullfighter that McCormick quotes is looking through his own eyes at the ritual. Hemingway looks from multiple vantages, not least from the vantage of the one whose dying is preordained. Whose death is referred to in the book's title?

3. The bullfight is not a competition or a sport, and the "playing field" is not equal. Some scholars argue that the justice of war depends on the equality of the status of the participants, and the proportion between the amounts of force that the various combatants use. Does this mean that the bullfight is unjust?

4. In order to allow the reader to see the bullfight, Hemingway explains the roles played by all the actors participating in the bullfight, including the *toro*, the *torero*, the *ganadero*, the *apoderado*, and the aficionado. In his book *On Killing*, David Grossman argues that humans do not like to kill, and that much time and effort is poured into supporting roles (supplying those actually fighting) or into fighting ineffectively. Who are the participants in wars and what roles do they play?

5. Why does Hemingway characterize the bullfight as a "rebellion against death"? By this he means that killing is a rebellion against accepting the necessity of death, and that some of us take a "Godlike" pride in meting out life and

death. Is killing ever just? Can it be done in full knowledge of necessity, rather than as a rebellion against necessity?

6. What is "pundonor"? Is it an excessive desire for honor? For that matter, is there such a thing as "reasonable honor"?

7. Is "A Natural History of the Dead" more than a digression? "A Natural History of the Dead" equates so-called natural and unnatural deaths. In arguing that all deaths are indecorous, Hemingway turns on its head the bitter phrase of Wilfred Owen, who criticized the old maxim that it is sweet and decorous to die for one's country (*dulce et decorum est pro patria mori*). Are all human deaths natural or are all human deaths unnatural? If we are all to die sometime, is there a difference between dying well and dying badly that means more than dying painfully or painlessly?

# Works Cited

Abram, David. *The Spell of the Sensuous.* New York: Vintage Books, 1996.
American Psychiatric Association. *Diagnostic and Statistical Manual of Mental Disorders,* 4th ed. (*DSM-4*). Washington, D.C.: American Psychiatric Association, 1994.
Anand, Mulk Raj. *Across the Black Waters.* 1939. New Delhi, India: Orient Paperbacks, 2000.
Anthony, David W. *The Horse, the Wheel, and Language: How Bronze-Age Riders from the Eurasian Steppes Shaped the Modern World.* Princeton: Princeton UP, 2007.
Aristotle. "The Poetics." In *Aristotle, The Poetics; Longinus, On the Sublime; Demetrius, On Style,* by Aristotle: 1–118. Cambridge, MA: Harvard UP, 1927.
Arnold, Aerol. "Hemingway's 'The Doctor and the Doctor's Wife.'" *Explicator* (March 1960): Item 36. Reprinted in *Critical Essays on Hemingway's In Our Time.* Ed. Michael S. Reynolds. Boston: Hall, 1983. 146–47.
Baker, Carlos. *Ernest Hemingway: A Life Story.* New York: Scribner, 1969.
———. *Hemingway: The Writer as Artist.* Princeton: Princeton UP, 1980.
Barnouw, Dagmar. *Weimar Intellectuals and the Threat of Modernity.* Bloomington: Indiana UP, 1988.
Beegel, Susan. "Ernest Hemingway's 'Lack of Passion.'" In *Hemingway: Essays of Reassessment,* ed. Frank Scafella. New York: Oxford UP, 1991. 62–78.
Beevor, Antony. *The Battle for Spain: The Spanish Civil War, 1936–1939.* New York: Penguin, 2006.
Benjamin, Jessica. *The Bonds of Love: Psychoanalysis, Feminism, and the Problem of Domination.* New York: Pantheon, 1988.
Bluemel, Kristin. *George Orwell and the Radical Eccentrics.* New York: Palgrave, 2004.
Bourke, Joanna. *An Intimate History of Killing.* Great Britain: Granta Books, 1999.
Carroll, Peter. "Ernest Hemingway, Screenwriter: New Letters on *For Whom the Bell Tolls.*" *The Antioch Review* 53.3 (1995): 261–83.
Caruth, Cathy. Introduction. *Trauma: Explorations in Memory.* Ed. Cathy Caruth. Baltimore: Johns Hopkins UP, 1995. 3–12.
Cecchin, Giovanni. *Hemingway: G. M. Trevelyan e il Friuli: Alle origini di Addio alle armi.* Lignano Sabbiadoro: Commune di Lignano Sabbiadoro, 1986.
Clark, Miriam Marty. "Hemingway's Early Illness Narratives and the Lyric Dimensions of 'Now I Lay Me.'" *Narrative* 12:2 (May 2004): 167–78.

Cohen, Milton A. "Vagueness and Ambiguity in Hemingway's 'Soldier's Home': Two Puzzling Passages." *Hemingway Review* 30.1 (Fall 2010): 158–64.

Cole, David. "Storytelling Mystique in *For Whom the Bell Tolls* and *The Treasure of the Sierra Madre.*" *Nebraska English Journal* 37.2 (1992): 22–30.

Conley, Tom. *Cartographic Cinema*. Minneapolis: U of Minnesota P, 2007.

Crane, Stephen. *The Red Badge of Courage*. New York: Random House, 1951.

Cuomo, Chris J. "War Is Not Just an Event: Reflections on the Significance of Everyday Violence." *Hypatia* 11.4 (Fall 1996): 31–45.

Das, Santanu. *Touch and Intimacy in First World War Literature*. Cambridge, UK: Cambridge UP, 2005.

Davis, R. M. "Hemingway's 'The Doctor and the Doctor's Wife.'" *Explicator* (Sept. 1966): Item 1. Reprinted in *Critical Essays on Hemingway's* In Our Time. Ed. Michael S. Reynolds. Boston: Hall, 1983. 148–49.

DeFalco, Joseph. *The Hero in Hemingway's Short Stories*. Pittsburgh: U of Pittsburgh P, 1963.

DiMarco, Louis A. *War Horse: A History of the Military Horse and Rider*. Yardley: Westholme Publishing, 2008.

Donahue, Peter. "The Genre Which Is Not One: Hemingway's *In Our Time*, Difference, and the Short Story Cycle." In *The Postmodern Short Story: Forms and Issues*. Ed. Farat Iftekharrudin et al. Westport, Conn.: Praeger, 2003. 161–70.

Dos Passos, John. Letter to *The New Republic*, published as "The Death of José Robles." *The New Republic* (19 July 1939). Reprinted in his *John Dos Passos: Travel Books and Other Writings, 1916–1941*. New York: Library of America, 2003.

Downhill, Jack. Phone conversation with Peter Hays. 30 Sept. 2011.

Dragunoiu, Dana. "Hemingway's Debt to Stendhal's Armance in *The Sun Also Rises*." *Modern Fiction Studies* 46.4 (2000): 868–92.

Dyer, Geoff. *The Missing of the Somme*. New York: Vintage, 1994.

Eby, Carl. *Hemingway's Fetishism: Psychoanalysis and the Mirror of Manhood*. Albany, NY: SUNY Press, 1998.

Elliott, Ira. "Performance Art: Jake Barnes and 'Masculine' Signification in *The Sun Also Rises*." *American Literature* 67 (1995): 77–94. Humanities Full Text (H. W. Wilson). Web. 2 Dec. 2012.

Fieve, Ronald. *Moodswing*. New York: William Morrow, 1975.

Florczyk, Steven. *Hemingway, the Red Cross, and the Great War*. Kent, OH: Kent State UP, 2014.

Fore, Dana. "Life Unworthy of Life? Masculinity, Disability, and Guilt in *The Sun Also Rises*." *Hemingway Review* 26:2 (Spring 2007): 74–88.

Forter, Greg. *Gender, Race, and Mourning in American Modernism*. Cambridge, UK: Cambridge UP, 2011.

Foucault, Michel. *The History of Sexuality*. New York: Pantheon, 1978.

———. *Power*. Ed. James D. Faubion. New York: New Press, 1994.

———. *Power/Knowledge: Selected Interviews and Other Writings, 1972–1977*. Ed. Colin Gordon. New York: Pantheon, 1980.

Freud, Sigmund. *Group Psychology and the Analysis of the Ego*. Trans. and ed. James Strachey. Bartleby.com. 2010. Web. <http://www.bartleby.com/290/5.html>.

Gajdusek, Robert. "Sacrifice and Redemption: The Meaning of the Boy/Son and Man/ Father Dialectic in the Work of Ernest Hemingway." *North Dakota Quarterly* 62.2 (Spring 1994–95): 166–80.

Gandal, Keith. *The Gun and the Pen: Hemingway, Fitzgerald, Faulkner and the Fiction of Mobilization.* Oxford: Oxford UP, 2008.

Garrington, Abbie. *Haptic Modernism: Touch and the Tactile in Modernist Writing.* Edinburgh: Edinburgh UP, 2013.

George, C. J. *Mulk Raj Anand: His Art and Concerns, a Study of His Non-Autobiographical Novels.* New Delhi, India: Atlantic Publishers, 1994.

Gilbert, Sandra M. "Soldier's Heart: Literary Men, Literary Women, and the Great War." In Sandra M. Gilbert and Susan Gubar, *No Man's Land: The Place of the Woman Writer in the Twentieth Century.* Vol. 2, *Sexchanges.* 3 vols. New Haven, CT: Yale UP, 1989. 258–323.

Girard, Rene. *Violence and the Sacred.* Baltimore: Johns Hopkins UP, 1977.

Gold, Mike. "Change the World." *Sunday Worker* 8 Dec. 1940.

Goodman, Paul. *Speaking and Language: Defence of Poetry.* New York: Random House, 1971.

Gottlieb, Werner. Phone conversation with Peter Hays. 8 June 2011.

Grimes, Larry E. "William James and 'The Doctor and the Doctor's Wife.'" *Hemingway: Up in Michigan Perspectives.* Ed. Frederic J. Svoboda and Joseph J. Waldmeir. East Lansing: Michigan State UP, 1995. 47–57.

Hagemann, E. R. "'Only Let the Story End as Soon as Possible': Time-and-History in Ernest Hemingway's *In Our Time.*" *Modern Fiction Studies* (Summer 1980): 255–62. Reprinted in *Critical Essays on Hemingway's* In Our Time. Ed. Michael S. Reynolds. Boston: Hall, 1983. 52–60.

Harris, Mark. *Five Came Back: A Story of Hollywood and the Second World War.* New York: Penguin Press, 2014.

Hediger, Ryan. "Animals." In *Hemingway in Context.* Ed. Debra A. Moddelmog and Suzanne Del Gizzo. Cambridge, UK: Cambridge UP, 2013. 217–26.

Hemingway, Ernest. *Across the River and into the Trees.* New York: Simon and Schuster, 1996.

———. *By-Line: Ernest Hemingway.* Ed. William White. New York: Scribner, 2003.

———. *Collected Poems.* Nicholas Gerogiannis, University of Nebraska Press, 1983 edited by Nicholas Gerogiannis, University of Nebraska Press, 1983. Ed. Nicholas Gerogiannis. Lincoln: U of Nebraska P, 1983.

———. *The Complete Short Stories of Ernest Hemingway: The Finca Vigía Edition.* New York: Scribner, 1987.

———. *Death in the Afternoon.* New York: Touchstone, 1960.

———. *Death in the Afternoon.* New York: Simon and Schuster, 1996.

———. *Ernest Hemingway: Selected Letters, 1917–1961.* Ed. Carlos Baker. New York: Scribner, 1981.

———. *A Farewell to Arms.* New York: Simon and Schuster, 1995.

———. *The Fifth Column and Four Stories of the Spanish Civil War.* New York: Scribners Paperback Fiction, Simon and Schuster, 1969.

———. *For Whom the Bell Tolls*. New York: Simon and Schuster, 1995.
———. *The Garden of Eden*. New York: Scribner, 1986.
———. *In Our Time*. New York: Boni and Liveright, 1925.
———. *Islands in the Stream*. New York: Scribner, 1970.
———. *The Letters of Ernest Hemingway. Vol. 1, 1907–1922*. Ed. Sandra Spanier et al. Cambridge, UK: Cambridge UP, 2011.
———, ed. *Men at War: The Best War Stories of All Time*. New York: Crown, 1942.
———. *A Moveable Feast*. 1964. New York: Simon and Schuster, 1996.
———. *Selected Letters: 1917–1961*. Ed. Carlos Baker. New York: Scribner, 1981.
———. *The Sun Also Rises*. New York: Simon and Schuster, 1954.
Hemingway, Valerie. *Running with the Bulls: My Years with the Hemingways*. New York: Ballantine, 2005.
Herbst, Josephine. *The Starched Blue Sky of Spain and Other Memoirs*. Boston: Northeastern UP, 1991.
Herlihy-Mera, Jeffrey. "He Was Sort of a Joke, In Fact: Ernest Hemingway in Spain." *Hemingway Review* 31.2 (2012): 84–100.
Herman, Judith. *Trauma and Recovery: The Aftermath of Violence—from Domestic Abuse to Political Terror*. New York: Basic, 1997.
Herndl, Diane Price. "Invalid Masculinity: Silence, Hospitals, and Anesthesia in *A Farewell to Arms*." *Hemingway Review* 21.1 (Fall 2001): 38–54.
Hirsch, Marianne. *The Generation of Postmemory: Writing and Visual Culture after the Holocaust*. New York: Columbia UP, 2012.
Hitchens, Christopher. "Young Men and War." *Vanity Fair* Feb. 1997: 38–50.
Hüppauf, Bernd. "Experiences of Modern Warfare and the Crisis of Representation." *New German Critique* 59 (1993): 41–76.
Hynes, Samuel. *A War Imagined: The First World War and English Culture*. New York: Atheneum, 1991.
"Into the Breach: *Saving Private Ryan*." Dir. Chris Harty. HBO, 1998. HBO First Look, season 5, episode 8 (documentary television series).
James, William. *A Pluralistic Universe*. 1909. Lincoln: U of Nebraska P, 1996.
Jameson, Fredric. "War and Representation." *PMLA* 124.5 (2009): 1532–47.
Johnson, Samuel. Annotations on William Shakespeare's *Hamlet* III.i. In vol. 1 of *The Plays of William Shakespeare*. Ed. Samuel Johnson. Samuel Johnson8 vols. London: J. and R. Tonson, 1765.
Josephs, Allen. *For Whom the Bell Tolls: Ernest Hemingway's Undiscovered Country*. New York: Macmillan, 1994.
———. "Hemingway and the Spanish Civil War or the Volatile Mixture of Politics and Art." In *Rewriting the Good Fight: Critical Essays on the Literature of the Spanish Civil War*. Ed. Frieda S. Brown, Malcolm A. Compitello, Victor M. Howard, and Robert S. Martin. East Lansing: Michigan State UP, 1989. 175–84.
Jünger, Ernst. *Copse 125: A Chronicle From the Trench Warfare of 1918*. New York: Howard Fertig, 2003.
———. *Storm of Steel*. Translated by Michael Hofmann. London: Allen Lane, 1961.
Keegan, John. *A History of Warfare*. New York: Vintage Books, 1993.

Kemp, Janet E. "Suicide Rates in VHA Patients through 2011, with Comparisons with Other Americans and other Veterans through 2010." Veterans Health Administration. Web. <http://www.mentalhealth.va.gov/docs/Suicide_Data_Report_Update_January_2014.pdf>.
Kennedy, A. L. *On Bullfighting*. New York: Anchor Books, 1999.
Koch, Stephen. *The Breaking Point: Hemingway, Dos Passos, and the Murder of José Robles*. Cambridge, MA: Counterpoint, 2005.
Kojève, Alexandre. "The Idea of Death in the Philosophy of Hegel." *Interpretation* (1973): 114–56.
Leigh, S. J., and David J. Leigh. "*In Our Time:* The Interchapters as Structural Guides to a Psychological Pattern." *Studies in Short Fiction* 12 (Winter 1975): 1–8. Reprinted in *Critical Essays on Hemingway's* In Our Time. Ed. Michael S. Reynolds. Boston: Hall, 1983. 130–37.
Lessing, Doris. *Landlocked*. New York: Plume, 1966.
Lieb, Michael. "S.B.'s 'In Paradisum Amissam': Sublime Commentary." *Milton Quarterly* 19.3 (1985): 71–79.
Liptak, Adam. "Reticent Justice Opens Up to a Group of Students." *New York Times* 13 April 2009. Web. <http://www.nytimes.com/2009/04/14/us/14bar.html?_r=0>.
Lisca, Peter. "The Structure of Hemingway's *Across the River and into the Trees*." *Hemingway: Five Decades of Criticism*. Ed. Linda W. Wagner. East Lansing: Michigan State UP, 1974. 288–306.
Lukacs, Georg. *Writer and Critic and Other Essays*. London: Merlin, 1978.
Mansfield, Katherine. "The Fly." *The Short Stories of Katherine Mansfield*. 1937. New York: Knopf, 1967. 597–602.
McClellan, Edwin N. *The United States Marine Corps in the World War*. Washington, D.C.: GPO, 1920; facsimile reprint, Washington, D.C.: Historical Branch, G-3 Division, Headquarters, U. S. Marine Corps, 1968. Web. <http://community.marines.mil/news/publications/Documents/The%20United%20States%20Marine%20Corps%20in%20the%20World%20War%20%20PCN%2019000411300.pdf>.
McCormick, John. *Bullfighting: Art, Technique, and Spanish Society*. New Brunswick: Transaction Publishers, 1998.
McLean, D. R. Letter to Father. 29 June 1915. *D. R. McLean's ANZAC Letters*. N.p. 6 June 2010. Web. <http://drmcleansanzacletters.blogspot.com/2010/06/dardanelles-29-june-1915-gallipoli.html>. 3 Jan. 2013.
McLoughlin, Kate. "War and Words." *The Cambridge Companion to War Writing*. Cambridge, UK: Cambridge UP, 2009.
Meredith, George. *The Ordeal of Richard Feverel*. 1878. New York: New American Library, 1961.
Messent, Peter. "'The Real Thing'? Representing the Bullfight and Spain in *Death in the Afternoon*." In *A Companion to Hemingway's* Death in the Afternoon. Ed. Miriam Mandel. Rochester, NY: Camden House, 2004. 123–42.
Meyers, Jeffrey. *Hemingway: A Biography*. New York: Da Capo Press, 1985.
Michener, James A. *Iberia*. New York: Ballantine Books, 1984.
Mieszkowski, Jan. "Watching War." *PMLA* 124.5 (Oct. 2009): 1648–61.

Milton, John. *Paradise Lost*. In *The Complete Poetry and Essential Prose of John Milton*. Ed. William Kerrigan, John Rumrich, and Stephen M. Fallon. New York: Random House, 2007. 250–630.

Moddelmog, Debra. *Reading Desire: In Pursuit of Ernest Hemingway*. Ithaca, NY: Cornell UP, 1999.

Monbiot, George. "George Orwell Was Hailed a Hero for Fighting in Spain: Today He'd Be Guilty of Terrorism." *The Guardian* 10 Feb. 2014. Raw Story. Web. <http://www.rawstory.com/2014/02/george-orwell-was-hailed-a-hero-for-fighting-in-spain-today-hed-be-guilty-of-terrorism/>. 10 Feb. 2014.

Müller, Timo. "The Uses of Authenticity: Hemingway and the Literary Field, 1926–1936." *Journal of Modern Literature* 33.1 (n.d.): 28–42. Humanities Full Text. Web. 13 Nov. 2012.

Murphy, Sara. "Traumatizing Feminism: Prevention Discourse and the Subject of Sexual Violence." In *Traumatizing Theory: The Cultural Politics of Affect In and Beyond Psychoanalysis*. Ed. Karyn Ball. New York: Other Press, 2007.

National Institute of Mental Health. "Post-Traumatic Stress Disorder (PTSD)." Web. NIMH website. <http://www.nimh.nih.gov/health/topics/post-traumatic-stress-disorder-ptsd/index.shtml>.

Newton, Adam Zachary. *Narrative Ethics*. Cambridge, MA: Harvard UP, 1995.

Nuffer, David. *The Best Friend I Ever Had: Revelations about Ernest Hemingway from Those Who Knew Him*. NP: Exlibris, 2008.

Ong, Walter. *Orality and Literacy: The Technologizing of the Word*. London: Methuen, 1982.

Owen, Wilfred. *The Collected Poems of Wilfred Owen*. Ed. C. Day Lewis. New York: New Directions, 1964.

Payne, Stanley G. *The Spanish Civil War, the Soviet Union, and Communism*. New Haven, CT: Yale UP, 2011.

Phelan, James. *Experiencing Fiction: Judgments, Progressions, and the Rhetorical Theory of Narrative*. Columbus: Ohio State UP, 2007.

Plath, James. "Barking at Death: Hemingway, Africa, and the Stages of Dying." In *Hemingway and Africa*. Ed. Miriam B. Mandel. Rochester: Camden House, 2011. 299–319.

Pozorski, Aimee. "Infantry and Infanticide in *A Farewell to Arms*." *Hemingway Review* 23.2 (2004): 75–98.

Quick, Robert. Letter to Mother. 8 June 1917. *ACR-7 USS Colorado/USS Pueblo*. Rootsweb. Ed. Joe Hartwell. 30 June 2011. Web. <http://freepages.military.rootsweb.ancestry.com/~cacunithistories/USS_Colorado.html>. 3 Jan. 2013.

Reynolds, Michael S. *Hemingway: The Paris Years*. New York: W. W. Norton, 1999.

———. *Hemingway's Reading, 1910–1940: An Inventory*. Princeton: Princeton UP, 1981.

———. *The Young Hemingway*. Oxford: Basil Blackwell, 1986.

Rich, Adrienne. *Of Woman Born: Motherhood as Experience and Institution*. 10th anniversary ed. New York: Norton, 1986.

Rimmon-Kenan, Schlomith. *Narrative Fiction: Contemporary Poetics*. London: Methuen, 1983.

Rudat, Wolfgang. "The Other War in *For Whom the Bell Tolls*: Maria and Miltonic Gender Role Battles." *Hemingway Review* 11.1 (1991): 8–24.

Ruddick, Sara. *Maternal Thinking: Toward a Politics of Peace*. Boston: Beacon Press, 1989.

Sander, Libby. "Veterans Tell Elite Colleges: 'We Belong.'" *The Chronicle of Higher Education.* 7 Jan 2013.
Sassoon, Siegfried. *Counter-Attack and Other Poems.* New York: Dutton, 1918.
Scarry, Elaine. *The Body in Pain.* New York: Oxford UP, 1985.
Scheff, Thomas J. *Bloody Revenge: Emotions, Nationalism, and War.* Boulder, CO: Westview Press, 1994.
———, and Suzanne M. Retzinger. *Emotions and Violence: Shame and Rage in Destructive Conflicts.* Lexington, MA: Lexington Books, 1991.
Schlieffen, Alfred von. *Alfred von Schlieffen's Military Writings.* Trans. Robert T. Foley. London: Frank Cass Publishers, 2003.
Schwartz, Delmore. "Ernest Hemingway's Literary Situation." In *Ernest Hemingway: The Critical Tradition.* Ed. Jeffrey Meyers. London: Routledge, 1982. 243–56.
Schwartz, Nina. "Lovers' Discourse in *The Sun Also Rises:* A Cock and Bull Story." *Criticism* 26.1 (1984): 49–69.
Seed, David. "'The Picture of the Whole': *In Our Time.*" In *Ernest Hemingway: New Critical Essays.* Ed. A. Robert Lee. Totowa, NJ: Barnes and Noble, 1983. 13–35.
Shay, Jonathan. *Achilles in Vietnam: Combat Trauma and the Undoing on Character.* New York: Scribner, 1994.
Smith, Adam. *The Theory of Moral Sentiments.* Ed. Knud Haakonssen. Cambridge, UK: Cambridge UP, 2002.
Smith, Paul. *A Reader's Guide to the Short Stories of Ernest Hemingway.* Boston: G. K. Hall, 1989.
Smith, Ronald. "Nick Adams and Post-Traumatic Stress Disorder." *War, Literature, and the Arts* 9.1 (1997): 39–48.
Solow, Michael K. "A Clash of Certainties, Old and New: *For Whom the Bell Tolls* and the Inner War of Ernest Hemingway." *Hemingway Review* 29.1 (2009): 103–22.
*The Spanish Earth.* Script: Ernest Hemingway and Joris Ivens. Dir. Joris Ivens. Photog. John Ferno. Film ed. Helen van Dongen. Nar. Ernest Hemingway. Contemporary Historians, Inc., 1937.
Strychacz, Thomas. "In Our Time, Out of Season." In *The Cambridge Companion to Hemingway.* Ed. Scott Donaldson. New York: Cambridge UP, 1996. 55–86.
"Suggested Essay Topics: *For Whom the Bell Tolls.*" Sparknotes. 3 Apr. 2013. Web. <http://www.sparknotes.com/lit/belltolls/study.html>.
Suits, Bernard. *The Grasshopper: Games, Life and Utopia.* Peterborough, Canada: Broadview Press, 2005.
Svoboda, Frederic Joseph. *Hemingway and* The Sun Also Rises: *The Crafting of a Style.* Lawrence: UP of Kansas, 1983.
Sylvester, Bickford. "Hemingway's Italian Waste Land: The Complex Unity of 'Out of Season.'" In *Hemingway's Neglected Short Fiction: New Perspectives.* Ed. Susan F. Beegel. Ann Arbor, MI: UMI Research Press, 1989. 75–98.
Tallack, Douglas, Diana Knight, Bernard McGuirk, and Steve Giles. "New Ways of Reading Old Texts." *English in Education* 20.2 (Summer 1986): 13–21.
Tetlow, Wendolyn E. *Hemingway's* In Our Time: *Lyrical Dimensions.* Lewisburg, PA: Bucknell UP, 1992.
Thomson, Captane. Phone conversation with Peter Hays. 5 May 2011.

Thomson, Rosemarie Garland. *Extraordinary Bodies: Figuring Physical Disability in American Culture and Literature*. New York: Columbia UP, 1997.

Thurston, Michael. "Genre, Gender, and Truth in *Death in the Afternoon*." *Hemingway Review* 17.2 (1998): 47–63.

Tomalin, Claire. *Katherine Mansfield: A Secret Life*. New York: St. Martin's Press, 1987.

———. *On the Battlefield of Memory: The First World War and American Remembrance, 1919–1941*. Tuscaloosa: U of Alabama P, 2010.

United Nations. "Report of the International Law Commission to the General Assembly, Part 3: Formulation of the Nürnberg Principles." *Yearbook of the International Law Commission, 1950*. Vol. 2. New York: United Nations, 1957. Available online at <http://legal.un.org/ilc/publications/yearbooks/Ybkvolumes(e)/ILC_1950_v2_e.pdf>.

Vernon, Alex. *Hemingway's Second War: Bearing Witness to the Spanish Civil War*. Iowa City: U of Iowa P, 2011.

———. *Soldiers Once and Still: Ernest Hemingway, James Salter, and Tim O'Brien*. Iowa City: U of Iowa P, 2004.

———. "*The Spanish Earth* and the Non-Nonfiction War Film." *Hemingway Review* 34.1 (Fall 2014): 30–46.

———. "War, Gender, and Ernest Hemingway." *Hemingway Review* 22.1 (2002): 34–55.

Vickroy, Laurie. *Trauma and Survival in Contemporary Fiction*. Charlottesville: U of Virginia P, 2002.

Villard, Henry Serrano, and James Nagel. *Hemingway in Love and War*. Boston: Northeastern UP, 1989.

Walpole, Hugh. *Fortitude*. New York: Grosset and Dunlap, 1913.

Warhol, Robyn R. "Neonarrative; or, How to Render the Unnarratable in Realist Fiction and Contemporary Film." In *A Companion to Narrative Theory*. Ed. James Phelan and Peter J. Rabinowitz. Malden, MA: Blackwell, 2005. 220–31.

Washington, Gene. "Hemingway, *The Fifth Column,* and the 'Dead Angle.'" *Hemingway Review* 28.2 (2009): 127–35.

Wharton, Edith. *A Son at the Front*. New York: Scribner, 1923.

Wilson, Edmond. *The Wound and the Bow: Seven Studies in Literature*. London: Methuen, 1942.

Wolfe, Cary. *Before the Law: Humans and Other Animals in a Biopolitical Frame*. Chicago: U of Chicago P, 2013.

Wolin, Richard, ed. *The Heidegger Controversy: A Critical Reader*. Trans. Joel Golb and Richard Wolin. New York: Columbia UP, 1991.

Woolf, Virginia. *Three Guineas*. New York: Harvest, 1938.

Wyatt, David. *Prodigal Sons: A Study in Authorship and Authority*. Baltimore: Johns Hopkins UP, 1980.

Wyschogrod, Edith. *Spirit in Ashes: Hegel, Heidegger, and Man-Made Mass Death*. New Haven: Yale UP, 1985.

Young, Philip. *Ernest Hemingway: A Reconsideration*. University Park: Pennsylvania State UP, 1966.

Zuckert, Catherine. *Natural Right and the American Imagination*. Savage, MD: Rowman and Littlefield, 1990.

# Selected Bibliography

Alisei, Tamara. "The Corrida and For Whom the Bell Tolls." *Neophilologus* 56.4 (1972): 487–92.
Anderson, Donald. "Soldier-Artists: Preserving the World." *War, Literature, and the Arts: An International Journal of the Humanities* (2013): 1–18.
Austin, J. L. *How to do Things with Words*. Cambridge, MA: Harvard UP, 1962.
Bacevich, Andrew. *Breach of Trust: How Americans Failed Their Soldiers and Their Country*. New York: Henry Holt, 2013.
Barker, Chris. "Hemingway's *Death in the Afternoon* and the Fear of Death in War." *War, Literature, and the Arts: An International Journal of the Humanities* 26 (2014): 1–19. Web. <http://wlajournal.com/wlaarchive/26/Barker.pdf>.
Barker, Jennifer M. *The Tactile Eye: Touch and the Cinematic Experience*. Oakland: U of California P, 2009.
Barloon, Jim. "Very Short Stories: The Miniaturization of War in Hemingway's *In Our Time*." *Hemingway Review* 24.2 (2005): 5–17.
Berger, John. *Ways of Seeing*. London: Penguin Books, 1990.
Black, Jeremy. *The Age of Total War, 1860–1945*. Lanham, MD: Rowman and Littlefield, 2010.
Broer, Lawrence. "Dangerous Families: A Midwestern Exorcism." *War + Ink: New Perspectives on Hemingway's Early Life and Writings*. Ed. Steve Paul, Gail Sinclair, and Steven Trout. Kent, OH: Kent State UP, 2014. 260–85.
Clifford, Stephen. "Hemingway's Fragmentary Novel: Readers Writing the Hero in *In Our Time*." *Hemingway Review* 13.2 (1994): 12–23.
Cohen, Milton A. "Beleaguered Modernists: Hemingway, Stevens, and the Left." In *Key West Hemingway: A Reassessment*, ed. Kirk Curnutt and Gail Sinclair. Tallahassee: U of Florida P, 2009. 77–90.
Confino, Alan, Paul Betts, and Dirk Schumann. *Between Mass Death and Individual Loss: The Place of the Dead in Twentieth-Century Germany*. New York: Berghahn Books, 2008.
Davies, Stephen, comp. Canadian Letters and Images Project. Canadian War Museum, n.d. Web. 3 Jan. 2013.
Dodman, Trevor. "'Going All to Pieces': *A Farewell to Arms* as Trauma Narrative." *Twentieth Century Literature* 52:3 (Fall 2006): 249–74.

Gee, James Paul. *What Video Games Have to Teach Us about Learning and Literacy.* New York: Palgrave Macmillan, 2007.

Grossman, David. *On Killing: The Psychological Cost of Learning to Kill in War and Society.* New York: Little, Brown and Co., 1995.

Grosz, Elizabeth. *Volatile Bodies: Toward a Corporeal Feminism.* Bloomington: Indiana UP, 1994.

Hays, Peter. "Hemingway's Clinical Depression: A Speculation." *Hemingway Review* 14.2 (Spring 1995): 50–63.

Haytock, Jennifer. "Hemingway's Soldiers and their Pregnant Women: Domestic Ritual in World War I." *Hemingway Review* 19.2 (Spring 2000): 57–72.

Heidegger, Martin. *Being and Time.* Albany: State U of New York P, 1996.

Hemingway, Ernest. "A Canary for One." In his *The Complete Short Stories of Ernest Hemingway: The Finca Vigía Edition.* New York: Scribner, 1987. 258–61.

———. *The Dangerous Summer.* New York: Charles Scribner's Sons, 1960.

———. *Green Hills of Africa.* New York: Scribner, 1935.

———. "The Heat and the Cold." In *The Spanish Earth.* Ed. Jasper Wood. Cleveland: J. B. Savage, 1938. 55–60.

———. *The Old Man and the Sea.* New York: Scribner, 1952. Edited by Nicholas Gerogiannis, University of Nebraska Press, 1983. edited by Nicholas Gerogiannis, University of Nebraska Press, 1983. edited by Nicholas Gerogiannis, University of Nebraska Press, 1983.

Hemingway, Mary Welsh. *How It Was.* New York: Knopf, 1976.

Jameson, Fredric. *The Political Unconscious: Narrative as a Socially Symbolic Act.* 1981; rpt., London: Methuen, 1983.

Jünger, Ernst. *The Adventurous Heart: Figures and Capriccios.* Trans. Thomas Friese, Eliah Bures, and Elliot Neaman. New York: Telos Press, 2012.

———. *On Pain.* Trans. David. C. Durst. New York: Telos Press, 2008.

———. "Total Mobilization." In *The Heidegger Controversy: A Critical Reader.* Trans. Joel Golb and Richard Wolin. New York: Columbia UP, 1991.

Keegan, John. *The Face of Battle: A Study of Agincourt, Waterloo, and the Somme.* New York: Penguin Books, 1983.

Kipling, Rudyard. *The Years Between.* London: Methuen, 1919.

LaCapra, Dominick. *Writing History, Writing Trauma.* Baltimore: Johns Hopkins UP, 2001.

Mandel, Miriam. *A Companion to Hemingway's* Death in the Afternoon. Rochester, NY: Camden House, 2004.

Marks, Laura. *The Skin of the Film: Intercultural Cinema, Embodiment, and the Senses.* Durham, NC: Duke UP, 2000.

McMahon, Laura. *Cinema and Contact: The Withdrawal of Touch in Nancy, Bresson, Duras, and Denis.* Oxford: Legenda, 2012.

Mellow, James. *Hemingway: A Life Without Consequences.* Cambridge, MA: Da Capo Press, 1992.

Messent, Peter. "Character and Agency: Teaching Mark Twain's 'A True Story.'" *Eureka Studies in Teaching Short Fiction* 4.1 (2003): 20–31.

———. *Ernest Hemingway*. Houndmills, Basingstoke: Macmillan, 1992.

———. "Liminality, Repetition, and Trauma in Hemingway's 'Big Two-Hearted River' and Other Nick Adams Stories." In *Mapping Liminalities: Thresholds in Cultural and Literary Texts*. Ed. Lucy Kay et al. Bern: Peter Lang, 2007. 136–65.

———. *New Readings of the American Novel: Narrative Theory and its Application*. Houndmills, Basingstoke: Macmillan, 1990.

Micale, Mark S., and Paul Lerner, eds. *Traumatic Pasts: History, Psychiatry, and Trauma in the Modern Age, 1870–1930*. Cambridge, UK: Cambridge UP, 2001.

Moddelmog, Debra. "'We Live in a Country Where Nothing Makes Any Difference': The Queer Sensibility of *A Farewell to Arms*." *Hemingway Review* 28.2 (2009): 7–24.

O'Brien, Tim. "Field Trip." In O'Brien, *The Things They Carried*. New York: Houghton Mifflin, 1990.

Orwell, George. *Homage to Catalonia*. London: Secker and Warburg, 1938.

"Principles of International Law recognized in the Charter of the Nürnberg Tribunal and in the Judgment of the Tribunal, with commentaries." United Nations Office of Legal Affairs. 1950. 28 Mar 2013. Web. <http://untreaty.un.org/ilc/texts/instruments/english/draft%20articles/7_1_1950.pdf>.

Quick, Paul S. "Hemingway's 'A Way You'll Never Be' and Nick Adams's Search for Identity." Web. <http://www.thefreelibrary.com/Hemingway's+%22A+Way+You'll+Never+Be%22+and+Nick+Adams's+search+for . . . -a0105518230>.

Roper, Michael. *The Secret Battle: Emotional Survival in the Great War*. Manchester: Manchester UP, 2009.

Rothberg, Michael. *Multidirectional Memory: Remembering the Holocaust in the Age of Decolonization*. Stanford, CA: Stanford UP, 2009.

Sassoon, Siegfried. *The Old Huntsman*. New York: Dutton, 1918.

Sempreora, Margot. "Nick at Night: Nocturnal Metafictions in Three Hemingway Short Stories." *Hemingway Review* 22.1 (Fall 2002): 19–26.

Shay, Jonathan. *Odysseus in America: Combat Trauma and the Trials of Homecoming*. New York: Scribner, 2003.

Shubert, Adrian. *Death and Money in the Afternoon: A History of the Spanish Bullfight*. Oxford: Oxford UP, 1999.

Sobchack, Vivian. *Carnal Thoughts: Embodiment and Moving Image Culture*. Oakland: U of California P, 2004.

Stoltzfus, Ben. "Sartre, Nada, and Hemingway's African Stories." *Comparative Literature Studies* 42.3 (2005): 205–28.

Strychacz, Thomas. *Dangerous Masculinities: Conrad, Hemingway, and Lawrence*. Gainesville: UP of Florida, 2008.

Thomas, Gregory M. *Treating the Trauma of the Great War: Soldiers, Civilians, and Psychiatry in France, 1914–1940*. Baton Rouge: Louisiana State UP, 2009.

Trotter, David. "Lynne Ramsay's Ratcatcher: Towards a Theory of Haptic Narrative." *Paragraph* 31.2 (2008): 138–58.

Trout, Steven. "Antithetical Icons? Willa Cather, Ernest Hemingway, and the First World War." *Cather Studies* 7 (2007): 269–87.

Wagner-Martin, Linda. "The Stein Subtext in *Death in the Afternoon*." In *A Companion to Hemingway's* Death in the Afternoon. Ed. Miriam Mandel. Rochester, NY: Camden House, 2004. 59–78.

"War and Sacrifice in the Post-9/11 Era: The Military-Civilian Gap." Pew Research Social and Demographic Surveys. 5 Oct. 2011. Web. <http://www.pewsocialtrends.org/2011/10/05/war-and-sacrifice-in-the-post-911-era/>.

# Contributors

Sarah Wood Anderson is associate lecturer of English at the University of Wisconsin-Madison, where she teaches courses in twentieth-century American literature and gender studies. She is the author of *Readings of Trauma, Madness, and the Body* (Palgrave, 2012). Her book *Understanding Claudia Emerson* is forthcoming.

Christopher Barker is a political theorist. He received his PhD from Claremont Graduate University, where he wrote his dissertation on the liberalism of John Stuart Mill. He has written published or forthcoming articles on Shakespeare's English history plays, Herodotean history, Hemingway's *Death in the Afternoon*, and the culture of game playing. He currently teaches constitutional history at Ohio University. He has previously held positions at Harvard University and Boston College.

Anna Broadwell-Gulde graduated from Hendrix College in 2013 with a double major in English literature and environmental communication. Recipient of a Fulbright fellowship, she spent the following year teaching English in northern Brazil and is excited to begin an interdisciplinary Master's program at the University of Chicago in fall 2015.

Milton A. Cohen is a professor of literary studies at the University of Texas at Dallas. He has written books on Hemingway (*Hemingway's Laboratory: The Paris in our time*, 2005), Cummings *(PoetandPainter: The Aesthetics of E. E. Cummings's Early Work*, 1987), and modernism (*Movement, Manifesto, Melee: The Modernist Group, 1910–1914*, 2004). His most recent book is *Beleaguered Poets and Leftist Critics: Stevens, Cummings, Frost, and Williams in the 1930s* (2010).

Zack Hausle graduated with a degree in philosophy from Hendrix College. Hausle's thesis work examined the utility of traditional frameworks of political philosophy in understanding surveillance policies and procedures in the United States. Hausle is currently a graduate student in biostatistics at the University of Michigan, Ann Arbor.

Peter L. Hays is professor emeritus at the University of California, Davis, where he still teaches a Hemingway course. His books on Hemingway, which provide the only concordance to Hemingway's fiction, include *A Concordance to Hemingway's* In Our Time (1990); *Teaching Hemingway's* The Sun Also Rises (2008); *The Critical Reception of Hemingway's* The Sun Also Rises (2011); and, most recently, *Fifty Years of Hemingway Criticism* (2014).

Ryan Hediger is assistant professor of English at Kent State University, Tuscarawas. His research focuses on violence, environment, animals, and U.S. literature after 1900. He has edited two essay collections, *Animals and War: Studies of Europe and North America* (2013) and, with Sarah McFarland, *Animals and Agency: An Interdisciplinary Exploration* (2009). He has also published essays in several journals, including the *Hemingway Review, Interdisciplinary Studies in Literature and Environment (ISLE)*, and *Animal Studies Journal*. He is currently writing a manuscript studying posthumanism, American literature, and homesickness.

Alexander Hollenberg is a professor of storytelling and narrativity at Sheridan College, specializing in American modernism and narrative ethics. His work has been published in the *Hemingway Review, Narrative, Style,* and *Studies in American Indian Literatures*. He is currently working on two book-length projects, "American Modernist Simplicity" and "Doctored Discourse: Modernism and Narrative Medicine."

Ruth A. H. Lahti is the assistant dean of writing and composition at Southern New Hampshire University. She earned her PhD in 2014 from the University of Massachusetts, Amherst. Her dissertation, "Transnational Gestures: Rethinking Trauma in U.S. War Fiction," remaps the ethics of American war writing through a focus on characters' bodily gestures as they evince the transnational dimensions of war. Her research interests include American war fiction, transnational fiction and theory, feminist theories of embodiment, and trauma theory. At the University of Massachusetts and Siena College, she taught classes on American literature and culture, the modern novel, and gender and sexuality in global literature. Her essays have appeared in the *Journal of Transnational American Studies* and *Current Writing: Text and Reception in Southern Africa*.

Peter Messent is emeritus professor of modern American literature at the University of Nottingham (UK). He has published several essays on Hemingway as well as the book, *Ernest Hemingway* (1992). He has also published widely on Mark Twain, notably the prize-winning study *Mark Twain and Male Friendship: The Twichell, Howells, and Rogers Friendships* (2009). His most recent book, *The Crime Fiction Handbook*, was published in 2013.

Steven A. Nardi has a PhD from Princeton University and was an assistant professor at the City University of New York. His publications include work on the Harlem Renaissance as well as essays on contemporary American poetry and Japanese postwar film. Currently, he is at work on a book manuscript titled "The Stars Pulled Down: Technology and Poetics in the American New Poetry and the Harlem Renaissance."

Mark P. Ott teaches at Deerfield Academy in Massachusetts. He is the author of *A Sea of Change: Ernest Hemingway and the Gulf Stream—a Contextual Biography* (Kent State

UP, 2008). Ott has presented academic papers at international Hemingway conferences in Cuba, Oak Park, Bimini, Italy, Key West, and Spain, and his scholarship has been published in the *Hemingway Review*. He has been awarded grants from the Ernest Hemingway Society, the Ernest Hemingway Collection at the John F. Kennedy Library, and the Arts and Sciences Advisory Council of the University of Hawaii–Manoa.

Josephine Reece graduated in 2013 in philosophy and English literature from Hendrix College, where her thesis investigated the boundaries of verbal and nonverbal communication in the early poetry of H.D. Recipient of a Fulbright scholarship, she has been fulfilling its terms as an English teaching assistant in South Korea. In fall 2015, she will become a PhD candidate in English literature at Harvard University.

Thomas Strychacz is a professor of American literature at Mills College, California. He is the author of three books: *Modernism, Mass Culture, and Professionalism* (1993), *Hemingway's Theaters of Masculinity* (2003), and *Dangerous Masculinities: Conrad, Hemingway, Lawrence* (2007). He also has contributed several essays to previous volumes in the Teaching Hemingway Series.

Lisa Tyler is a professor of English at Sinclair Community College in Dayton, Ohio, where she has taught for more than twenty years. She is the author of *Student Companion to Ernest Hemingway* (2001), as well as of more than two dozen essays in academic journals and edited collections. She also edited another essay collection in the Teaching Hemingway Series, *Teaching Hemingway's* A Farewell to Arms (2008).

Alex Vernon is professor of English at Hendrix College in Arkansas. He is the author of two war memoirs, *most succinctly bred* (2006) and *The Eyes of Orion: Five Tank Lieutenants in the Persian Gulf War* (1999), which won an Army Historical Foundation Distinguished Book Award; two books of literary criticism/history, *Soldiers Once and Still: Ernest Hemingway, James Salter, and Tim O'Brien* (2004) and *Hemingway's Second War: Bearing Witness to the Spanish Civil War* (2011); the cultural study *On Tarzan* (2008); and three edited collections, *Arms and the Self: War, the Military, and Autobiographical Writing* (2005), *Approaches to Teaching the Works of Tim O'Brien* (2010), and *Critical Insights: War* (2012).

# Index

*The 17th Parallel*, 2

Abraham Lincoln Brigade, 100–101, 105n7
Abram, David, 232, 236n2
*Across the River and into the Trees*, 10, 71, 172–86
*The Act of Killing*, 123
Afghanistan wars, 6, 10–11, 58, 77
Africa, 155
"[All armies are the same . . . ]," 8
*All Quiet on the Western Front* (film), 122–23, 125, 127
American Civil War, 123, 140
American Expeditionary Force, 1
American Occupational Therapy Association, 136
American Psychiatric Association, 135, 137, 139, 141
American Revolutionary War, 140
Anand, Mulk Raj, 8, 41–59
Anderson, Donald, 168n4
Anderson, Sarah, 10
Anthony, David W., 156n6
*Apocalypse Now*, 123
Aristotle, 162
Auden, W. H., 93
Austen, Jane, 237n6
Austin, J. L., 73n6

Baker, Carlos, 37, 101, 111, 135, 136, 163, 142n2, 184n4
Barker, Christopher, 10, 168n2
Barker, Jennifer M., 128n6
Barloon, Jim, 16
Barnouw, Dagmar, 160, 171n25
*The Battle of Algiers*, 123
"The Battler," 34, 134, 141
Benedict, Helen, 48
Benjamin, Jessica, 38

*The Best Years of Our Lives*, 123
Betts, Paul, 170n20
Bluemel, Kristin, 45
*The Big Parade*, 122
"Big Two-Hearted River," 7–8, 27–28, 60, 70; in Ernest Hemingway Seminar, 191; and trauma, 136, 140–41, 173–74, 183
Bourke, Joanna, 2, 169n5, 170n20
Broadwell-Gulde, Anna, 10, 194
Brenner, Gerry, 153, 174
bullfighting, 10, 16, 33–34. See also *Death in the Afternoon*
"The Butterfly and the Tank," 96

Canadian Letters and Images Project, 18–19
"A Canary for One," 149
Cannae, 157
Capa, Robert, 3, 127
Carnegie Hall, 95
Carroll, Peter, 112
Caruth, Cathy, 147, 172, 179–80
"Cat in the Rain," 19, 149
Catholicism, 165
Caudwell, Christopher, 105n7
Cecchin, Giovanni, 140
Chandrasekaran, Rajiv, 108–9
"chapter 2" (*In Our Time*), 19–21, 23
"chapter 6" (*In Our Time*), 36–37
"chapter 7" (*In Our Time*), 26–27
"chapter 15" (*In Our Time*), 34
"chapter 33" (*In Our Time*), 33–34
Chaucer, Geoffrey, 237n6
Chicotes, 96
Churchill, Winston, 141
Clark, Miriam Marty, 182
"A Clean, Well-Lighted Place," 69–70, 137
Clifford, Stephen, 21
Cohen, Milton, 9, 135, 140, 105n5
Cold War, 77

Cole, David, 236n1
Communist International (COMINTERN), 93–94, 114
Communist Party, 94, 100
Confino, Alan, 120n20
Conklin, Guy, 139
Conley, Tom, 129n7
Crane, Stephen, 5, 138
"Cross-Country Snow," 38, 40
Cummings, E. E., 8
Cuomo, Chris J., 36–37
Custer, George Armstrong, 140

*The Daily Worker*, 100–101
*The Dangerous Summer*, 170n16
Das, Santanu, 2, 43, 123–29
Davis, Peter, 127
Davis, R. M., 34
*Death in the Afternoon*, 10, 16–17, 157–71
DeFalco, Joe, 135
del Gizzo, Suzanne, 4, 9, 60
del Torro, Guillermo. See *The Devil's Backbone*
"The Denunciation," 96–97, 98
*The Devil's Backbone*, 122
Dimarco, Louis A., 156n6
"The Doctor and the Doctor's Wife," 34–35, 37, 85–86
Dodman, Trevor, 174, 185n7
Donahue, Peter, 21
Dos Passos, John, 93, 95, 101, 103, 137, 106n16, 121n1
Downhill, Jack, 139
Dragunoiu, Dana, 171n24
drones, 90
DuBois, W. E. B., 48
Dyer, Geoff, 2, 5

Eagleton, Terry, 192
Eby, Carl, 139–40, 141, 191
ecofeminism, 192
Elliott, Ira, 205
Elshtein, Jean Bethke, 170n20
Enlistment in Foreign Service (U.S. Code), 9
*Esquire*, 30

*A Farewell to Arms*, 5, 6–8, 10, 41–59, 63–64, 66–67, 78, 164; in Ernest Hemingway Seminar, 190–92, 194; and Foucault/biopower, 209–23; and language/rhetoric, 17, 111, 113; and trauma, 134, 140, 145–47, 154, 173–74, 179, 185n7
fascism, 87–91, 94
"Fathers and Sons," 37, 39

Faulkner, William, 45, 173
Fieve, Ronald, 141
*The Fifth Column*, 95, 97–99, 102, 216
First World War, 1–3, 4, 8, 122, 124–29, 133–42, 155, 157. See also *A Farewell to Arms*; "Big Two-Hearted River"; "Cross-Country Snow"; "In Another Country"; *In Our Time*; "A Natural History of the Dead"; "Now I Lay Me"; "A Pursuit Race"; "Soldier's Home"; "A Way You'll Never Be"; "Who Murdered the Vets?"
Fitzgerald, F. Scott, 173, 184n3
Fitzgerald, Zelda, 184n3
Florczyk, Steven, 4, 7
Ford (corporation), 104n1
Ford, Ford Maddox, 141
Fore, Diana, 186n16
Forter, Greg, 186n12
*For Whom the Bell Tolls*, 3–4, 5, 6, 8–9, 10, 11, 77–91, 99–104, 107–21, 224–37; and depression/trauma, 137, 144, 150–55, 173, 179; and Ernest Hemingway Seminar, 189–92, 194
Foucault, Michel, 10, 194, 209–23
France, 160
Freud, Sigmund, 182
Friend, Krebs, 135
Fussell, Paul, 2

Gadjusek, Robert, 32
Gallipoli, 19
Gandal, Keith, 173, 182–83, 184n5
*The Garden of Eden*, 6, 7, 152, 190–91
Garrington, Abby, 128n4
Gee, James, 9, 109–10, 120
Gellhorn, Martha, 3, 189, 105n8, 105n9
General Motors, 104n1
George, C. J., 46
"Get a Seeing-Eyed Dog," 9, 144, 147–50
Gilbert, Sandra M., 2, 30–31
Girard, René, 192, 208n2
Gold, Mike, 100
*Gone with the Wind*, 101
"To Good Guys Dead," 8
Goodman, Paul, 70
Gottlieb, Werner, 141
Graves, Robert, 158
Great War. See First World War
Greco-Turkish War, 3, 77. See also "On the Quai at Smryna"
*Green Hills of Africa*, 9–10, 141, 155
Grimes, Larry E., 35
Grossman, David, 245n4

Grosz, Elizabeth, 156n1
Gubar, Susan, 2, 30–31

Hageman, E. R., 36
Hannibal, 158
Hanks, Tom, 126
Harris, Mark, 157
Hausle, Zack, 10, 193–94
Hawkins, Ruth, 190
Hays, Peter L., 9, 36, 142n4, 142n5
H.D., 184n3, 193
"The Heat and the Cold," 125–27
Hediger, Ryan, 9, 156n5
Hellman, Lillian, 95
Hemingway, Clarence (father), 39, 134, 167
Hemingway, Grace Hall (mother), 135
Hemingway, Gregory (son), 40
Hemingway, John Hadley Nicanor (son), 37, 40
Hemingway, Leicester (brother), 134
Hemingway, Margaux (granddaughter), 134
Hemingway, Mary (wife), 191
Hemingway, Patrick (son), 40
Hemingway-Pfeiffer Home and Education Center, 190
Hemingway, Sean (grandson), 4
Hemingway, Ursula (sister), 134
Hemingway, Valerie (daughter-in-law), 142n1
Hendrix College, 189–94
Hendrix-Murphy Foundation in Language and Literature, 190
Herbst, Josephine, 105n12
Herlihy-Mera, Jeffrey, 158
Herman, Judith, 172, 176, 184n1
Herndl, Diane Price, 174, 212, 222, 184n2, 184n6, 223n1
Herodotus, 157
Hirsch, Marianne, 43–44
Hitler, Adolph, 35
Hollenberg, Alex, 7
Holocaust, 43–44
Hughes, Langston, 48
Huppauf, Bernd, 123–29
*The Hurt Locker*, 123
Hynes, Samuel, 2, 30–31

"In Another Country," 10, 173–75, 177
India, and the British Empire, 47–48
"Indian Camp," 22–23, 32, 83, 85–86, 141
*In Our Time*, 7–8, 15–29, 77–91, 133–42, 173; in Ernest Hemingway Seminar, 190. See also individual stories

International Brigades, 93–94, 96, 105n7. See also Abraham Lincoln Brigade
Iraq war, 6, 10–11, 58, 108–9, 137
*Islands in the Stream*, 173
Italy, 94, 103, 73n3
Ivens, Joris, 3, 9, 95, 122–29, 189

James, William, 23–24
Jameson, Frederic, 147, 73n9
Jin, Ha, 48
Johnson, Samuel, 4
Josephs, Allen, 110–11
Joyce, James, 141
Jünger, Ernst, 10, 159–60, 167

*Kansas City Star*, 20
Kashkin, Ivan, 161
Keegan, John, 156n6, 169n5
Kemp, Janet E., 157
*Ken* magazine, 95
Kennedy, A. L., 158, 162, 168n2
Key West, 95, 98
"Killed Piave—July 8—1918," 8
Kipling, Rudyard, 30, 31
Koch, Stephen, 105n4, 121n1
Kojeve, Alexandre, 166, 170n21
Komunyakaa, Yusef, 48
Korean War, 77
Kurowsky, Agnes von, 138, 139

LaCapra, Dominick, 48
"The Lady Poet with Foot Notes," 8
Lahti, Ruth, 8, 10
*Lebanon*, 123
Leclerc, Philippe, 3
Leed, Eric J., 2
Lessing, Doris, 36
Linker, Beth, 2
Liptak, Adam, 157
Lisca Peter, 178, 183, 186n14, 186n15
Lukacs, Georg, 72
Luria, A. R., 237n7

Maclean, Douglas, 19
MacLeish, Archibald, 95, 141
"The Malady of Power: A Second Serious Letter," 33
Mandel, Miriam, 158
Manifest Destiny, 85
Mansfield, Katherine, 31–32
Mayo Clinic, 134, 141
Marks, Laura, 128n6

Marvell, Andrew, 150
Marxism, 98
McAlmon, Robert, 137
McClellan, Edwin N., 11
McCormick, John, 158, 167, 168n2, 245n2
McKim, Kristi, 124
McLoughlin, Kate, 126, 237n8
McMahon, Laura, 128n6
*Men at War*, 3, 5, 10–11, 40, 70, 161, 169n6
*Men Without Women*, 174
Meredith, George, 38–39
Merleau-Ponty, Maurice, 232
Messent, Peter, 8, 166, 73n1, 73n7
*The Mexican Suitcase*, 127
Meyers, Jeffrey, 142n1
Michaels, Walter Benn, 191
Michener, James, 167
Michigan, 160
Mieszkowski, Jan, 128n2
Milestone, Lewis, 125, 127. See also *All Quiet on the Western Front* (film)
Mills College, 90
Milton, 226–28, 235–36
Moddelmog, Debra, 4, 9, 60, 181–82, 223n1
modernism/modernity, 57, 190
Monbiot, George, 9
Montgomery, Constance, 139
Moore, Marianne, 48
moral injury, 9, 133
Moreira, Peter, 4
Morrison, Toni, 48
Müller, Timo, 198, 202, 206, 208n1
Murphy, Sara, 180
Mutually Assured Destruction, 77
"My Old Man," 34

Nagel, James, 60, 134, 138–39, 141
Napoleonic wars, 128n2
Narayan, R. K., 45
National Institute of Mental Health, 135
"A Natural History of the Dead," 9, 151–52, 165–66, 171n22, 246n7
Nazi Germany, 87, 92, 94, 103
Nelson, Cary, 123
Nevinson, C. R. W., 30
New Deal, 98
*New Masses*, 94, 100
*The New Republic*, 93
Newton, Adam Zachary, 26
New Zealand Expeditionary Force, 19
"Night Before Battle," 96
Nin, Andrés, 105

Ninh, Bao, 48
"Notes on the Next War: A Serious Topical Letter," 33
"Now I Lay Me," 69, 134, 137, 141, 173–74, 182
Nuffer, David, 134
Nuremberg Principles, 117

Oak Park, 135
O'Brien, Tim, 2–3, 45, 150, 73n8
Oe, Kenzaburo, 48
"The Old Man and the Sea," 152
"The Old Man at the Bridge," 105n10
"On the Quai at Smyrna," 18, 27, 32, 83–87, 170n18
"On Writing," 191
O'Neill, Susan, 48
Ong, Walter, 194, 224–37
Orwell, George, 9, 45, 93, 158, 104n3, 105n7
Owen, Wilfred, 31, 126, 171n23, 246n7

Pakistan, 90
Payne, Stanley, 104n3, 105n13
Persian Gulf war, 6
Phelan, James, 24
Phrynicus, 157
Picasso, Pablo, 8–9, 77–91
Plath, James, 9–10, 155
Plath, Sylvia, 77
postmodernism, 190
post-traumatic stress disorder (PTSD), 9–10, 85, 133–42, 156n3
Pound, Ezra, 77, 141
Pozorski, Aimee, 221–22
"A Pursuit Race," 137

Quick, Paul S., 73n3
Quick, Robert, 18–19
Quintanilla, Luis, 4
Quintanilla, Pepe, 105n12

Rao, Raja, 45
Reece, Josephine, 10, 193–94
Remembrance Day, 15
Retzinger, Suzanne M., 35
*Restrepo*, 123
Reynolds, Michael, 4, 34, 134, 135, 137, 139, 183, 189
Rich, Adrienne, 38
Ricks, Thomas, 108–9
Rimmon-Kenan, Schlomith, 8, 61–74
Robles, Jose, 93
Rome, Harold, 141

Roosevelt, Eleanor, 105n9
Roosevelt, Theodore, 141, 183
Roper, Michael, 170n20
Rothberg, Michael, 43
Rousseau, Jean Jacques, 128n2
Rovit, Earl H., 153
Rudat, Wolfgang, 237n3
Ruddick, Sara, 36

Sander, Libby, 58
San Fermin, 160
Sargent, John Singer, 127
Sassoon, Siegfried, 31
*Saving Private Ryan*, 122, 126, 157
Scarry, Elaine, 194, 196–208
Scheff, Thomas J., 35, 37
Schlieffen, Alfred Graf von, 158
Scholes, Robert, 60
Schumann, Dirk, 170n20
Schwartz, Delmore, 111
Schwartz, Nina, 171n24
Second American Writers Congress, 95
Second World War, 3, 4, 37, 77–79, 99, 140, 157. See also *Across the River and into the Trees*; *Saving Private Ryan*
Sedgwick, Eve Kosofsky, 192
Seed, David, 34
Seymour, David, 127
Shakespeare, William, 3–4, 169n6
Shay, Jonathan, 9, 133, 162
shell shock. See moral injury; post-traumatic stress disorder (PTSD); suicide; traumatic brain injury (TBI)
Sherry, Vincent, 2
"Shock Troops," 8
"The Short Happy Life of Francis Macomber," 152, 190, 169n7
Shubert, Adrian, 169n11
"A Silent, Ghastly Process," 19–21
Sino-Japanese War, 3, 4
Smith, Adam, 158, 167
Smith, Paul, 60, 135
Smith, Ronald, 140
"The Snows of Kilimanjaro," 152, 190, 170n18
Sobchack, Vivian, 123, 128n6
"Soldier's Home," 1–2, 19, 24–26, 33; and trauma, 135–36, 140, 141, 173
Solow, Michael K., 153–54, 106n15
Sparknotes, 118
Spain, 160
Spanish Civil War, 3–5, 8–9, 11, 189. See also *For Whom the Bell Tolls*; *The Spanish Earth*

*The Spanish Earth*, 3, 9, 95, 122–29, 189
Spender, Stephen, 121n3
Stein, Gertrude, 135, 141
Structuralism, 60–74
Studebaker (corporation), 104n1
Sturgeon, Noel, 192
Strychacz, Thomas, 8–9, 35, 42
suicide, 16, 134, 157, 167
Suit, Bernard, 169n10
*The Sun Also Rises*, 10, 61–62, 64–65, 134; and bullfighting, 158, 160, 164, 196–208; in Ernest Hemingway Seminar, 190, 194; and trauma, 173, 182–83
Supreme Court of the United States, 157
Sylvester, Bickford, 32
Svoboda, Frederic, 204
Syria, 11

Tallack, Douglas, 61
Taro, Gerda, 127
Terrorism Act of 2006 (UK), 9
Tetlow, Wendolyn E., 37–38
Texas Oil Company, 104n1
*The Thin Red Line*, 123
Thomas, Clarence, 157
Thomas, Gregory, 170n20
Thompson, Captane, 140
Thomson, Judith Jarvis, 161
Thomson, Rosemarie Garland, 156n1
"The Three-Day Blow," 38–40
Thurston, Michael, 171n22
*To Have and Have Not*, 95
"Today is Friday," 97
Toer, Pramoedya Ananta, 48
*Toronto Star*, 19–21
trauma. See moral injury; post-traumatic stress disorder (PTSD); suicide; traumatic brain injury (TBI)
traumatic brain injury (TBI), 9, 133–42
Trevelyan, G. M., 140
Trotter, David, 128n6
Trout, Steven, 2, 8, 16
Trumbo, Dalton, 128
Turnegev, Ivan, 39
Tyler, Lisa, 8

*Under Kilimanjaro*, 155
"Under the Ridge," 96
United Nations, 117
"Up in Michigan," 37, 189, 192
USS *Pueblo*, 18–19
USSR, 93, 101, 104

Vernon, Alex, 111–12, 144–45, 156n7, 174, 221; and gender, 43, 175, 182, 183, 185n8, 185n9, 223n1; and the Spanish Civil War, 104n2, 105n9, 121n2, 128n1
"A Very Short Story," 27
Veterans Day, 15
"A Veteran Visits the Old Front," 5
Vickroy, Laurie, 184n2, 185n11
Vietnam war, 3–4, 77
Villard, Henry Serrano, 134, 138–39
Vonnegut, Kurt, 43, 150

Wagner-Martin, Linda, 4, 60
Walpole, Hugh, 39–40
*Waltz with Bashir*, 123
*War Witch*, 123
Washington, Gene, 216–17

"A Way You'll Never Be," 8, 60–74, 134, 140–41
Welsh, Thomas, 160–61
Wharton, Edith, 32
"Who Murdered the Vets?," 94
Wilson, Edmund, 9, 173, 121n3
Winter, Jay, 2
Wolfe, Cary, 156n2
Wolin, Richard, 160
Woodward, Bob, 108–9
Woolf, Virginia, 38
Wyatt, David, 62

Young, Philip, 9, 60, 134, 173

Zuckert, Catherine, 166, 169n13

www.ingramcontent.com/pod-product-compliance
Lightning Source LLC
Chambersburg PA
CBHW021821300426
44114CB00009BA/276